AutoCAD® LT ...
For Dummie...

M000290913

Ten Top AutoCAD LT 2000 Drawing and Editing Commands

Button	ToolTip	Purpose
	Line/Polyline	Draw line segments as separate objects/ single object
	Arc	Draw circular arcs
	Circle	Draw circles
	Multiline Text	Create and edit multiple lines of text; apply special formatting to characters
	Linear Dimension	Draw horizontal, vertical, and rotated dimensions
	Erase	Delete objects
	Copy Object	Create one or more copies of objects
	Move	Move objects
	Stretch	Stretch, shorten, or move objects
	Trim/Extend	Shorten or lengthen objects using other objects

Ten Top AutoCAD LT 2000 Dialog Boxes

Button/Menu Item	Dialog Box Name	Purpose
	Plot	Control plot devices, plot settings, layouts, and page setups; preview plots; plot (which means the same thing as print in AutoCAD LT)
	AutoCAD DesignCenter	Copy named objects (layers, block definitions, and so on) between drawings; search for drawings
	Properties	Set options, such as layer, color, linetype, lineweight for objects; additional options depend on the type of object selected
	Layer Properties Manager	Create, set options for layers
	Insert Block	Insert a block
	Hatch	Create hatching inside boundaries
SNAP	Drafting Settings	Control snap and grid, tracking, and object snaps (right-click SNAP button and choose Settings)
	Dimension Style Manager	Set options for dimensioning; includes preview of the options' effects
Insert⇨Xref Manager		Attach and manage external reference files
Format⇨Drawing Units	drawing units	Manage and change linear and angular unit settings

Cheat Sheet $2.95 value. Item 0600-5.

For more information about IDG Books, call 1-800-762-2974.

For Dummies®: Bestselling Book Series for Beginners

Drawing Scale and Limits Charts: Feet and Inches

Drawing Scale	81/2" x 11"	11" x 17"	24" x 36"	30" x 42"	36" x 48"
1/16" = 1'–0"	136' x 176'	176' x 272'	384' x 576'	480' x 672'	576' x 768'
1/8" = 1'–0"	68' x 88'	88' x 136'	192' x 288'	240' x 336'	288' x 384'
1/4" = 1'–0"	34' x 44'	44' x 68'	96' x 144'	120' x 168'	144' x 192'
1/2" = 1'–0"	17' x 22'	22' x 34'	48' x 72'	60' x 84'	72' x 96'
3/4" = 1'–0"	11'–4" x 14'–8"	14'–8" x 22'–8"	32' x 48'	40' x 56'	48' x 64'
1" = 1'–0"	8'–6" x 11'	11' x 17'	24' x 36'	30' x 42'	36' x 48'
11/2" = 1'–0"	5'–8" x 7'–4"	7'–4" x 11'–4"	16' x 24'	20' x 28'	24' x 32'
3" = 1'–0"	2'–10" x 3'–8"	3'–8" x 5'–8"	8' x 12'	10' x 14'	12' x 16'

Drawing Scale and Limits Charts: Millimeters

Drawing Scale	210 x 297 mm	297 x 420 mm	420 x 594 mm	594 x 841 mm	841x 1,189 mm
1 = 200	42,000 x 59,400 mm	59,400 x 84,000 mm	84,000 x 118,800 mm	118,800 x 168,200 mm	168,200 x 237,800 mm
1 = 100	21,000 x 29,700 mm	29,700 x 42,000 mm	42,000 x 59,400 mm	59,400 x 84,100 mm	84,100 x 118,900 mm
1 = 50	10,500 x 14,850 mm	14,850 x 21,000 mm	21,000 x 29,700 mm	29,700 x 42,050 mm	42,050 x 59,450 mm
1 = 20	4,200 x 5,940 mm	5,940 x 8,400 mm	8400 x 11,880 mm	11,880 x 16,820 mm	16,820 x 23,780 mm
1 = 10	2,100 x 2,970 mm	2,970 x 4,200 mm	4,200 x 5,940 mm	5,940 x 8,410 mm	8,410 x 11,890 mm
1 = 5	1,050 x 1,485 mm	1,485 x 2,100 mm	2,100 x 2,970 mm	2,970 x 4,205 mm	4,205 x 5,945 mm

Drawing Scale and Text Height Chart: Feet and Inches

Drawing Scale	Drawing Scale Factor	1/8" Text Height	3/32" Text Height
1/16" = 1'–0"	192	24"	18"
1/8" = 1'–0"	96	12"	9"
1/4" = 1'–0"	48	6"	4 1/2"
1/2" = 1'–0"	24	3"	2 1/4"
3/4" = 1'–0"	16	2"	1 1/2"
1" = 1'–0"	12	1 1/2"	1 1/8"
1 1/2" = 1'–0"	8	1"	3/4"
3" = 1'–0"	4	1/2"	3/8"

Drawing Scale and Text Height Chart: Millimeters

Drawing Scale	Drawing Scale Factor	3 mm Text Height	2.5 mm Text Height
1 = 200	200	600 mm	500 mm
1 = 100	100	300 mm	250 mm
1 = 50	50	150 mm	125 mm
1 = 20	20	60 mm	50 mm
1 = 10	10	30 mm	25 mm
1 = 5	5	15 mm	12.5 mm

AutoCAD® LT 2000
FOR
DUMMIES®

AutoCAD® LT 2000 FOR DUMMIES®

by Bud Smith and Mark Middlebrook

IDG BOOKS WORLDWIDE

IDG Books Worldwide, Inc.
An International Data Group Company

Foster City, CA ◆ Chicago, IL ◆ Indianapolis, IN ◆ New York, NY

AutoCAD® LT 2000 For Dummies®

Published by
IDG Books Worldwide, Inc.
An International Data Group Company
919 E. Hillsdale Blvd.
Suite 400
Foster City, CA 94404
www.idgbooks.com (IDG Books Worldwide Web site)
www.dummies.com (Dummies Press Web site)

Library of Congress Catalog Card No.: 99-66700

ISBN: 0-7645-0600-5

Printed in the United States of America

10 9 8 7 6 5 4 3 2

1O/QX/RR/QQ/IN

Distributed in the United States by IDG Books Worldwide, Inc.

Distributed by CDG Books Canada Inc. for Canada; by Transworld Publishers Limited in the United Kingdom; by IDG Norge Books for Norway; by IDG Sweden Books for Sweden; by IDG Books Australia Publishing Corporation Pty. Ltd. for Australia and New Zealand; by TransQuest Publishers Pte Ltd. for Singapore, Malaysia, Thailand, Indonesia, and Hong Kong; by Gotop Information Inc. for Taiwan; by ICG Muse, Inc. for Japan; by Intersoft for South Africa; by Eyrolles for France; by International Thomson Publishing for Germany, Austria and Switzerland; by Distribuidora Cuspide for Argentina; by LR International for Brazil; by Galileo Libros for Chile; by Ediciones ZETA S.C.R. Ltda. for Peru; by WS Computer Publishing Corporation, Inc., for the Philippines; by Contemporanea de Ediciones for Venezuela; by Express Computer Distributors for the Caribbean and West Indies; by Micronesia Media Distributor, Inc. for Micronesia; by Chips Computadoras S.A. de C.V. for Mexico; by Editorial Norma de Panama S.A. for Panama; by American Bookshops for Finland.

For general information on IDG Books Worldwide's books in the U.S., please call our Consumer Customer Service department at 800-762-2974. For reseller information, including discounts and premium sales, please call our Reseller Customer Service department at 800-434-3422.

For information on where to purchase IDG Books Worldwide's books outside the U.S., please contact our International Sales department at 317-572-3993 or fax 317-572-4002.

For consumer information on foreign language translations, please contact our Customer Service department at 1-800-434-3422, fax 317-572-4002, or e-mail rights@idgbooks.com.

For information on licensing foreign or domestic rights, please phone +1-650-653-7098.

For sales inquiries and special prices for bulk quantities, please contact our Order Services department at 800-434-3422 or write to the address above.

For information on using IDG Books Worldwide's books in the classroom or for ordering examination copies, please contact our Educational Sales department at 800-434-2086 or fax 317-572-4005.

For press review copies, author interviews, or other publicity information, please contact our Public Relations department at 650-653-7000 or fax 650-653-7500.

For authorization to photocopy items for corporate, personal, or educational use, please contact Copyright Clearance Center, 222 Rosewood Drive, Danvers, MA 01923, or fax 978-750-4470.

About the Authors

Mark Middlebrook's *AutoCAD LT 2000 For Dummies* is his fourth book on AutoCAD, and his third book with Bud Smith. Mark used to be an engineer, but gave it up when he discovered that he couldn't handle a real job. He is now principal of Daedalus Consulting, an independent CAD and computer consulting company in Oakland, California. (Daedalus was the guy in ancient Greek legend who built the labyrinth on Crete. In a demonstration of the sad consequences of over-education, Mark named his company after Daedalus before he realized that few of his clients would be able to pronounce it, and even fewer spell it.) Mark is also a contributing editor for *CADALYST* magazine and proprietor of markcad.com, his own new San Francisco Bay Area .com startup. Visit `markcad.com` before Mark — the cad — gets too lonely there.

Bud Smith's *AutoCAD LT 2000 For Dummies* makes more than ten books he's written and his third book with Mark Middlebrook. Non-AutoCAD-related work includes authorship of the hit book, *Creating Web Pages For Dummies*, now in its fourth edition. Bud first realized he might have a talent for structural design during junior high school, when his model of the Hoover Dam was judged the best project in the class. But that sounded too much like real work to Bud, who has built a career in computing and writing instead. Bud is Producer of the Technology Channel at AltaVista Company and has worked as a data entry clerk, computer programmer, technical writer, computer journalist, and marketer. In order to avoid dealing with all the new features in AutoCAD 2000 and AutoCAD LT 2000 himself — what he calls the "A2K problem" — he asked Mark to co-author *AutoCAD 2000 For Dummies* and this book with him.

ABOUT IDG BOOKS WORLDWIDE

Welcome to the world of IDG Books Worldwide.

IDG Books Worldwide, Inc., is a subsidiary of International Data Group, the world's largest publisher of computer-related information and the leading global provider of information services on information technology. IDG was founded more than 30 years ago by Patrick J. McGovern and now employs more than 9,000 people worldwide. IDG publishes more than 290 computer publications in over 75 countries. More than 90 million people read one or more IDG publications each month.

Launched in 1990, IDG Books Worldwide is today the #1 publisher of best-selling computer books in the United States. We are proud to have received eight awards from the Computer Press Association in recognition of editorial excellence and three from Computer Currents' First Annual Readers' Choice Awards. Our best-selling ...*For Dummies*® series has more than 50 million copies in print with translations in 31 languages. IDG Books Worldwide, through a joint venture with IDG's Hi-Tech Beijing, became the first U.S. publisher to publish a computer book in the People's Republic of China. In record time, IDG Books Worldwide has become the first choice for millions of readers around the world who want to learn how to better manage their businesses.

Our mission is simple: Every one of our books is designed to bring extra value and skill-building instructions to the reader. Our books are written by experts who understand and care about our readers. The knowledge base of our editorial staff comes from years of experience in publishing, education, and journalism — experience we use to produce books to carry us into the new millennium. In short, we care about books, so we attract the best people. We devote special attention to details such as audience, interior design, use of icons, and illustrations. And because we use an efficient process of authoring, editing, and desktop publishing our books electronically, we can spend more time ensuring superior content and less time on the technicalities of making books.

You can count on our commitment to deliver high-quality books at competitive prices on topics you want to read about. At IDG Books Worldwide, we continue in the IDG tradition of delivering quality for more than 30 years. You'll find no better book on a subject than one from IDG Books Worldwide.

John Kilcullen
Chairman and CEO
IDG Books Worldwide, Inc.

*Eighth Annual
Computer Press
Awards* ≥*1992*

*Ninth Annual
Computer Press
Awards* ≥*1993*

*Tenth Annual
Computer Press
Awards* ≥*1994*

*Eleventh Annual
Computer Press
Awards* ≥*1995*

Dedication

From Bud: This book is for my late maternal grandparents, Jim and Maxine Myers. You showed me that a life of hard work and dedication to family could reap lasting rewards. You also left a couple dozen direct descendants to carry on for you (and carry on we do).

From Mark: To the engineers at Middlebrook + Louie, and especially to Hardip Pannu, who first prodded me into writing about AutoCAD LT. They helped me realize that AutoCAD LT is every bit as interesting — and peculiar — as AutoCAD, and that many LT users do different things than AutoCAD users.

Authors' Acknowledgments

The management and staff at Dummies Press had the foresight to encourage us to bring the Dummies approach to AutoCAD LT and help us create a book that would meet the real needs of all kinds of LT users. Our Project Editor, John Pont, was relentlessly patient, cheerful, and encouraging. (We're not sure what's in the water back east, John, but please bottle up some and send it out here.) The eagle eye of Tech Editor Dave Byrnes kept us relentlessly honest and saved us from several embarrassing mistakes. Steve Hayes signed us to the book contract and supported the effort through to the result you hold in your hands.

Publisher's Acknowledgments

We're proud of this book; please register your comments through our IDG Books Worldwide Online Registration Form located at http://my2cents.dummies.com.

Some of the people who helped bring this book to market include the following:

Acquisitions, Editorial, and
Media Development

Project Editor: John W. Pont

Acquisitions Editor: Steven H. Hayes

Technical Editor: David Byrnes

Editorial Manager: Leah P. Cameron

Senior Editor, Freelance: Constance Carlisle

Editorial Assistant: Beth Parlon

Production

Project Coordinator: E. Shawn Aylsworth

Layout and Graphics: Brian Drumm, Clint Lahnen, Barry Offringa, Tracy Oliver, Jill Piscitelli, Brent Savage, Brian Torwelle, Maggie Ubertini

Proofreaders: Laura Albert, Vickie Broyles, Sally Burton, Rebecca Senninger, Charles Spencer, Ethel M. Winslow

Indexer: Sharon Duffy

Special Help
Jerelind Charles, Tonya Maddox, Pam Wilson-Wykes

General and Administrative

IDG Books Worldwide, Inc.: John Kilcullen, CEO; Bill Barry, President and COO; John Ball, Executive VP, Operations & Administration; John Harris, CFO

IDG Books Technology Publishing Group: Richard Swadley, Senior Vice President and Publisher; Mary Bednarek, Vice President and Publisher; Walter R. Bruce III, Vice President and Publisher; Joseph Wikert, Vice President and Publisher; Mary C. Corder, Editorial Director; Andy Cummings, Publishing Director, General User Group; Barry Pruett, Publishing Director

IDG Books Manufacturing: Ivor Parker, Vice President, Manufacturing

IDG Books Marketing: John Helmus, Assistant Vice President, Director of Marketing

IDG Books Online Management: Brenda McLaughlin, Executive Vice President, Chief Internet Officer; Gary Millrood, Executive Vice President of Business Development, Sales and Marketing

IDG Books Packaging: Marc J. Mikulich, Vice President, Brand Strategy and Research

IDG Books Production for Branded Press: Debbie Stailey, Production Director

IDG Books Sales: Roland Elgey, Senior Vice President, Sales and Marketing; Michael Violano, Vice President, International Sales and Sub Rights

◆

The publisher would like to give special thanks to Patrick J. McGovern, without whom this book would not have been possible.

◆

Contents at a Glance

Cartoons at a Glance

By Rich Tennant

page 187

page 9

page 333

page 321

page 51

Fax: 978-546-7747
E-mail: richtennant@the5thwave.com
World Wide Web: www.the5thwave.com

Table of Contents

Introduction

• •

AutoCAD is an amazing thing. It was dreamed up in the early '80s at a time when most people thought that personal computers weren't all that big of a deal, when even someone who liked PCs would hardly dream of pushing them to do something as hard as CAD (which can stand for computer-aided design, computer-aided drafting, or both, depending on whom you talk to). After all, CAD could run only on the most powerful graphical computers of the day. But AutoCAD, to the surprise of many, was a hit from its first day, and it has grown to define a whole new way of creating architectural, mechanical, geographical, and other kinds of drawings.

AutoCAD LT, in its own way, is even more amazing. In its newest version, AutoCAD LT 2000, it has most of the capabilities of "full" AutoCAD, at a fraction of the price. (For details on the differences, see Chapter 2.) Given the high price of full AutoCAD, AutoCAD LT 2000 may be the best deal in software today.

The only problem with LT, as those familiar with the product call it, is that sometimes it's a little too much like full AutoCAD. While AutoCAD and LT 2000 are more consistent and easier to use than earlier versions, they still have unusual features like a command line that you must deal with in order to get any work done. And the total number of features in AutoCAD and LT, with their rich array of options, is so large that figuring out either program is a chore. That's where *AutoCAD LT 2000 For Dummies* comes in. With this book, you have an excellent chance of creating an attractive, usable, and printable drawing on your first or second try without putting a T-square through your computer screen in frustration.

About This Book

This book is not designed to be read straight through, from cover to cover. It's designed as a reference book so that you can dip in and out of it as you run into new topics. Look for the part that contains the information you want, narrow your search down to a specific chapter, find out what you need to know, and then get back to work. This book also is not designed to be completely comprehensive. Thousands of pages of documentation are required to describe completely how to use AutoCAD LT, and the resulting proliferation of manuals, online documents, and third-party books just leaves many people confused. With this book, you're able to get right to work.

How to Use This Book

AutoCAD LT 2000 is bound to leave you wondering what's going on at some point. If you're new to the program, the first time you click an icon and get only a prompt on a command line as a response, you may wonder whether something's wrong with your computer. Slightly more experienced users are likely to trip up on the intricate relationship among setup, drawing, and printing. And sometimes even experts may stumble over the details of paper space, setting up dimensions properly, or mastering the completely revamped AutoCAD LT 2000 Plot dialog box.

Use the table of contents and the index in this book to find the topic that stumps you. Go to the appropriate section and read up on the topic. Usually, you find a set of steps, a picture, or a description of how to do the task that's troubling you — and often, you find all three. (How's that for service?) Use that section to get yourself back on track and then close the book and go on.

What's Not in This Book

Unlike many other *For Dummies* books, this one does tell you to consult the documentation sometimes, especially the online documentation that's part of AutoCAD LT. AutoCAD LT 2000 is just too big and complicated for a single book to attempt to describe it. The manual set is so big that Autodesk doesn't even print all of it; in AutoCAD LT 2000, several manuals are included only in online help.

This book focuses exclusively on AutoCAD LT 2000, the newest and easiest-to-use version of the program. It also points out differences between AutoCAD LT 2000 and full AutoCAD 2000, so you can work productively with others who use either program.

Please Don't Read This!

Sprinkled through the book are icons labeled *Technical Stuff.* These icons alert you to discussions of minute detail that are unlikely to concern you unless you're a confirmed AutoCAD LT techno-nerd. As you slowly advance to expert status, however, you may find yourself going back through the book to read all that technical stuff. (At that point, you may also want to ask your boss for a vacation, because you just may be working a little too hard!)

Who Are — and Aren't — You?

AutoCAD and AutoCAD LT have a large, loyal, and dedicated group of long-time users. This book may not meet the needs of all these long-time members of the AutoCAD faithful. This book is probably not for you if

- ✔ You were an early recipient of the famous Information Letter in which Autodesk cofounder John Walker first suggested something like AutoCAD LT.

- ✔ You have lectured at Autodesk University.

- ✔ You founded Autodesk University.

- ✔ You read all those 1,000-page-plus technical tomes about AutoCAD and AutoCAD LT for pleasure.

- ✔ You sent suggestions for changes in AutoCAD LT 2000 to the AutoCAD Wish List and saw them incorporated in the new release of the program.

- ✔ After your suggestion was incorporated into the program, you sent e-mail to Autodesk explaining how the developers did it wrong.

If you don't fall into any of these categories, well, this definitely is the book for you.

However, you do need to have some idea of how to use your computer system before tackling AutoCAD LT — and this book. You need to have a working computer system on which to run LT and have it connected to a monitor, printer, and network, as well as the World Wide Web. If you don't already have this kind of complete setup and need to purchase and set it up yourself, pick up *PCs For Dummies,* 6th Edition, by Dan Gookin (from IDG Books Worldwide, Inc.).

You also need to know how to use Windows 98, Windows 95, or Windows NT to copy and delete files, create a subdirectory (the DOS word for it) or folder (the official Windows term), and find a file. You need to know how to use a mouse to select (highlight) objects or to choose (activate) commands, how to close a window, and how to minimize and maximize windows. If you don't know how to do these things, run — don't walk — to your nearest bookstore and get IDG Books' *Windows 95 For Dummies,* 2nd Edition, or *Windows 98 For Dummies,* both by Andy Rathbone, or *Windows NT 4 For Dummies* by Andy Rathbone and Sharon Crawford, and try to master some basics before you start with AutoCAD LT. (At least have those books handy as you start using this book.)

How This Book Is Organized

This book is really well organized. Well, at least it's organized. Well, okay, we drew some circles on the floor, threw scraps of paper with different ideas and topics written on them toward the circles, and organized the book by which scrap landed in which circle.

Seriously, the organization of this book into parts is one of the most important, uh, *parts* of this book. We have taken the unusual step of creating separate parts about working with existing drawings (Part II) and creating new drawings (Part III). This structure mirrors the real-world use of AutoCAD LT by some people for touching up existing drawings, plotting, and other light tasks, and by others for full-scale production work at a lower cost per desktop than full AutoCAD.

The following sections describe the parts of the book.

Part I: LT for Me, See

Need to know your way around the AutoCAD LT 2000 screen? Why does AutoCAD even exist, anyway? What's the difference between AutoCAD 2000 and AutoCAD LT 2000, besides those two little capital letters in the middle of the name? Is everything so slooow because it's supposed to be slow, or do I have too wimpy a machine to truly use this wonder of modern-day computing? And why am I doing this stuff in the first place? Part I answers all these questions — and more.

Part II: Working with Existing Drawings

Here's where we help those of you who just want to use AutoCAD LT 2000 to print an existing drawing and the drawing comes out too small, the text is too large, and the whole thing takes six hours to print on that weird plotter someone is making you use. Are you ready for the printer to laugh at you as you make your "witching hour" attempt to print the final version of the drawings due the next day at 9 a.m.? (And let us tell you, a Hewlett-Packard inkjet plotter can slide its ink cartridges back and forth in a rhythm eerily reminiscent of a head-wagging "nyah-nyah-nyah-nyah-nyah.") Read this stuff.

Chapter 4 is a must-read for all users, covering the new plotting architecture in AutoCAD 2000 and AutoCAD LT 2000. Chapters 5 and 6 tell you how to mark up and edit existing drawings — just what you need to know for light AutoCAD LT 2000 work, and to avoid causing problems in the drawings you're working with. Chapters 7 and 8 show you how to share information between AutoCAD LT and other programs and how to get the most information superhighway mileage out of your drawings. This part has you covered.

Part III: Creating Your Own Drawings

AutoCAD LT has more ways to create a drawing and then gussy it up than you could ever imagine — and maybe more than you need. First, you need to set up the new drawing. Then you need to draw and edit in it until it represents something — no mean feat. Then add text, dimensions, and hatch patterns to contribute to the appearance of your drawings. Use blocks and external references to manage repetitive parts of your drawings. This part helps you find your way through the maze of possibilities to a good solution with a minimum of headaches.

Part IV: The Part of Tens

Everyone loves lists, unless it's the overdue list at the local library. This part contains pointers to AutoCAD LT resources and a To Do list that will make you a savvy pro, or at least someone who acts like a savvy pro, in no time. Are the Part-of-Tens chapters information-packed nutrition or junk food foisted on the reader by self-indulgent authors? You be the judge.

Part V: Appendix

Yes, this book has an appendix, and we'd prefer that you not have it removed! The appendix gives you a relentlessly and thoroughly updated glossary of AutoCAD LT terms.

Icons Used in This Book

Icons, previously confined to computer screens, have escaped and are now running amok in the pages of this book. (Yeah, we know that icons started out in print in the first place, but computer people stole them fair and square. Now we writers are getting even.) These icons are like the ones in AutoCAD LT 2000 except that they're fewer, simpler, easier on the eyes, and used more consistently. (What, us, an attitude problem?) The icons used in this book are described next.

This icon tells you that a pointed insight lies ahead that can save you time and trouble as you use AutoCAD LT. For example, maybe finding out how to hit the spacebar with your nose would help increase your speed in entering commands and moving the mouse at the same time. (And maybe not. . . .)

The Technical Stuff icon points out places where you may find more data than information. Unless you're really ready to find out more about AutoCAD LT — much more — steer clear of these paragraphs the first time you read a given section of the book.

This icon tells you how to stay out of trouble when living a little close to the edge. Failure to heed its message may have disastrous consequences for you, your drawing, your computer — and maybe even all three.

Remember when Spock put his hand over McCoy's face and implanted a suggestion in his brain that later saved Spock's life? This icon is like that: helpful reminders of things you already know but that may not be right at the tip of your brain — or whatever.

This icon tells you how to do things from the keyboard instead of by using menus, toolbars, or random mouse clicks. The keyboard stuff is usually harder to remember but quicker to use.

This icon points to new stuff in AutoCAD LT 2000. It's mostly designed for those of you who know AutoCAD LT pretty well already and just want to find out what's new in this release, but new AutoCAD users starting out their CAD working lives with AutoCAD LT 2000 may find this stuff interesting, too.

A Few Conventions — Just in Case

You probably can figure out for yourself all the information we're about to impart in this section, but just in case you want to save that brain power for AutoCAD LT, here it is in cold type.

Text you type into the program at the command line, in a dialog box, text box, and so on appears in **boldface type**. Examples of AutoCAD LT commands and prompts appear in a `special typeface`, as does any other text in the book that echoes a message, a word, or one or more lines of text that actually appear on-screen. (Longer segments also have a shaded background.)

Sidebars also are set off in their own typeface, with a fancy head all their own, and are surrounded by a shaded box, much like this:

This is a sidebar head

And this is how the text in a sidebar appears. Neat, huh? Well, different at least. Hey, two-column text can be pretty nifty all on its own, even without peripheral AutoCAD LT material to occupy its space! What? You don't buy that? Oh, well, back to our main event, then.

Regarding menus and menu items or commands: If you're told to open a menu or choose a command, you can use any number of methods to do so — pressing a shortcut key combination on the keyboard, clicking the corresponding toolbar button, or clicking the menu or command name with the mouse, highlighting the name by moving over it with the cursor arrow keys, and then pressing Enter — whatever way you're most comfortable with. Sometimes we tell you to do it a certain way, because that's how we, as the AutoCAD LT authorities du jour, think it's done best. But if you already know what we're talking about, feel free to do it your way instead. (And if it doesn't work, of course, you didn't hear this from us.)

Anytime you see a menu name or command name with an underlined letter, such as File, it means that the underlined letter is the Windows shortcut key for that menu name or command. Hold down the Alt key and press the first underlined key to select the menu. Then, continue to hold down the Alt key and press the second underlined key to select the command. (You can let up on the Alt key after you select the menu if you'd like and then press the command's shortcut key to access it. But don't press the Alt key down a second time, or Windows will select a different menu instead of the command you want.) Oh, and often in this book you see phrases such as "choose File⇨Save As from the menu bar." The funny little arrow (⇨) separates the main menu name from the specific command on that menu. In this example, you would open the File menu and choose the Save As command. Again, the underlined letters are the *hot keys* — keys you can press in combination with the Alt key to open menus and activate commands.

AutoCAD LT has an interesting convention for command-line shortcuts: The shortcut letters appear in capital letters, whereas the rest of the command appears in lowercase. So when you see a sentence like "enter **DimLInear** for a linear dimension," it means "for a linear dimension, enter **DIMLINEAR**, or **DLI** for short, at the command line." Because you will be seeing this convention used in AutoCAD LT's Help files and printed documentation, we use it in this book as well.

Well, that covers the basics. The details — ah, those are yet to come. And believe us when we tell you with the utmost sincerity that you have much to look forward to . . . . (Cue lightning, thunder, and a low moan from the nether regions of your computer.)

Where to Go from Here

If you've read this Introduction, you're probably at least a little bit like us: You like to read. (People who don't like to read usually skip this front-matter stuff and scurry to the index to get to exactly, and only, the part they need at that moment.) So take a few more minutes to page through and look for interesting stuff. And pick up a pen and some stick-on notes; the icons and headings in this book are only a start. Personalize your book by circling vital tips, drawing a smiley face if you like a joke, even X-ing out stuff that you disagree with. (And we've hidden plenty of our own opinions in this book, so get those Xs ready.)

Part I
LT for Me, See

The 5th Wave — By Rich Tennant

Larry the Balloon Man employs AutoCAD LT software into his balloon animal act.

LARRY the BALLOON MAN

In this part . . .

AutoCAD LT is more than just another application program; it's a complete environment for drafting and
design. So if you're new to AutoCAD LT, you need to know
several things to get off to a good start. We describe these
key facts in this part of the book.

If you're an experienced AutoCAD LT user, you'll be most
interested in the high points of the new release and a
quick look at how to get productive on it fast. All that is
here, too. (*Tip:* Look for the 2K icons, which point out
AutoCAD LT 2000 highlights.)

Chapter 1

Why AutoCAD LT 2000?

In This Chapter

▶ Finding where CAD fits

▶ Comparing AutoCAD LT to other programs

AutoCAD LT 2000 is one of the best deals around — a shining example of the old 80/20 rule: roughly 80 percent of the capabilities of AutoCAD 2000 for roughly 20 percent of the money. Like AutoCAD 2000, AutoCAD LT 2000 runs on mainstream personal computers and doesn't require any additional hardware devices. With AutoCAD LT, you can be a "player" in the world of AutoCAD, the world's leading CAD program, for a very low starting cost.

AutoCAD LT 2000 is a very close cousin to AutoCAD 2000. Autodesk, the company that makes the two programs, created AutoCAD LT 2000 by starting with the AutoCAD 2000 program, taking out a few features to make the program a little simpler to use (and to justify a lower price), adding a couple of features to enhance ease of use compared to "full" AutoCAD, and then testing the result.

AutoCAD LT 2000, shown in Figure 1-1, is almost identical to AutoCAD 2000 in the way it looks and works. The opening screen and menus of the two programs are nearly indistinguishable, with LT missing a small number of the commands found in the AutoCAD 2000 menus.

In fact, the major difference between the programs has nothing to do with the programs themselves. The major difference is that AutoCAD LT lacks support for several programming languages that software developers and even some advanced users employ to create utilities and industry-specific applications for AutoCAD. AutoCAD supports add-ons written in Microsoft's Visual Basic for Applications (VBA), in a specialized AutoCAD programming language called AutoLISP, and in a specialized version of the C programming language called the AutoCAD Runtime Extension (ARX).

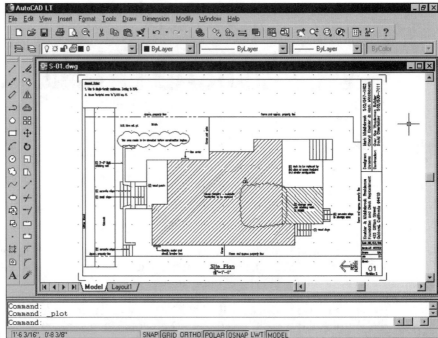

Figure 1-1:
AutoCAD LT
2000 is
"real"
AutoCAD.

Software developers, including Autodesk's own programmers, use AutoCAD's support for these programming languages to develop add-on programs that work with AutoCAD. For example, AutoCAD includes a set of handy utility commands called the Express Tools, and Autodesk used AutoLISP and other AutoCAD programming languages to create them. Other software developers create specialized applications for architectural drafting or other industry-specific needs.

AutoCAD LT doesn't support any of these programming languages, so most of the utilities and applications developed for AutoCAD don't work with LT. AutoCAD LT does include the same menu and script customization features that AutoCAD has. As a result, a few very simple AutoCAD add-ons do work with LT. For example, you can purchase or download *block libraries* — collections of drafting symbols — that work with LT.

AutoCAD LT also has only limited 3D support. You can view and edit 3D objects in AutoCAD LT, so you can work with drawings created in AutoCAD that contain 3D objects. You also can extrude a 2D object, which gives you a limited ability to create 3D models. (CAD people call this ability "2½D" because it's limited to giving 2D objects depth in one direction.) However, you cannot create 3D surfaces or solids.

The lack of 3D object creation in LT is not as big a negative for many users as you might think. For most users, creating 3D objects takes a great deal of time, and figuring out how to do it well requires lots of training or trial and error. Only if you are in the minority of users who really need 3D object creation capability would you even want to get started in this area. So, the limited nature of AutoCAD LT 2000's 3D support may be a blessing in disguise for many LT users.

Besides lacking add-on programs and support for creating most kinds of 3D objects, the other major concern in using AutoCAD LT 2000 is the same as the major concern for users of "full" AutoCAD: the steep learning curve required to do much in any version of AutoCAD. AutoCAD was originally designed for maximum power and then modified somewhat to add ease of use. AutoCAD LT shares this same heritage.

But never fear; *AutoCAD LT 2000 For Dummies* is here! We designed this book to help you use the capabilities you need from AutoCAD LT 2000 with a minimum of time and effort. We build up from the simple to the powerful, one step at a time, making it as easy as possible for you to get your work done.

Letting the CAD Out of the Bag

If you have some experience using AutoCAD, even a version previous to AutoCAD 2000, you will have a pretty easy time getting started with AutoCAD LT. (One major area that is much-changed in AutoCAD 2000 is printing; see Chapter 4 for details.)

If you're new to AutoCAD, though, you need to get oriented before starting your journey with AutoCAD LT 2000. After you know the lay of the land, you can accomplish many tasks in LT with a quick, hit-and-run foray into the program. If you start out without this knowledge, however, you may need to slog through a full-scale assault just to accomplish one or two simple tasks. So, this chapter introduces you to the world of CAD and AutoCAD LT 2000's place in that world.

Depending on whom you ask, CAD stands for computer-aided drafting or computer-aided design. Most people use CAD programs for drafting — creating and modifying drawings that guide the construction of something. A design task, by contrast, involves making decisions like "how many veeblefetzers can I cram into this crawl space?" These decisions are part of your CAD work, too, so computer-aided design is not a bad name. Just remember that you'll probably use AutoCAD LT primarily for drafting.

CAD programs have some similarities to other kinds of programs used for drawing, as shown in Figure 1-2. Here's a quick rundown on some major types of drawing programs that you may recognize, and how they relate to CAD programs:

Figure 1-2:
Paint and
draw
programs
share some
features
with CAD
software.

✔ **Paint programs.** You use these simple programs for creating *bit-mapped images*. A bit-mapped image is recorded as a bunch of *pixels* (short for "picture elements," the little dots on your screen). The standard format for bit-mapped images in Windows is a *BMP* (BitMaP) file. The Paint program that comes free with Windows is, as you might expect, a proto-typical example of a simple paint program. Adobe Photoshop, for all its sophistication, is just a grown-up paint program.

The biggest difference between a paint program and CAD is that you can't modify objects in a paint program; after you draw a line, for exam-ple, you can't select it again as a line — just as a bunch of pixels. If the line crosses other lines or images, it's nearly impossible to select it again just as a line. So, creation is easy in a paint program, but editing is hard, and precision is next to impossible.

Within AutoCAD LT 2000, paint-type images are referred to as *raster images*.

✔ **Draw programs.** You use a draw program for creating *vector-based images.* Vector-based images are stored as a set of geometrical objects (such as lines and arcs), using any of a variety of formats. Adobe Illustrator and CorelDraw are draw programs; Visio and Autodesk's Actrix are examples of a specialized form of draw program called a *diagramming program,* pioneered by Visio.

The biggest difference between a CAD program and a draw or diagramming program is the degree of support for precision. In a draw program, you can easily create an image, but creating a precise one is difficult. In a CAD program, creating an image can be somewhat difficult, but making it precise doesn't require much additional work. CAD programs also offer robust support for CAD-specific features like dimensioning and hatching.

If you only have experience using a paint program, AutoCAD LT presents a fairly steep learning curve for you — you'll have to "think different," to quote the ads of a large computer company named for a fruit. Follow the steps in this book carefully, and don't assume you know how to do something until you've tried it.

If you've used a draw program or a diagramming program, and especially if you've used one to do complicated, precise work, you don't face such a steep learning curve. After you understand how to select objects, enter commands, and print, you can get rolling.

In either case, figuring out how to use AutoCAD LT 2000 offers many rewards. AutoCAD is the best-selling CAD program in the world, and billions of dollars worth of drawings have been created with it. By using AutoCAD LT, you inherit much of the AutoCAD infrastructure. You also gain the ability to create precise, well-documented drawings that can be used, edited, and reused by literally millions of other designers and drafters.

LT's Greatest Hits

We need to make something clear up front: AutoCAD LT is not the most intuitive program in the world to use. That's because it works in almost exactly the same way as "full" AutoCAD, a program designed for power first and ease of use second. (Don't feel bad — in the not-too-distant past, power came first, compatibility with early versions of AutoCAD was second, and ease of use was third.)

However, for anyone who works with AutoCAD users (and for many other people, as well), the advantages of using AutoCAD LT certainly justify the effort of mastering those parts of AutoCAD LT that you need for doing your work. We describe some of those advantages here.

The importance of being DWG

We can think of at least two reasons why using AutoCAD LT, despite its somewhat steep learning curve, is very often a great idea. The first involves the DWG file format. AutoCAD stores its files in a format called *DWG* — short, we assume, for "drawing."

For complicated intellectual property reasons, companies no longer like to say that their acronyms and abbreviations stand for anything, so we're left to guess what they mean. To many people, DWG means drawing.

AutoCAD LT's key advantage is its use of the same DWG file format as "full" AutoCAD, as shown in Figure 1-3. AutoCAD LT reads and writes DWG files using almost exactly the same computer code as in AutoCAD, because the same company creates both programs and uses much of the same programming work for both. Thanks to this common parentage, an AutoCAD user and an AutoCAD LT user can share files smoothly, while users of any other pair of CAD programs probably can't share files without bumping into compatibility problems.

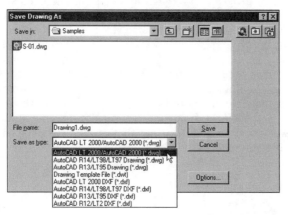

Figure 1-3:
AutoCAD LT
and
AutoCAD
share a
common
DWG file
format.

To understand the importance of smooth DWG exchange, think of a similar problem involving word processing (clearly a subject near and dear to the hearts of book writers — CAD experts or not). If you take a Microsoft Word file and try to use it in an early version of WordPerfect, you get lots of gibberish on-screen. (More recent versions convert the file automatically.) Even converting from a newer Word file back to an old version of Word is likely to cause formatting errors. Fixing the problems can cost lots of time and money.

Think how much more important file exchange can be, though, for CAD programs. Creating CAD files can take dozens or even hundreds of hours, so any process that even has a chance of introducing errors requires a great deal of checking and, frequently, rework. And companies use CAD files to create parts, build buildings, even design medical instruments such as pacemakers; clearly, an error can cause serious problems.

To quickly sum up years of technical work by Autodesk and its competitors, as well as discussions, articles, online debates, and even lawsuits, DWG compatibility is notoriously hard to achieve. The only program that offers nearly flawless file compatibility with AutoCAD is AutoCAD LT.

The rich history (and herstory) of AutoCAD

AutoCAD and the company that makes it, Autodesk, are true Silicon Valley-type success stories. (Actually, Autodesk is based in Marin County, just north of San Francisco, over an hour's drive from the epicenter of Silicon Valley, which is, we assert, Bud Smith's otherwise unremarkable home in Cupertino.) AutoCAD evolved from humble beginnings into a robust program that ran on DOS, UNIX, and the Macintosh, and now to a program that works well with Windows — and is only updated for the Windows platform.

Autodesk's early leader, John Walker, has written a book, *The Autodesk File,* that gives his opinions and insights into the development of AutoCAD through about 1996. You can find this book online, in its entirety, at www. fourmilab.ch. It includes early discussions of an AutoCAD LT-like product and a few notes on LT itself.

John Forbes is another important Autodesk figure — a former product manager for AutoCAD. After some internal dissension at Autodesk, he moved on to Visio, a competing company, and swore publicly to beat Autodesk in its major markets. This effort has not been an overall winner so far, but it has provided some needed competition for Autodesk. In late 1999, Microsoft announced its intention to purchase Visio.

The third key personality in AutoCAD history is Carol Bartz, who has been CEO of Autodesk since the early 90s. She refocused the company on AutoCAD, first abandoning several money-losing projects, then bringing to market such winners as AutoCAD LT and Actrix — a diagramming program that, perhaps by coincidence, competes directly with Visio. The continued success of AutoCAD and related products comes, in part, from her relentless focus on the importance of keeping the company's AutoCAD product line front and center.

Why workalike works

In addition to DWG compatibility, another, subtler reason exists for viewing AutoCAD LT as your best choice for a lower-priced CAD program. And, like DWG compatibility, this reason relates to AutoCAD's position as the industry standard for CAD. Choosing AutoCAD LT makes sense because of all the industry experience and products that exist for AutoCAD and therefore, to a large extent, for AutoCAD LT.

This book is a great example of how LT benefits from "full" AutoCAD. The authors of this book first worked together on a book about AutoCAD Release 12. Based on that experience, we've worked together on other AutoCAD books — *AutoCAD LT 2000 For Dummies* is the most recent — and finally convinced several people that an LT book is a good idea. If not for LT's AutoCAD connection, we probably wouldn't have written this book at this time.

Similar reasoning applies to many books, articles, courses, and products related to AutoCAD and AutoCAD LT. The AutoCAD connection provides the base for AutoCAD LT-related products, and AutoCAD itself provides an upgrade path in case LT can't meet all your needs.

As we mention earlier in this chapter, not all AutoCAD-compatible products work with AutoCAD LT. You can't use the add-on programs and utilities developed using one of the AutoCAD customization programming languages, such as AutoLISP or the AutoCAD Runtime Extension (ARX). Before you buy any product that was developed to work with AutoCAD, make sure that it supports AutoCAD LT, too.

The final, but perhaps most important, AutoCAD-related advantage of AutoCAD LT is all the AutoCAD knowledge that's likely to be in the heads of your coworkers. If you have colleagues with AutoCAD experience, you have an experienced technical support staff on call nearby. Although you don't want to wear out your welcome (using this book can help you answer the easy questions yourself), this informal support network, plus any formal AutoCAD support in your organization, is an invaluable resource. And as your LT knowledge grows, you can help other LT and AutoCAD users with their problems in return.

Working with AutoCAD veterans

Watching an experienced AutoCAD user work can be a bewildering experience. In all likelihood, the old pro moves quickly and unpredictably between the program's menus, the toolbars on the side of the screen, the command line at the bottom of the screen, and perhaps even outdated control interfaces like the old side-screen menu or a drawing tablet with AutoCAD commands on it. You may see that person start a command or process in one part of the screen, continue it in another, and complete it in a third.

Also, you may see AutoCAD veterans using a program that looks a lot different from your version of AutoCAD LT. They may have an old version of AutoCAD; they may be running one or more add-on programs (mostly not compatible with LT); or, they may be using a version of AutoCAD that they've customized and rearranged beyond recognition — or all three.

AutoCAD veterans use a confusing mixture of very fast, efficient approaches and old hangovers from previous versions that are no longer the best way to work. A novice AutoCAD or LT user can't easily distinguish which is which when getting help from an experienced user.

Unless you have an unusually thoughtful, patient, and otherwise unoccupied AutoCAD veteran nearby, you probably shouldn't get most of your beginning AutoCAD instruction from a veteran. Turn to this book as a resource for the basics of using AutoCAD LT and save your questions for when you need to know how your company does things, or for when no other source — neither this book, the AutoCAD LT Help files (which we describe in Chapter 2), nor your own trials and tribulations — provides a quick, satisfactory answer. You'll get brownie points for going it alone as much as you can — and will then be more likely to get a quick, helpful answer just when you need it.

Chapter 2

Le Tour de AutoCAD LT 2000

- -

In This Chapter

▶ Checking out the title bar and the menu bar

▶ Starting a new drawing

▶ Fiddling with the drawing area

▶ Discovering the status bar

▶ Fooling with toolbars

▶ Commanding the command line

▶ Setting system variables and using dialog boxes

▶ Getting help

- -

A new user of AutoCAD LT probably can't fully appreciate the beauty of the AutoCAD LT 2000 screen. To a new user, the LT screen just looks like an unusually complicated Windows application. But as a new user, you're missing out on years of ugly, DOS-based screens and hard-to-enter commands. Lucky you! But do be ready to hear some war stories from the grizzled AutoCAD and AutoCAD LT users with whom you talk.

All is not well in Denmark, however. (Nor anyplace else people are just getting started with AutoCAD LT.) That's because AutoCAD LT 2000 is still different from any Windows program you've ever seen. The main difference is the command line, which we describe in detail a bit later in this chapter. Regardless of whether you really want to, you have to use the command line, at least to finish entering commands that you start by choosing a menu item. One of the main purposes of this book is to help you work around the command line as much as you can, and work with it when you have to.

Like the rest of the book, this chapter is written for someone who has used other Windows programs but has never used AutoCAD LT before, and also includes pointers and insights for experienced users who are upgrading to AutoCAD LT 2000. If you're new to AutoCAD LT or new to a Windows version, read this chapter carefully — while running AutoCAD LT if you can. Try things that are new or seem as though they may be confusing. An hour invested in poking around now can greatly improve your productivity later. And if you still aren't fully used to Windows, check out *Windows 95*

For Dummies, 2nd Edition, by Andy Rathbone; *Windows 98 For Dummies,* by Andy Rathbone, or *Windows NT 4 For Dummies,* by Andy Rathbone and Sharon Crawford (all published by IDG Books Worldwide, Inc.).

If you're experienced with Windows versions of AutoCAD LT, especially AutoCAD LT 98, most of this chapter is likely to be old hat for you. Just scan through it and read the parts marked with the AutoCAD LT 2000 icon, which indicates something truly new.

Commanding AutoCAD LT

Finding your way around AutoCAD LT 2000 can be an odd experience. You recognize from other Windows applications much of the appearance and workings of the program, such as its toolbars and pull-down menus, which you use for entering commands or changing system settings. But other aspects of the program's appearance — and some of the ways in which you work with it — are quite different from nearly any other program.

You can, in many cases, tell the program what to do in at least four ways — the menu bar, the command line, keyboard shortcuts, or right-click menus — none of which is necessarily the best method to use for all tasks. The experience is much like that of having to act as several different characters in a play; you're likely to forget your lines (or even who "you" are at the time!) at least every now and then.

To get started with AutoCAD LT 2000, focus on using the menus at the top of the screen. These menus enable you to access most of the program's functions and are the easiest–to–remember method of issuing commands. You can safely delay committing to memory the other, faster ways of making AutoCAD LT do your bidding until after you master these handy little menus.

Getting AutoCAD LT installed

Those grizzled AutoCAD and LT veterans we keep mentioning no doubt can curl your hair — if you still have all your hair, unlike one of the authors — with horror stories about days and weeks wasted trying to get old versions of AutoCAD and LT to work with plotters, tablets, and especially the thrice-cursed network. These days, the AutoCAD LT installation process is easier, is much better integrated with the Windows environment, and is fairly well documented in the "Installing LT 2000" chapter in the *Getting Started* book that comes with the product. We assume that you have AutoCAD LT installed and running already. If you are having trouble, the *Getting Started* book is your first resource.

Actually making things happen in the drawing area is a bit different, too. For instance, say you want to draw two rectangles, select them, and move them. The process of doing this is much more complex than in a regular draw or paint program. You'll find that you can start the rectangle command from a menu, from a toolbar button, or from the command line. You can continue it by drawing directly on-screen or by entering coordinates at the command line. No matter what, you must finish the command on the command line. See Chapter 5 for more on entering commands.

Then, in selecting the two rectangles, you don't click one, hold down the Shift key, and then click the other — at least, not if you're using AutoCAD LT the way it's set up when you first install it. Instead, every time you select something, it's added automatically to any existing selection; you hold down Shift to *remove* an item from a set of selected objects. And after you select an item, little boxes appear on it for you to grab, but don't expect to then just drag the item; AutoCAD LT has several different kinds of *grips* (the little boxes), and almost a half-dozen things you can do once you click them. See Chapter 6 for details.

We aren't trying to scare you by pointing out that many of your habits from using Windows and from other drawing or painting programs are not going to automatically carry you through in the AutoCAD LT environment. However, to learn AutoCAD LT you'll have to experiment, read this book, try some additional things, and read this book some more. And then unlearn your new, AutoCAD-specific habits when you go back to using Windows and other programs! The upside is that AutoCAD LT's way of doing things is very fast and powerful once you get used to it. But the learning curve can be some-what of a roller-coaster ride.

The extensive Help system in AutoCAD LT is another saving grace; expect to spend a great deal of time using it, especially if you don't like referring to the printed manual. Because the LT Help system uses a Web-based engine (vrooommm!), you may already know how to use it — or at least be able to quickly figure it out, using your existing Web knowledge to good advantage.

The AutoCAD LT 2000 Help system differs noticeably from the AutoCAD 2000 Help system. AutoCAD LT 2000 uses a Web-type help engine as opposed to the traditional WinHelp engine used by AutoCAD 2000 and many of the Windows applications you know and love (or at least tolerate). So using the Help system is one area where you can't share knowledge with your AutoCAD 2000-using friends. See the last section in this chapter for more on AutoCAD LT 2000 Help.

The Magnificent Seven

The starting screen for AutoCAD LT 2000 has seven parts, as shown in Figure 2-1. The screen displays all the elements found in other modern Windows programs, plus a few more. Make no mistake about it — this screen is busy. And that's even before you start using it!

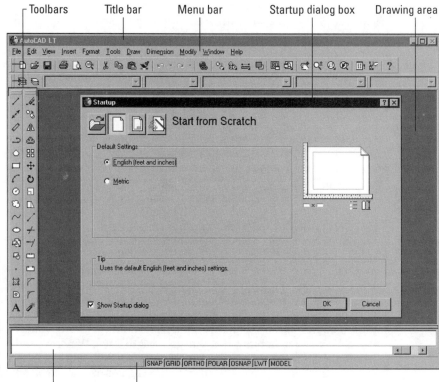

Toolbars   Title bar   Menu bar   Startup dialog box   Drawing area

Figure 2-1:
Starting
with seven
parts to the
AutoCAD LT
screen.

Command line area   Status bar

But don't worry; for now, you can just ignore that pesky command line and most of those enigmatic buttons. (Later, they become key to your productivity.) The most important elements you need in order to get started are the *title bar* and *menu bar* at the top of the screen, the *status bar* at the bottom, and the *Startup dialog box* and the *drawing area* in the middle. The buttons on the *toolbars* are accelerators that help you do your work faster after you master the basics. The *command line* gives you a lot of power and control in using AutoCAD LT's commands, at the expense of added keystrokes and complexity. All the pieces of the screen make sense — really, they do! — and this chapter gets you well on your way to understanding exactly what they all do.

The title bar — where everybody knows your (drawing's) name

Okay, so the title bar is where you go to order a royal coat of arms on the rocks, right? No, nothing so esoteric, we're afraid. The title bar is simply the little bar across the top of the screen that shows you the program's name (and, if you have a single drawing open and maximized, the drawing's name). This information is useful when you're running several programs simultaneously in Windows.

 Something new in AutoCAD LT 2000 is the ability to have multiple drawings open in a single session of LT — no, we're not kidding, even though this has been a standard feature of other programs for years. If you open more than one drawing, each one has its own menu bar with the drawing's name in it that takes up precious space in the overall AutoCAD LT window. The Window menu, also new in AutoCAD LT 2000, helps you manage multiple drawing windows at the same time.

 Don't click the X, or Close, button when you actually want to minimize the overall window. The X closes the program — but only after you get a helpful warning message asking if you want to save any changed files first. Click Cancel at this point to avoid leaving the program.

Bellying up to the menu bar

The *menu bar* contains the names of all the primary menus in your version of AutoCAD LT. The AutoCAD LT 2000 menu bar looks just like the menu bars in other Windows programs.

Figure 2-2 shows the menu bar for AutoCAD LT 2000 with the Draw menu open. If you spend a few minutes in AutoCAD LT 2000 touring the menus, opening dialog boxes, and so on, you quickly notice that AutoCAD LT 2000 makes considerable use of submenus and dialog boxes to expand your range of choices. (*Submenus* are menus you access from the primary menus at the top of the AutoCAD LT screen, not what you use to order your lunch at a sandwich shop.)

Getting started in the Startup dialog box

 The *Startup dialog box,* shown in Figure 2-3, is the first thing you see when you start AutoCAD LT without selecting a drawing. The dialog box appears when you start AutoCAD LT by double-clicking it; a similar dialog box called Create New Drawing appears when you are running LT and then choose File⇨New. (If you start AutoCAD LT by double-clicking a drawing, neither the Startup dialog box nor the Create New Drawing dialog box appears; LT just loads the drawing.)

 If you don't see the Startup dialog box when you start AutoCAD LT, someone turned it off. Turn it back on again by choosing Tools⇨Options⇨System and checking Show Startup Dialog.

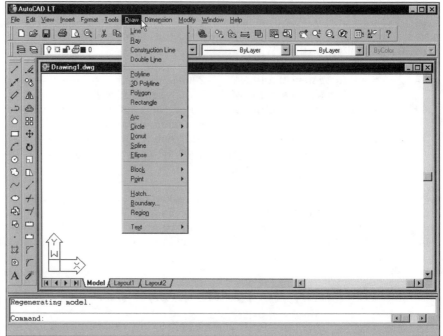

Figure 2-2:
Taking a
look in the
AutoCAD LT
menus.

Figure 2-3:
A close-up
view of the
Startup
dialog box.

Hot-wiring the menu bar

Some standard tips and tricks for Windows are especially useful in AutoCAD LT. Control-key shortcuts for the most popular functions — CTRL+S to save, CTRL+O to open a file, CTRL+P to print — work the same way in LT as in Microsoft programs. Use them! If all you glean from this book is to frequently press Ctrl+S to save, you've learned more than all-too-many other users.

Also worth using are the Alt+key shortcuts, which are available for all menu choices, not just the most popular ones. To fly around the menus, just press and hold the Alt key and then press the letters on your keyboard that correspond to the underlined letters on the menu bar and in the menu choices. Using the Alt key shortcuts this way can speed up your work.

As mentioned in the Introduction, we give the shortcut keys in this book whenever we mention an AutoCAD LT or Windows menu name and command name. The names are given in the right order for you to enter them from the keyboard. For example, to open a new drawing by using the File menu's New command, hold down the Alt key and then choose F, N for File⇨New. The Create New Drawing dialog box appears.

The Startup and Create New Drawing dialog boxes are there to help you create a new drawing that works the way you want — that is, a drawing that fits on the page, with text in proportion to the drawing, and that easily scales to larger or smaller paper. Unfortunately, these dialog boxes really don't help much. After you create a new drawing with either dialog box, you must perform additional drawing setup steps as described in Chapter 9. Alternatively, you can use a template that is already set up like the result that you want (also described in Chapter 9).

Drawing on the drawing area

Although the AutoCAD LT drawing area seems to just sit there, it's actually the program's most important and valuable piece of on-screen real estate. The drawing area is where the images you create in LT take shape. And the drawing area can actively help you do your work. If you do the correct drawing setup work, as described in Chapter 9, the drawing area can almost magically take on the dimensions and other characteristics you need to help you create the exact drawing you want. Two important configuration settings help determine the drawing area's effectiveness:

✔ **Limits:** The first key setting is the limits of the drawing you're working on. To draw a football field and football stadium, for example, you may set the limits at about 500 units (yards or meters) in the horizontal direction and 300 units (yards or meters) in the vertical direction. After you set these limits, the drawing area acts as a 500-×-300-unit grid into which you can place objects. (Footballs, hot dog vendors, and rabid fans excepted, of course.) Figure 2-4 shows an example.

✔ **Snap setting:** The second important setting for the drawing area is the snap setting, which causes the mouse pointer to gravitate to certain points on-screen. If you're working on your football stadium and set the snap setting to ten units, for example, you can easily draw end lines and sidelines that fall on 10-yard intervals. To draw in the seating area, however, you may want to set snap to a finer setting, such as one unit, or turn off snap altogether so that you can start your lines anywhere you want. No matter what changes you make, the point is to make the drawing area help you do your work.

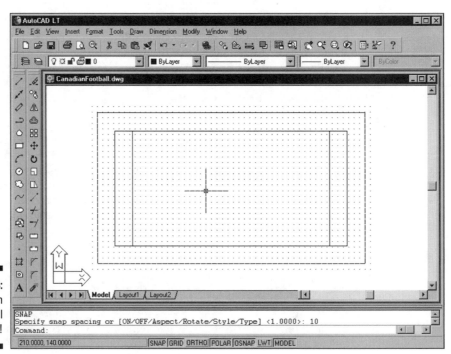

Figure 2-4:
Canadian
football
rules!

As you can see, you can make the drawing area work absolute wonders for your drawings — but only if you set up AutoCAD LT drawings correctly in the first place. If you don't configure these settings correctly, the drawing area can become really, really mad at you and may even fight back — with potentially devastating results to your drawings. Wrong settings can, for example, turn perfectly acceptable on-screen text into microscopic — and unreadable — ant tracks on paper. But don't freak out just yet: Valuable setup information awaits your discovery in Chapter 9 of this book.

Looking for Mr. Status Bar

The *status bar,* at the very bottom of the screen, tells you several important bits of information about the drawing you're working on, some of which may not make sense at first glance. These elements include the current *coordinates* of the mouse cursor; whether *snap, grid, ortho,* and *polar tracking* modes are on or off; whether running *object snaps* are on or off; whether *lineweights* are shown; and whether you're in *model space* or *paper space.* (What all these things mean is explained briefly in the next few paragraphs and in depth throughout the book.)

You can maximize the screen space available for AutoCAD LT and other programs by setting the Windows taskbar to auto-hide. Choose Start➪Settings➪ Taskbar to bring up the Taskbar Properties dialog box. In the Taskbar Options tab, click the Auto Hide option to put a check in the check box. Then click Apply. The taskbar will disappear; to bring it back, just move the mouse pointer down to the area formerly occupied by the taskbar. The taskbar will pop back up, ready to use.

Brand new in AutoCAD LT 2000 is the capability to reach settings dialog boxes for LT options by right-clicking the corresponding status bar button. This feature makes accessing important settings much easier and removes the need to remember command-line commands or menu locations for quickly changing them. This is just one example of how much easier the proliferation of right-click menus in AutoCAD LT 2000 makes learning and using LT.

Figure 2-5 pinpoints the buttons on the status bar. If you're new to the program, these areas bear some explanation. The following list does just that:

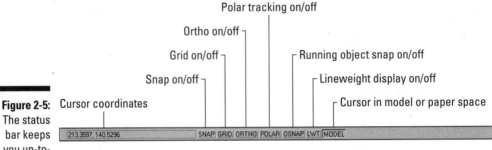

Polar tracking on/off

Ortho on/off ¬

Grid on/off ¬

Snap on/off ¬

Running object snap on/off

Lineweight display on/off

Figure 2-5: Cursor coordinates

Cursor in model or paper space

The status bar keeps you up-to-date.

213.3597, 140.5296   SNAP GRID ORTHO POLAR OSNAP LWT MODEL

✔ **Coordinates of the cursor:** The current *cursor coordinates* are extremely important in CAD (computer-aided design or drafting, as you may recall) because they relate the drawing to the real-world object or scene the drawing represents. The cursor coordinates aren't the coordinates on-screen or on paper; they're the real-world location of a point on or between objects. In a CAD drawing of a soft drink can, for example, the top of the can should be about 5 inches, or 12.5 centimeters, from the bottom of the can. After you set up your drawing correctly, the cursor coordinates on the status bar reflect the real-life dimensions of the object or scene you're drawing.

If you're new to AutoCAD LT, try rolling the cursor around the drawing area to watch the cursor coordinates update. (After that, you can go out and watch the grass grow for even more excitement!) If the coordinates don't change as you move the cursor around the drawing area, click in the coordinates area to turn on live coordinate read-out.

✔ **SNAP, GRID, and ORTHO mode buttons:** As described in Chapters 9 and 10, you can bring order to the AutoCAD LT drawing area in three ways: first, by telling it to *snap* the cursor to certain regularly spaced hot spots, enabling you to more easily draw objects a fixed distance apart; second, by making the drawing area display a *grid* of dots to align objects with; and third, by setting *Ortho* mode, which makes drawing straight horizontal and vertical lines easy. The SNAP, GRID, and ORTHO buttons appear to be "out" or "raised" if the mode is off, and "in" or "recessed" if the mode is on. Right-clicking the SNAP or GRID button and choosing Settings brings up the Snap and Grid tab of the Drafting Settings dialog box.

✔ **POLAR tracking mode button:** Polar tracking causes the cursor to "prefer" certain angles when you draw and edit objects. By default, the preferred angles are multiples of 90 degrees, but you can specify other angle increments. Clicking the POLAR button toggles polar tracking on or off. If you right-click the POLAR button and choose Settings, AutoCAD LT displays the Polar Tracking tab of the Drafting Settings dialog box, in which you can specify preferred angles and other polar tracking settings.

✔ **Running Object Snap (OSNAP) button:** A *running object snap* is a setting that causes the cursor to jump to specific locations on objects that you've drawn, such as corners and centers of shapes. This feature is nice to have turned on sometimes and a real pain to have on at other times. (For example, if you're trying to click a point near but not on a corner, and AutoCAD LT keeps jumping to the corner, you're going to get frustrated.) In AutoCAD LT 2000, you can easily set the features you want to pinpoint and then turn the whole set on or off by clicking the OSNAP button. This capability makes using running object snaps much more practical.

✔ **Lineweight (LWT) display mode button:** In AutoCAD LT 2000, you have the option of having LT display the *lineweight* of your lines — lines appear thicker on-screen if they're thick, thinner on-screen if they're thin. These lineweights also appear on printed drawings by default. However, having this option on makes updating the screen slower, and may make your drawing dense and hard to read. Turn it off if it bothers you. Right-clicking this button brings up a menu that opens a Lineweight Settings dialog box for setting lineweight display options.

✔ **MODEL/PAPER space:** Briefly, *model space* is where you create and modify objects; *paper space* enables you to arrange elements in your drawing for printout. A *layout* is a specific display on your model based on specific paper space settings. (Paper space has been in AutoCAD and AutoCAD LT for almost a decade, but layouts are a new embellishment of paper space in AutoCAD LT 2000.) Stick with model space until you master it; then turn to Chapter 9 for instructions on how to use paper space to create layouts — multiple views on the objects you've drawn. The MODEL/PAPER button indicates whether you're working in model or paper space. The default setting is MODEL. Right-clicking this button does *not* bring up a settings dialog box; see Chapters 4 and 9 for fuller descriptions — in excruciating detail — of these settings.

It's hard to tell whether the appearance of the different status bar buttons as either raised or depressed means "on" or "off." Depressed, or down, means on; raised, or up, means off. To quickly check, click the GRID button; its mode will change, and the change will be reflected on the command line — <Grid off>, for instance. Also, depending on the size of the grid setting and how far you're zoomed in, the grid may appear or disappear in your drawing. Click again to restore the previous on or off setting.

Better living with power toolbars

The most important elements in making AutoCAD LT 2000 do your bidding are the various *toolbars* that enable you to enter commands quickly and control how you draw, what you draw, and maybe even whether you're quick on the draw. In this section, we describe how to use toolbars in the default setup that's standard for AutoCAD LT, how to move the toolbars, and how to customize the toolbars.

All the AutoCAD LT 2000 toolbars provide *ToolTips,* an indispensable feature that identifies each button by its function . . . if you lean on it a bit. Simply hold the mouse pointer over a button — no need to click it — and, like magic, the name of the button appears in a little yellow box below the button. The ToolTip feature incorporates yet another component that can be easy to miss: A longer description of the button's function appears in the status bar, at the very bottom of the screen. (ToolTips work for status mode buttons, but the longer descriptions don't appear.) If the identifying name and the description at the bottom of the screen aren't enough to tell you what the button does, you can always bring in a little out-of-town muscle — in other words, look it up in the Help system, which is described in the section "Fun with F1," later in this chapter.

Figure 2-6 shows the ToolTip, tool description, and help for the Match Properties button on the Standard toolbar. The ToolTip identifies the button, and the tool description in the status bar gives a longer explanation of the button's function. If AutoCAD LT were to suddenly talk when you were stuck and say, "Button help!," it wouldn't be exaggerating much!

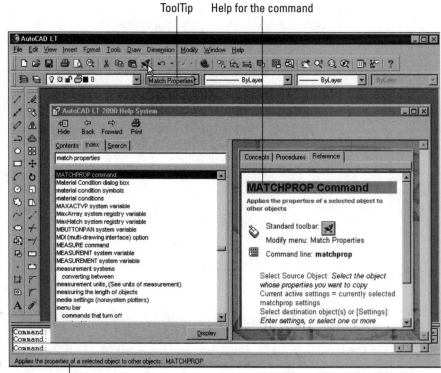

Figure 2-6:
You can get help from the ToolTip, the tool description, and the LT Help system for every AutoCAD LT toolbar button.

Use the AutoCAD LT 2000 menus as your first stop in getting to know the program. Then begin clicking buttons for the functions you use most and right-clicking for option settings. Finally, move on to the command line equivalents for the fastest power use.

AutoCAD LT ships with toolbars in a default setup:

- ✔ Standard toolbar on top, just below the menu bar
- ✔ Object Properties toolbar beneath the Standard toolbar
- ✔ Draw toolbar (vertical) on the far-left edge of the screen
- ✔ Modify toolbar vertically aligned just to the right of the Draw toolbar

The picture of the AutoCAD LT screen in Figure 2-1 back at the start of this chapter shows the default toolbar setup. You can drag the toolbars all over the place and, by right-clicking any toolbar, bring up a list of 18 toolbars you can turn on and off. Use Figure 2-1 for reference in case you change your toolbar setup and then want to go back to the original.

The Standard toolbar helps you quickly access a number of file management, drawing management, and view functions. Using the Standard toolbar enables you to perform common file operations by clicking the New, Save, and Open buttons, fix a mistake by clicking the Undo or Redo button, and move around in your drawing by clicking the Pan button or several useful Zoom buttons.

The Object Properties toolbar actually consists of several different elements lumped together. By using the drop-down lists that appear on the Object Properties toolbar, you can change the current layer and modify any layer's characteristics, change the colors used to draw objects, and change the line-type used to draw objects. You also can edit two characteristics that are new in AutoCAD LT 2000: lineweights and plot styles. Not only can you change the *current* settings for all these properties (that is, the properties LT applies to objects as you draw them), you can also select existing objects and change *their* properties with these drop-down lists. Although all these capabilities are highly desirable, the ways in which their functions differ can be highly confusing. (See Chapter 10 for more information.) The capability to change layers quickly, however, is well worth the price of admission by itself. (See the sidebar "Looking at layers" for a somewhat technical description of AutoCAD LT layers.)

The Draw toolbar roughly matches the functions available in the AutoCAD LT Draw menu. The Draw toolbar may be the one you use most when creating objects in a new drawing; it pulls together frequently used drawing functions into a single place. It gives you quick access to several kinds of lines, basic shapes, hatching, and text.

Looking at layers

In AutoCAD LT, a drawing consists of one or more *layers*. Layers are like slices across the complete object being created, each with its own specific kind of content. You can use layers to separate different kinds of geometry (electrical, plumbing, and so on) and to isolate documentary information such as text comments and dimensions. Layers are the most important organizational tool for your drawing, and knowing which layer you're currently working on is vitally important. The layer drop-down list on the Object Properties toolbar shows the names of all layers in the current drawing, along with icons (lightbulb, sun, snowflake, padlock, and the like) that indicate some settings for each layer. The initial layer in a drawing that hasn't yet had layers added to it is named *0* (zero).

Like the Draw toolbar, the Modify toolbar is patterned after its namesake, the Modify menu. In use, the Modify toolbar is the kissing cousin of the Draw toolbar and may be the toolbar you use most frequently when you edit an existing drawing. The Erase button is right at the top, followed by different options for creating new geometry from existing parts of the drawing and for adjusting lines and shapes that you have already added to the drawing.

The default toolbar setup is intended to expose as many of the frequently used commands in AutoCAD LT as possible in a convenient and easy-to-access yet unobtrusive format. Although you can move and even customize the toolbars, you may not want to; part of the value of the toolbars is that you become accustomed to clicking key buttons quickly and without conscious effort. If you move the toolbars and their buttons around, your muscle memory of where your most-used buttons are must be retrained each time.

The buttons in the default setup of the AutoCAD LT 2000 toolbars reflect some of the new and changed functions in this version of LT. For example, the Standard toolbar has a Properties button, for quick access to this new feature (see Chapter 10), and the Object Properties bar embodies new capabilities such as the ability to change displayed and printed lineweights.

Toolbars to the nth degree

You can easily move the toolbars around the screen — just grab a corner and drag. You can move toolbars into either a *docked* or a *floating* position. If you move a toolbar right up against any edge of the drawing area, it docks; otherwise it floats over the program window, getting in your way. If you need to access more (or fewer) toolbars, right-click any toolbar and turn toolbars on and off by clicking their names in the cursor menu that appears.

Commanding the command line

The *command line* is a unique feature of AutoCAD and AutoCAD LT and is probably the hardest for new users to get used to. Windows users who thought that they had escaped the dreaded DOS command line may be especially surprised to find a command line still lurking smack dab at the heart of AutoCAD LT. Yet the command line is actually a very handy tool for increasing speed and productivity in AutoCAD LT. Figure 2-7 shows the command line as it appears after you first open LT, skulking away down at the bottom of the screen, hoping you don't notice it below that big, open drawing area.

Figure 2-7:
The
AutoCAD LT
2000
command
line.

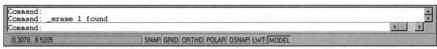

In the very early days of CAD, back in the '60s, CAD users used one text-only screen for communicating with the program; a second, graphics-only screen showed the results of the commands they entered. The command line is the direct descendant of the old command screen.

If you have an 800 x 600 screen or larger and like to use the command line, you can make the command line taller. If you have the Windows taskbar hidden, you can make the command line six lines rather than its normal three without obscuring any of the buttons in the default toolbar set. To make the command line bigger, just rest the mouse pointer over the top edge of the command line; the pointer turns into a vertical, two-headed arrow. Click the mouse button and hold, and then drag the top edge of the command line upward.

The major use of the command line for new users is to finish commands. When you draw a line, for instance, the line command just keeps going, asking you to draw more line segments; to terminate the line command, you need to look at the command line and know that you need to press Enter (or spacebar) to complete the command. As you get more experienced with AutoCAD LT, you may also want to start some commands from the command line as well as finish them there; it's quicker, once you know the commands, than using menus or toolbar buttons.

AutoCAD LT makes finding out how to use the command line fairly easy. After you choose a command from the menus, for example, LT echoes that command on the command line. Watch the command line as you use the menus and dialog boxes and memorize those commands that you use most — or write 'em down if you're a card-carrying member of the MTV generation (short attention span and all that, you know. . .). Then enter the command directly from the command line whenever you need to use that function swiftly.

In recent releases of AutoCAD and AutoCAD LT, along with making the strongest possible commitment to Windows, Autodesk has actually improved the command line. You can now use the arrow keys to move up in the list of commands that you have previously entered; each time you press the up-arrow key, another previously entered command appears. When the command you want is in your sights, edit it if needed and then press Return to execute it (so to speak). This function should further improve command-line productivity.

New with AutoCAD LT 2000, you can right-click the command line to bring up the six most recent commands and other useful options. Try it!

You can also bring up a large text window with command line contents in it. (You can panic really inexperienced AutoCAD and AutoCAD LT users by pulling this trick on their screens when they're not looking!) Just press F2 at any time and a large text window will appear, as shown in Figure 2-8; press F2 again and it will vanish.

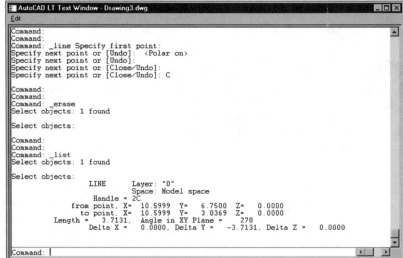

Figure 2-8:
The command line that ate Detroit.

Creature features

Two additional features of AutoCAD LT 2000 deserve mention in this tour; one is old, and the other is truly ancient. The *aerial view* is a pop-up window that gives you a bird's-eye view of your drawing that you can use to "drive" what appears in the drawing window. Most users now use real-time pan and zoom instead, as described in Chapter 5. But if you want to try the aerial view (it's most useful for very large, complex drawings), go to the menus and choose View⇨Aerial View (Alt+V+V). Or from the command line, enter **DSVIEWER** or **AV** to make the aerial view come and go.

The *screen menu*, or *side-screen menu*, is not even available in AutoCAD LT — but you may see it on an AutoCAD user's screen. The screen menu was a primitive menuing system used before AutoCAD had true menus like other Windows programs. Some users still turn it on in AutoCAD so they can run old utility programs that drive their commands through the screen menu. Because most such utilities don't run in AutoCAD LT, it would truly make no sense to have the screen menu as an AutoCAD LT 2000 feature.

What Really Makes AutoCAD LT Tick?

In reading about and using AutoCAD LT 2000, you encounter two topics frequently: *system variables,* which are very old, and *dialog boxes,* which in their current, highly usable forms are relatively new. System variables and dialog boxes are closely related, because they both affect the settings that control the way AutoCAD LT works. Understanding them and how they work together will dramatically speed your ascent to proficiency in LT.

Most modern Windows programs use dialog boxes very heavily; any place you see an item on a menu that ends in ellipses (three dots in a row. . .), that item leads to a dialog box. You'll see many dialog boxes described in detail in this book. There are two odd but cool things about dialog boxes in AutoCAD LT 2000: The first is that you can start dialog boxes from the command line. Just click the Help button in a dialog box to see how to start that dialog box from the command line. (Try entering **DSETTINGS** at the command line if you really want to experiment right now.)

The other cool thing about AutoCAD LT dialog boxes is that they aren't the only way to change program settings in the program. You can get right at these settings using *system variables*.

System variables are the settings that AutoCAD LT checks before it decides how to do something. If you set the system variable SAVETIME to 10, for example, LT automatically saves your drawing file every ten minutes; if you set SAVETIME to 60, the time between saves is one hour. Hundreds of system variables control the operations of AutoCAD LT.

Of these hundreds of system variables in AutoCAD LT, almost 70 system variables control dimensioning alone. (*Dimensioning* is the process of labeling objects with their lengths, angles, or special notes. Different professions have very different standards for how dimensions on their drawings should look. Using dimensions is described in detail in Chapter 13; triskaidekaphobics beware.)

To change the name of a system variable, just type its name at the AutoCAD LT command prompt. For instance, use the SAVETIME system variable to change the number of minutes between automatic saves.

The capability to change a system variable directly is powerful, and knowing the names and appropriate range of settings for a few key system variables that you use regularly may be worth the time and effort. But expecting you to remember hundreds of variables, how they work, and how they interact with one another is just too much — even for all you "power users" out there. This is where dialog boxes come in.

"Full" AutoCAD versus AutoCAD LT

You may already know that AutoCAD LT 2000 is nearly identical to AutoCAD 2000; but what, exactly, are you missing out on? Really not that much. The highlights of the differences (or lowlights, if you wish you had full AutoCAD):

✔ **Limited customizability.** AutoCAD LT 2000 lacks a whole bunch of programming interfaces that full AutoCAD has. This means a huge number of add-on programs for AutoCAD don't run on LT, from trivial helper programs to full architectural or mechanical drafting and design environments. If your colleagues or others in your profession use helper programs with AutoCAD that you can't use from LT, this is the single biggest negative for you about LT.

✔ **Limited 3D.** 3D is a very "sexy" feature, and yes, it's the wave of the future. However, 3D features are very time-consuming to run and require expertise to use effectively. In LT, you can view and edit 3D objects; you just can't create them. If you don't have well-understood, specific uses for 3D, you're probably almost as well off without it.

✔ **Raster disaster.** AutoCAD 2000 has a powerful IMAGE command for importing image files (Windows BMP files, GIF files, and so on). You can see such files in LT if they're in a DWG file you're working on, but you can't modify them much. No problem for most of the people, most of the time; a big problem if this is an important part of your work.

Surveys of AutoCAD users say that roughly half of them use add-on programs sparingly or not at all. The majority of such users also probably use either 3D or raster images on an occasional basis or never. Such users might as well be running AutoCAD LT and saving thousands of dollars.

The same surveys say that most "full" AutoCAD users run AutoCAD around 30 hours a week; most LT users, 15 hours or less. If you are an occasional user or don't need add-on programs, 3D, or raster features, LT is a great fit. But if you do need one of these missing features, consider upgrading to full AutoCAD.

Fun with F1

AutoCAD LT 2000 features a powerful Help system. It's different, though, from the Windows Help you may be familiar with in other Windows programs. The new Web-based help system is a lot like a Web browser for help. See Figure 2-9 for a look at this new Help system.

AutoCAD LT 2000 includes a full documentation set, accessible through the Help system. Click the Contents tab in Help to see the documents available, which include a guide to using the Help system, a *User's Guide,* and guides on customization, commands, system variables, and utilities. In addition to the online guides, LT has a help index and help search.

To use Help, press F1 at any point in the program, or click the Help button found in all dialog boxes. Help appears quickly. After you've acquainted yourself with the Contents tab, you can use the Index tab to look for topics or the Search tab to search for specific words.

You can figure out how to use AutoCAD LT's Help on your own, but the important thing is that you take the time to become familiar with its contents. You will become a much more effective AutoCAD LT user if you check Help regularly when you're stuck, somewhat confused, or simply curious.

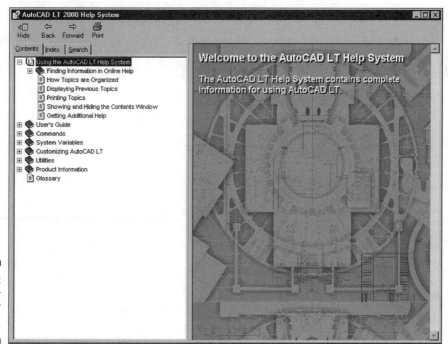

Figure 2-9:
Your
AutoCAD LT
SOS.

AutoCAD LT 2000 even goes beyond the bounds of the LT program and Windows to give you help. You can install a CD-ROM called *AutoCAD LT Learning Assistance* that comes with AutoCAD LT. You choose AutoCAD LT Learning Assistance from the AutoCAD LT 2000 Help menu, but it actually runs as a separate program. Also available from the Help menu is an Autodesk on the Web option. It links you to an Autodesk Web site with frequently updated help information about AutoCAD LT 2000.

Though linked, Help runs as a separate task from AutoCAD LT itself. Any time you use Help in AutoCAD LT 2000, you can keep Help open in the background and return directly to the main AutoCAD LT screen by pressing the Alt+Tab key combination to cycle through your currently running tasks.

If you have experience with earlier versions of AutoCAD or AutoCAD LT, the What's New feature of Help is pretty useful for becoming familiar with new features of the program. You can access this feature by choosing Help⇨What's New. Then select from the topics listed. Each topic describes the feature and provides a link to one or more relevant areas in the online documentation. Figure 2-10 shows the What's New page for the Lineweight topic.

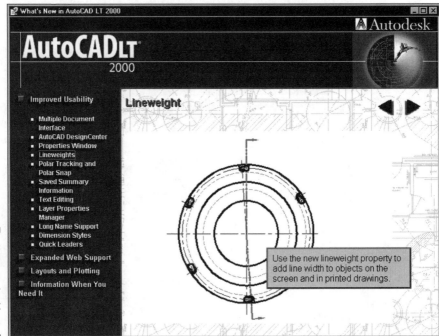

Figure 2-10: Get help throwing your (line)weight around.

Chapter 3

Learning to Drive

· ·

In This Chapter

▶ Setting up snappily

▶ Starting a drawing from scratch

▶ Setting snap and grid

▶ Setting the scale

▶ Drawing and inspecting home plate

· ·

*I*f you've never used AutoCAD LT before, you're in for a treat, and you're in for a shock. Kind of like eating those super-strong lemon drops — the ones that are wonderfully spicy but, when you first taste them, almost too strong to keep in your mouth. (Kids love to give these candies to adults and then watch them try to figure out what to do.)

AutoCAD LT 2000 is an extremely powerful program, and you can and will create wonderful results with it — either from scratch or through editing, commenting on, and printing others' work. When you're getting started, however, AutoCAD LT may be the most frustrating program that you will ever encounter. When you use a menu command to start drawing a line segment or arc, you then have to respond to prompts on the command line, of all places, to finish drawing the object. And when you finish by printing out your drawing, the results — unless you've set up the drawing very carefully — may be anywhere from odd to unusable.

This chapter is a quick introduction to using AutoCAD LT 2000 that quickly exposes you to the power and the pitfalls, for the new user, of this highly capable program. If you've ever used AutoCAD or AutoCAD LT before, you probably don't need to read through this chapter, though skimming it might be good review. But if LT is new to you, roll up your sleeves and plunge in. You'll become comfortable with the program faster than you can get the taste of one of those super lemon drops out of your mouth.

Making Setup a Snap

The easiest way to set up your drawing correctly is to use an existing drawing that's as similar as possible to the one you're going to create. That way, you do less wheel reinvention. This book goes into great detail about how to print, edit, and otherwise work with existing drawings (see Chapters 4 through 8).

However, at some point in your life, you just may, possibly, have to start a drawing from scratch. (Of course, this actually happens all the time.) Starting a drawing from scratch is easy and isn't likely to cause problems if you think about one factor right at the beginning: the *drawing scale factor*.

You see, in AutoCAD LT 2000 (and in all versions of AutoCAD), you don't draw images in the size that they're eventually going to be printed, then zoom in and out to add detail. You draw images in the size that matches their appearance in the real world. This approach gives you a great deal of control and precision.

However, working in real-world sizes does cause problems for things like text labels, which aren't really part of the objects you're putting in your image, but which have to be at a reasonable size so they're readable when you print out your drawing. And in general, whenever you print your drawing, you can have problems with it not translating well to a printout.

The drawing scale factor helps you solve this problem. The drawing scale factor is just the conversion factor between your drawing's size and its final printed size. If you're working at a scale of 1 cm = 1 m, the drawing scale factor is 100. If you're working at a scale of ¼ inch = 1 mile, the drawing scale factor is 253,440. You need to use the drawing scale factor to set up correct heights for text, hatching, and so on.

Chapter 4 has detailed background information about drawing scales and drawing scale factors; Chapter 9 summarizes how to choose a reasonable drawing scale. (Chapters 4 through 8 deal with existing drawings, which already have a drawing scale factor built into them.) If you're not accustomed to using a drawing scale factor, refer to Chapter 9 for more details.

Scratch where it itches

Starting a drawing from scratch seems simple at first, but actually is a challenge to do right in AutoCAD LT. Follow these steps to quickly make the initial decisions for your drawing:

1. **Start AutoCAD LT 2000.**

   The Startup dialog box appears. If the Startup dialog box does not appear, or if you're already running AutoCAD LT 2000, choose File⇨New.

2. **If it's not already chosen, click the Start from Scratch button.**

   The dialog box contents change to show Start from Scratch, as shown in Figure 3-1.

3. **Choose a units setting — English (the default of feet and inches) or Metric. Then click OK.**

   A new drawing window appears, titled `Drawing1.dwg` (or some number larger than 1, if this isn't the first drawing that you've created during this LT session).

4. **Click the Maximize box in the drawing window (not in AutoCAD LT 2000 itself).**

   This optional step makes the drawing window fill the available area, maximizing the space available for your drawing.

5. **Choose Format⇨Units.**

   The Drawing Units dialog box appears.

6. **Use the pull-down menu to choose the type of units. Click OK when done.**

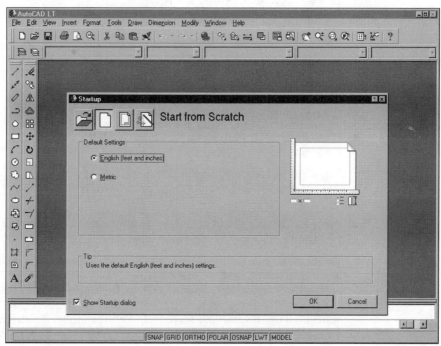

Figure 3-1:
Just Start
from
Scratch.

Your choices are

- **Architectural:** Feet and inches, with partial inches displayed as fractions

- **Engineering:** Feet and inches, with partial inches displayed as decimals

- **Decimal:** Unitless decimal numbers

- **Fractional:** Unitless numbers, with partial units displayed as fractions

- **Scientific:** Unitless powers of 10

See Table 3-1 for a quick look at how AutoCAD LT formats each type of unit.

In AutoCAD LT, *unitless* means that *you,* rather than LT, choose what a single unit means — millimeters, yards, fathoms, or whatever you like.

You can also set other options in this dialog box, such as the precision of unit display and the type of angular units, but in most cases the defaults are fine.

7. **Choose Format⇨Drawing Limits.**

   A prompt appears in the command line area:

   ```
   Reset Model space limits:
   Specify lower left corner or [ON/OFF] <0'-0",0'-0">:
   ```

   This is the infamous AutoCAD LT command line making an appearance. Usually, you want the lower-left corner of your drawing to be the 0,0 location, at least initially.

8. **Press Return for (0,0) or enter the lower-left corner coordinates you want.**

   A new prompt appears in the command line area:

   ```
   Specify upper right corner <12.0000,9.0000>:
   ```

9. **Press Return for (12,9) or enter the upper-right corner coordinates you want.**

   The default coordinates (12,9) correspond to a weird architectural paper size that almost no one uses and a 1 = 1 drawing scale that's pretty uncommon, too. Often, you'll set the upper-right limits coordinate to the X and Y dimensions of the paper that you'll eventually plot on, multiplied by the drawing scale factor. For example, if you want to create a 1 = 100 drawing (drawing scale factor = 100) on an 11-x-17-inch piece of paper in landscape mode, you would enter 1700,1100.

Table 3-1	Pick Your Units		
	Fractions	*Decimals*	*Exponents*
Feet and Inches	Architectural (0'–0 ¹⁄₁₆)	Engineering (0 ¹⁄₁₆)	N/A
Metric, Other	Fractional (0 ¹⁄₁₆)	Decimal (0.0000)	Scientific (0.0000E+01)

If you haven't yet selected a paper size or aren't sure whether your drawing will fit on a particular paper size, you'll need to block out your drawing (perhaps in a hand-drawn sketch), figure out the paper size and drawing scale, and then calculate the limits using the drawing scale factor. See Chapter 9 for details and a helpful table.

Setting the limits correctly is one of the good CAD habits that you should practice when using AutoCAD LT. With the limits set correctly, you can easily zoom to an overall view of your drawing (see the next section), manage your on-screen drawing so it prints well, and generally have an easier life. The settings in the next two sections also can make your life easier.

U got the look

After you have the drawing limits set correctly, as described in the previous section, you can take advantage of them to quickly zoom to an overall view of your drawing, and to set the snap and grid settings so they help you create an accurate drawing. The following steps quickly take you through setup information that we cover in more detail in Chapter 9:

1. **With your drawing open and limits set (as described in the previous set of steps), choose View⇨Zoom⇨All.**

   AutoCAD LT 2000 zooms to your drawing's limits.

2. **To set snap and grid settings, choose Tools⇨Drafting Settings. If the Snap and Grid tab is not selected, select it.**

   The Drafting Settings dialog box appears, with the Snap and Grid tab selected, as shown in Figure 3-2.

3. **Click the Grid On checkbox to set it, and set the Grid spacing to a reasonable distance.**

   The grid is a rectangular array of visible dots in your drawing. The grid can be very helpful for orienting you relative to the limits of your drawing and how tightly zoomed in (or loosely zoomed out) you are at any given time. You can use the grid spacing to set the grid to mark square inches on your printout, or to represent some reasonable interval within your drawing's geometry.

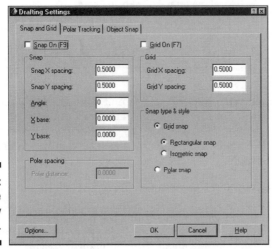

4. **If you want to have an additional, invisible grid of snappable points in your drawing, click the Snap On checkbox to set it, and set the snap spacing to a reasonable distance.**

   The snap grid is really nice if you're drawing objects that align to an even, rectangular array, but it can also give you too many things to snap to. Leave the snap grid off for now unless you're sure you need it.

5. **Click OK to close the Drafting Settings dialog box.**

Work for scale

One sign of true AutoCAD aficionados is their ability to do the little things up front that make work easier all the way through a project, and a good example of this kind of preparation is using the drawing scale factor to set the linetype scale and dimension scale. (In childhood, this was explained to one of the authors as the Five Ps — Prior Planning Prevents Poor Performance. In actual use, this expression is often made more colorful with additional letters representing unprintable words.) If you follow these steps, you will earn the admiration — or at least avoid the pity — of the AutoCAD masters among your coworkers:

1. **At the command line, type** LTScale.

   LTScale is the line type scale, which controls the spacing between dots and dashes in linetypes that are not continuous. Setting the linetype scale correctly prevents the dashes and dots from looking crammed together or too spaced out.

   A prompt appears in the command line area:

   ```
   Enter new linetype scale factor <1.0000>:
   ```

2. **Enter the drawing scale factor for the current drawing as the linetype scale.**

   For a drawing whose scale is 1 = 100, the drawing scale factor is 100.

3. **Choose Format⇨Dimension Style from the menu bar.**

   The Dimension Style Manager dialog box appears, with Standard as the default dimension style.

4. **Click the Modify button and then the Fit tab.**

5. **In the text box next to** Use overall scale of, **type the drawing scale factor for the current drawing.**

   This setting — the dimension scale or *dimscale* — controls the display and print size of dimensions.

6. **Click OK and then click Close.**

   Lines that you put in your drawing that are not continuous, and dimension text, will now look right when you print your drawing. Other programs try, with more or less success, to handle these kinds of settings for you; but AutoCAD and AutoCAD LT allow you direct control of the underlying settings. Though this makes for more initial setup, it also allows you to get excellent results when it comes time to print and use your drawing.

Get the Drawing Basics

Drawing in AutoCAD or AutoCAD LT is very powerful and significantly different from any other drawing program. The differences can seem like a hassle, but they are directly related to the powerful capabilities that differentiate AutoCAD and AutoCAD LT from other drawing programs.

This section steps you through drawing a simple shape. The remaining chapters of this book demonstrate the many cool things that you can do with simple *or* complicated objects, such as inspecting or changing properties, manipulating overall dimensions, dimensioning, and hatching.

If you follow the steps in this section to the letter, you will be drawing on Layer 0 of your drawing. This is okay for practice, but all "real" AutoCAD LT drawings use layers, as we describe in Chapter 10. In your "real" drawings, create layers and put the objects you create on them, not on Layer 0.

Safe at home

Follow these steps to draw a simple shape in AutoCAD LT: home plate of a baseball diamond. (You can see the official dimensions of a U.S. Major League Baseball home plate at www.majorleaguebaseball.com/u/baseball/mlbcom/headquarters/rules1.htm.) In the following steps, you draw the home plate at full scale (1 = 1, drawing scale factor = 1) for plotting on a 22-x-34-inch sheet:

1. **Open a new drawing in AutoCAD LT 2000. Use File⇨New or click the Start from Scratch button.**

   The Start from Scratch option of the Create New Drawing dialog box appears.

2. **Choose English (feet and inches) and click OK.**

   A blank drawing area appears.

3. **Set up the new drawing according to the instructions earlier in this chapter. Leave Type of Units set to Decimal, set 34,22 as the upper-right corner of the limits, set grid to one inch, and leave linetype scale and dimension scale set to their default values of 1. Then choose View⇨Zoom⇨All to display the full area defined by the new limits onscreen.**

4. **Click the Line button on the Draw toolbar.**

   A prompt appears:

   ```
   Specify first point:
   ```

5. **Enter 2,2.**

   Throughout this example, "Enter *something*" means "type *something* and then press the Enter key."

   You place the corner of home plate a little to the right and up from the bottom-left corner of the sheet.

   A prompt appears:

   ```
   Specify next point or [Undo]:
   ```

6. Enter @17,0.

A baseball home plate is 17 inches along its front edge. (You're using the unitless decimal type of units, and you set the base unit to one inch.) The @ sign indicates *relative* coordinates — that is, AutoCAD LT selects the point that's 17 units to the right and 0 units up from the previous point (2,2). For more on using coordinates in AutoCAD LT, see Chapter 10.

The prompt repeats:

```
Specify next point or [Undo]:
```

7. Enter @0,8.5.

A baseball home plate has short sides 8½ inches long at a right angle to the front edge, and 45-degree angled sides approximately 12 inches long that meet 17 inches from the middle of the front edge.

A prompt appears:

```
Specify next point or [Close/Undo]:
```

The prompt is different because the shape now has two sides. It's now possible to close the shape by typing C for Close.

8. Enter @-8.5,8.5.

The prompt repeats:

```
Specify next point or [Close/Undo]:
```

9. Enter @-8.5,-8.5.

The prompt repeats:

```
Specify next point or [Close/Undo]:
```

10. Enter C.

The shape closes and the command completes. The screen should look as it does in Figure 3-3.

You can choose <u>V</u>iew, <u>Z</u>oom, <u>E</u>xtents to make home plate fill the screen.

11. If you want to save your work, choose <u>F</u>ile⇨Save <u>A</u>s, enter a name (such as HomePlate.dwg) in the File <u>n</u>ame edit box, and click the <u>S</u>ave button.

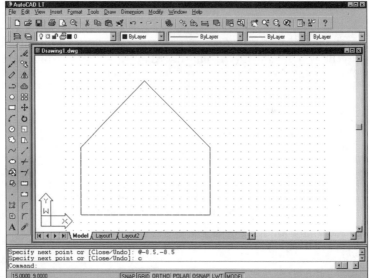

Figure 3-3:
Home, home
on the
plate . . .

Inspect the best

As we explain in much more detail later in this book, AutoCAD LT doesn't just create simple, geometrical objects. All objects have a number of interesting and useful properties, such as layer, color, linetype, and lineweight. For example, you can use the layer property to control the visibility and plot characteristics of a group of related objects. AutoCAD LT tracks these properties and lets you change them.

In the following steps, you check the properties for the baseball home plate that was created in the previous section. However, you can follow the same steps to check — and change — properties of the objects in any drawing:

1. Click an object in a drawing.

The object *ghosts* (that is, appears dashed) to indicate that it's selected, and boxes called *grips* appear on the object. Chapter 6 tells you more about grips.

2. Right-click anywhere in the drawing area.

A context-sensitive menu appears with options such as Rotate and Properties.

3. **Choose Properties.**

   The properties for the selected object appear, as shown in Figure 3-4. (The Properties window may appear in a different location on your screen.) Note that not only general properties such as color and layer appear, but also specific geometric properties such as the length of the selected line.

4. **Click another object.**

   The properties that are common to the selected objects appear. For instance, if the objects share the same color, the color appears; if they start at a different Y coordinate, though, the Start Y field is left blank.

For more on these topics, and additional topics such as dimensioning, see Part III of this book, starting with Chapter 9. Also, take the time to experiment while you're reading this chapter; it's easier to understand when you have time to do so, and then you'll have more skills in your bag of tricks when a deadline looms.

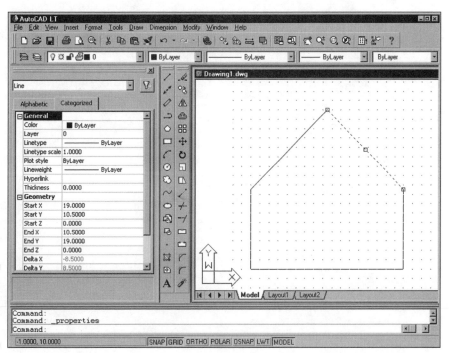

Figure 3-4:
Check the properties of a line.

Part II
Working with Existing Drawings

The 5th Wave   By Rich Tennant

"I COULDN'T SAY ANYTHING—THEY WERE IN HERE WITH THAT PROGRAM WE BOUGHT THEM THAT ENCOURAGES ARTISTIC EXPRESSION."

In this part . . .

Many AutoCAD LT users get started by plotting, reviewing, adding comments to, and making changes to existing drawings created by other users of AutoCAD or LT. This part shows you how to do those tasks with a minimum of preliminaries or extra fuss. This part also shows you how to use AutoCAD LT with other Windows programs and with the Internet. Whether your goal is to tap into drawings that others create or extend what you can do with your own drawings, this part will help you get there quicker and with fewer mishaps.

Chapter 4

Plotting: Waiting for Your Prints to Come In

- -

In This Chapter

▶ Plotting the simple way

▶ Plotting different paper layouts

▶ Plotting to scale

▶ Plotting lineweights and other fancy effects

▶ Plotting in color

▶ Troubleshooting plotting

- -

Despite the increasing number of offices with a computer (or two) on every desk, many people still need to or want to work with printed drawings. In fact, you might have purchased AutoCAD LT just so you could make your own hard-copy prints of drawings. Maybe you got tired of always depending on the CAD department people — or maybe the CAD manager threatened to harm you if you asked for "just one more check print"!

Perhaps you bought AutoCAD LT so you *wouldn't* have to rely on hard-copy versions of drawings, but could view them on-screen instead. Even if that's true, you might need to give hard-copy prints to your less savvy colleagues who don't have AutoCAD LT. You might want to make some quick prints to pore over during your bus ride home. You might find that checking drawings the old-fashioned way — with a hard-copy print and a red pencil — turns up errors that managed to remain hidden on the computer screen.

Whatever the reason, you'll want to print drawings at some point — probably sooner rather than later. Most CAD books and classes save plotting for late in the game, after you learn all about drawing and editing. We cover it first in this part of the book, because it's often one of the first things that people who work with existing drawings need to do. We take as a given that someone else has created some DWG files in AutoCAD or AutoCAD LT and sent them to you or made them available on the network. This chapter answers the question, "What do I do now?"

You Say Printing, I Say Plotting

Plotting originally meant creating hard-copy output on a device that was capable of printing on larger sheets, such as D size or E size, that measure several feet on a side. These plotters often used pens to draw, robot-fashion, on large sheets of vellum or mylar, which then could be run through *diazo blueline machines* — copying machines that create blueprints — in order to create less-expensive copies. *Printing* meant creating hard-copy output on ordinary printers — dot matrix or laser, in those days — that used ordinary sized paper, such as A size (letter size, 8½ x 11 inches) or B size (ledger size, 11 x 17 inches).

In early versions, AutoCAD had different software drivers and commands for plotting and printing. Nowadays, the PLOT and PRINT commands take you to the same dialog box, and AutoCAD LT 2000 makes no distinction between plotting and printing.

Now that you have the lingo down, you must face the unfortunate fact that plotting an AutoCAD LT drawing is considerably more complicated than printing a word processing document or a spreadsheet. CAD has a larger range of different plotters and printers, drawing types, and output procedures than most other computer applications do. AutoCAD LT 2000 tries to help you tame the vast jungle of plotting permutations, but you'll probably find that you have to take some time to get the lay of the land and clear a path to your desired hard-copy output. This chapter can help, and reading it is a lot less dangerous than swinging a machete around.

Plotting received a major facelift — and heart and brain transplants — in AutoCAD 2000 and AutoCAD LT 2000. The Plot dialog box and many plotting concepts differ completely from earlier versions. AutoCAD LT 2000 plotting is more flexible, powerful, and rational than plotting in previous versions. However, simple it is not.

Get with the system

One of the complications you face in your attempts to create hardcopy is that AutoCAD LT has two distinct ways of communicating with your plotters and printers. Operating systems, and the programs that run in them, use a special piece of software called a *printer driver* to format data for printing and then send it to the printer or plotter. When you configure Windows to recognize a new printer connected to your computer or your network, you're actually installing the printer's driver. ("Bring the Rolls around front, James. And bring me a gin and tonic and a D-size plot while you're at it.") AutoCAD LT, like other Windows programs, works with the printers you've configured in Windows. AutoCAD LT calls these *system printers* because they're part of the Windows system.

But AutoCAD LT, unlike other Windows programs, can't leave well enough alone. It turns out that some output devices, especially some larger plotters, aren't controlled very efficiently or very well by Windows system printer drivers. For that reason, AutoCAD LT comes with specialized *nonsystem drivers* (that is, drivers that are not installed as part of the Windows system) for plotters from companies such as Hewlett-Packard, Xerox, and Océ. These drivers are kind of like nonunion workers. They ignore the nice, tidy rules for communicating with Windows printers in order to get things done a bit more quickly and effectively.

Using already-configured Windows system printer drivers usually is easiest, and they work well with many devices — especially devices that print on smaller paper, such as laser and inkjet printers. However, if you have a large plotter, you may be able to get faster plotting, better plot quality, or more plot features by installing a nonsystem driver. Appendix A of the AutoCAD LT 2000 *Getting Started Guide* tells you how.

AutoCAD LT 2000 has a major exception to the old "nonsystem drivers give better results than system drivers" rule. HP plotters now work better with the new Windows system driver that Autodesk includes on the AutoCAD LT 2000 CD. For instructions on installing the new system printer driver, navigate to the \Windows System Drivers\HP folder on the CD, choose the subfolder corresponding to your language and operating system, and read the Readme.Txt file contained therein.

Configure it out

For now, you simply should make sure that AutoCAD LT recognizes the devices that you want to use for plotting. The following procedure shows you how:

1. **Launch AutoCAD LT and open an existing drawing or start a new, blank drawing.**

2. **Choose Tools⇨Options to open the Options dialog box, and click the Plotting tab.**

3. **Click the drop-down arrow to view the list just below the Use As Default Output Device option, as shown in Figure 4-1.**

   Notice that the list includes two kinds of devices, designated by two tiny, difficult-to-distinguish icons to the left of the device names. A little laser printer icon, with a sheet of white paper coming out the top, indicates a Windows system printer configuration. A little plotter icon, with a piece of paper coming out the front, indicates a nonsystem (that is, AutoCAD-specific) configuration.

The nonsystem configuration names always end in *pc3,* because they're stored in special AutoCAD Printer Configuration version 3 files. So, if you can't tell the difference between the icons, look for the *pc3* at the end of the name.

System printers   List of devices

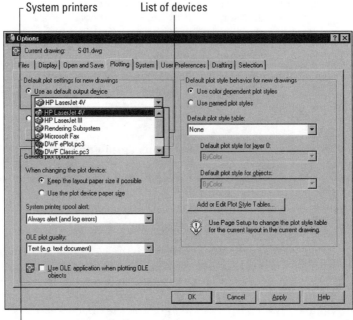

Figure 4-1:
System and
nonsystem
printers.

Nonsystem printers

4. **Verify that the list includes the printers and plotters that you want to have available in AutoCAD LT.**

    If not, choose Start➪Settings➪Printers, launch the Add Printer wizard, and follow the instructions. If your printer isn't in the default Windows list, cancel the wizard and hunt down a driver disk that came with your printer, or download the current driver from the printer manufacturer's Web site.

5. **Choose the output device that you want to make the default for new drawings.**

6. **Click OK to close the dialog box and retain any change that you made in the previous step.**

You use the AutoCAD LT 2000 Plotter Manager Add-A-Plotter wizard to create nonsystem driver configurations. This wizard is similar to the Windows Add Printer wizard, so if you can handle adding an ordinary printer in Windows, you probably can handle adding a nonsystem plotter configuration to AutoCAD LT 2000. When you complete the wizard steps, AutoCAD LT 2000 saves the information in a PC3 (Plot Configuration version 3) file. The wizard can import some settings from older AutoCAD LT 98 PC2 (version 2) and AutoCAD LT 95 PCP (version 1) files.

A Simple Plot

Okay, so you believe us. You know that you're not going to master AutoCAD LT 2000 plotting in five minutes. That doesn't change the fact that your boss, employee, wife, husband, construction foreman, or 11-year-old son is demanding a quick check plot of your drawing — and is sneering at you for not being able to do it.

The 18 steps to plotting success

Here's the quick, cut-to-the-chase procedure for plotting a simple drawing — a mere 18 steps! This procedure assumes that you plot in model space — that is, that the tab labeled Model at the bottom of the drawing area shows the drawing in a way that you want to plot. (We cover plotting paper space layout tabs later in this chapter.) This procedure doesn't deal with plotting to a specific scale, controlling plotted lineweights, or any of the other weird and wonderful options that you'll eventually have to grapple with (see the rest of this chapter for details). It should, however, result in a piece of paper that bears some vague resemblance to what AutoCAD LT displays on your computer monitor.

Many changes you make in the Plot dialog box also make hidden changes to plot settings in the drawing. If you're plotting someone else's drawing, and that someone else plans to use the drawing again in the future, make your own "plotting copy" of the DWG file. Fiddle around with the plot settings in your copy, so you don't mess up the drawing owner's plot settings.

Follow these steps to make a simple, not-to-scale plot of a drawing:

1. **Open the drawing in AutoCAD LT.**

2. **Click the Model tab at the bottom of the drawing area to ensure that you're plotting the model space contents.**

   We explain model space and paper space layouts in the section "Plotting the Layout of the Land," later in this chapter.

3. **Zoom to the drawing's current extents (choose View⇨Zoom⇨Extents) so you can verify the area you're going to plot.**

   A drawing's *extents* are the lower-left and upper-right corners of an imaginary rectangle that just surrounds all the objects in the drawing.

4. **To display the Plot dialog box, click the Plot button on the Standard toolbar.**

   The Plot dialog box appears, as shown in Figure 4-2.

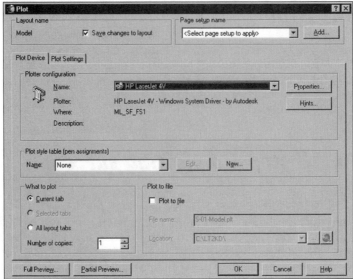

Figure 4-2:
The Plot
Device tab
in the Plot
dialog box.

5. **Make sure the Plot Device tab is selected.**

6. **In the Plotter Configuration area, select a device that you're used to printing to from other Windows applications.**

   For example, choose the laser or inkjet printer that you customarily use to print word processing documents. Stick to system printer devices (those that display the little printer icon next to their names). Avoid for now any nonsystem printer configurations (those whose names end in *pc3*).

7. **Set the remaining Plot Device settings as shown in Figure 4-2:**

   • Plot Style Table (Pen Assignments): None

   • What to Plot: Current Tab

   • Plot to File: Leave unchecked

8. **Click the Plot Settings tab, shown in Figure 4-3.**

9. **In the Paper Size And Paper Units area, select a paper size that's loaded in your printer.**

10. **In the Plot Area area (sponsored by the Department of Redundancy Department — with apologies to Monty Python), choose Extents.**

11. **In the Drawing Orientation area, choose either Portrait or Landscape.**

   If your drawing is longer than it is tall, such as a side view of a typical ranch house, choose Landscape; if your drawing is taller than it is long, such as a side view of a typical skyscraper, choose Portrait.

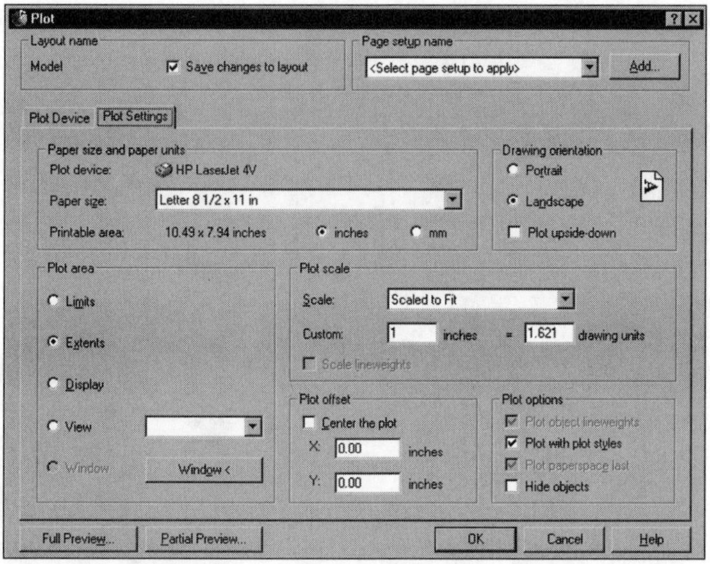

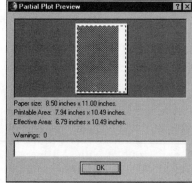

Figure 4-3:
The Plot
Settings tab
in the Plot
dialog box.

12. **In the Plot Scale area, choose Scaled to Fit from the Scale drop-down list.**

13. **Set the Plot Offset and Plot options settings as shown in Figure 4-3.**

14. **Click Partial Preview and check that the plot orientation and size fit the paper, as shown in Figure 4-4; then click OK to return to the Plot dialog box.**

Figure 4-4:
The partial
plot
preview.

15. **Click Full Preview and check that the entire drawing displays on the "paper," as shown in Figure 4-5; right-click and choose Exit to return to the Plot dialog box.**

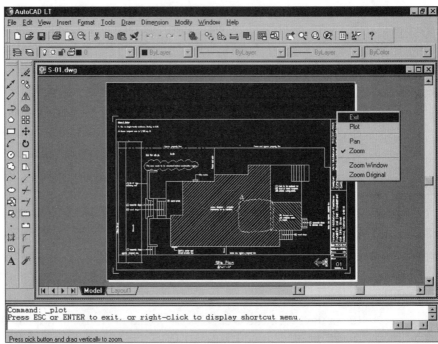

Figure 4-5:
The full plot
preview.

16. **If you found any problems with the partial or full plot previews, adjust the Plot Settings (for example, Drawing Orientation) and repeat the full preview until the plot looks right.**

17. **Make sure that Save Changes to Layout (in the Layout Name area at the top of the Plot dialog box) is turned on.**

     This option saves the plot setting changes you made, so they become the default the next time you plot this drawing.

18. **Click OK to create the plot.**

If for some reason your plot didn't work, well, we warned you that AutoCAD LT plotting was complicated and temperamental! Read the rest of this chapter for all the details about the numerous other plotting options that can cause plotting to go awry. If you're in a big hurry, turn directly to the troubleshooting section at the end of the chapter ("Troubles with Plotting").

Preview one, two

One of the keys to efficient plotting is liberal use AutoCAD LT's Partial Preview and Full Preview buttons, which are always available at the bottom of the Plot dialog box. (To maintain political fairness, we recommend conservative use of some other LT options elsewhere in the book.)

The partial preview is a quick reality check to make sure your plot fits on the paper and is turned in the right direction. AutoCAD LT 2000 displays the paper size, *printable area* (that is, paper size minus a small margin), and *effective area* (that is, the amount of space that your plotted drawing takes up). The paper size appears as a white sheet, the printable area as a dashed rectangle, and the effective area as a blue box. AutoCAD LT 2000 displays warnings such as the one shown in Figure 4-6 when it detects that something is wrong.

Figure 4-6:
A partial preview with warnings.

> Paper size: 8.50 inches x 11.00 inches.
> Printable Area: 7.94 inches x 10.49 inches.
> Effective Area: 7.86 inches x 10.49 inches.
> Warnings: 1
> Origin forced effective area off paper.

The full preview takes a bit longer to generate but shows exactly how your drawing lays out on the paper and how the various lineweights, colors, and other object plot properties will appear. You can zoom and pan around the preview by using the right-click menu, as shown previously in Figure 4-5. (Any zooming or panning that you do does not affect what area of the drawing gets plotted — zooming and panning is just a way to get a better look at different areas of the plot preview.)

You should get in the habit of doing a partial preview and then a full preview before each plot (especially if you've made any changes to plot settings). The partial preview ensures that you're in the ballpark and helps you fix drawing orientation or scale problems quickly. The full preview makes sure that you're in the right seat in the ballpark and gives you the best chance that your view of the game is just what you desire.

Plotting the Layout of the Land

In the previous section we show you how to plot the model space representation of your drawing by making sure that the Model tab is active when you open the Plot dialog box. In some drawings, you want to plot a paper space layout instead.

About paper space layouts

Layouts are an extension of the paper space concept from previous versions of AutoCAD LT. *Paper space* is a separate "space" for composing a printed version of your drawing. You create the drawing itself, called the *model,* in *model space.* No, this is not the alternate universe in which the *Sports Illustrated* swimsuit issue is created. To flesh out this analogy, model space is in the Bahamas; paper space is at your local newsstand.

AutoCAD LT 2000 allows more than one paper space *layout* per drawing and connects each layout with specific plot settings for that layout. Figure 4-7 shows a drawing in model space, and Figure 4-8 shows a paper space layout for plotting the same drawing with a title block.

We show you how to create paper space layouts in Chapter 9, but a summary of the process and concepts is in order here. A paper space layout begins life like a blank sheet of paper that covers your model and hides it from view. You create one or more *viewports* — like cutting a hole in the opaque piece of paper — to reveal the model "underneath." AutoCAD LT calls these openings *floating viewports* to distinguish them from the old-fashioned tiled viewports that are allowed in model space.

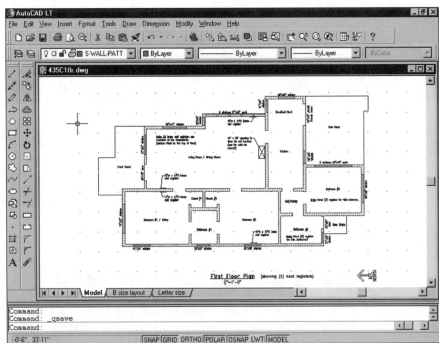

Figure 4-7:
Model
space.

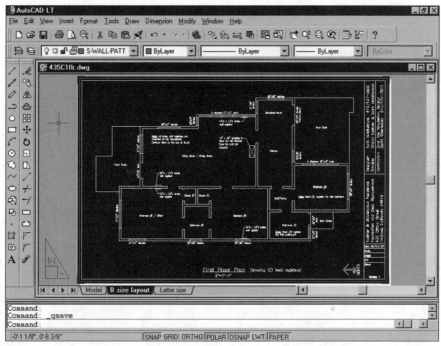

Figure 4-8:
A paper
space
layout.

Some users of AutoCAD LT versions before AutoCAD LT 2000 embraced paper space for all their drawings, some used it selectively, and many ignored it completely. With AutoCAD 2000 and AutoCAD LT 2000, Autodesk hopes to make paper space layouts the standard operating procedure for all (or at least most) drawings.

Whether you should plot model space or a paper space layout in an existing drawing depends entirely on how the creator of the drawing set it up. You can ask the creator, or you can do some investigation of your own to figure it out.

Five more steps to (paper space) plotting success

After someone has created a paper space layout in a drawing, plotting it is pretty much like plotting model space, except that you need to find the appropriate paper space layout and make sure that the MODEL / PAPER button on the status bar says PAPER:

1. **Open a drawing that contains, or that you suspect contains, a paper space layout.**

   If you don't have any paper space drawings handy, you can use one of the AutoCAD LT sample drawings, such as the architectural floor plan drawing stored in \Program Files\AutoCAD LT 2000\Sample\Home Floor Plan.DWG.

   The presence of a Layout1 tab next to the Model tab at the bottom of the drawing area doesn't necessarily mean that the drawing contains an already set up paper space layout. AutoCAD LT 2000 always displays a Layout1 tab when you open a drawing created in an earlier version of AutoCAD or AutoCAD LT, and displays a Layout1 and Layout2 tab when you open a drawing created in AutoCAD 2000 or AutoCAD LT 2000.

2. **Click the first tab to the right of the Model tab at the bottom of the drawing area (usually named Layout1).**

   AutoCAD and AutoCAD LT give the default names Layout1 and Layout2 to layouts, but the creator of the drawing may have renamed them to something more descriptive.

   Don't confuse the Model tab at the bottom of the drawing area with the MODEL / PAPER button on the status bar. The tabs control which view of the drawing (model space or a paper space layout) fills the drawing area. When a paper space layout fills the drawing area, the status bar button controls whether drawing, editing, and plotting take place in paper space or model space inside a viewport.

3. **If the Page Setup dialog box appears, click Cancel, and when the dialog box disappears, click the Undo button on the Standard toolbar to return to model space.**

   You guessed wrong — the current drawing doesn't contain a paper space setup! The Page Setup dialog box is AutoCAD LT's way of saying, "This paper space layout hasn't been set up yet; what do you want me to do?" We tell you what to do in Chapter 9. For now, skip the next step and plot model space instead.

   If the Page Setup dialog box doesn't appear, but instead you see a view of your drawing similar to Figure 4-8 (shown previously), you've found an already set up layout and you can continue with this set of instructions.

4. **Make sure that the MODEL / PAPER button on the status bar says** PAPER. **If it says** MODEL, **click it to change it to** PAPER.

   This step ensures that you're plotting the entire contents of the paper space layout, rather than just the model contents of a particular viewport.

5. **Jump to Step 3 in the section "The 18 steps to plotting success," earlier in this chapter.**

   From this point, the simple plotting procedure for a paper space layout is the same as for model space.

Fancy Plots

In previous sections of this chapter we help you gain some plotting confidence. Those sections show you how to create simple plots with a laser or inkjet printer on smaller sheets such as 8½-x-11 and 11-x-17-inch paper. Those skills may be all you need, but if you care about plotting drawings at a specific scale, controlling plotted lineweights and colors, or adding special effects such as screening (plotting shades of gray), then read on.

Scaling: To fit or not to fit?

Plotting a drawing scaled to fit, as we describe in "The 18 steps to plotting success" and "Five more steps to (paper space) plotting success," earlier in this chapter, works fine for some situations. But many kinds of technical drawings are created to be plotted at a specific scale, so people viewing a hard-copy version can measure distances with a special kind of ruler called, appropriately enough, a *scale*. (I'll bet you were afraid something fishy was going on here.)

A traditional architectural or engineering scale is triangular in cross section and about a foot long (no, it's not used for measuring hot dogs). It resembles a triangular prism, with three rectangular faces — one corresponding to each of the sides of the triangle. Each rectangular face has two long sides, and each of these sides is divided into gradations corresponding to a different drawing scale. It's like having six rulers in one, but with each ruler stretched or squeezed by a different amount.

Even if you work with drawings that are created to be plotted at a specific scale, plotting scaled to fit often is the most efficient way to make a reduced-size check plot. For example, drafters in your office might create drawings that get plotted on D size sheets (24 x 36 inch), while you have access to a laser printer with a B size (11 x 17 inch) paper tray. By plotting the D size drawings scaled to fit on B size paper, you end up with check plots that are slightly smaller than half size (¹¹⁄₂₄ size, to be exact). You won't be able to measure distances on the check plots with a scale, but you probably will be able to check them for overall correctness.

Drawing scale versus the drawing scale factor

CAD users employ two different ways of talking about a drawing's intended plot scale:

✔ *Drawing scale* is the traditional way of describing a scale — "traditional" in that it existed long before CAD came to be. Drawing scales are expressed with an equal sign or colon; for example 1=8 1:0, 1=20, or 2:1. Translate the equal sign or colon as "corresponds to." In all cases, the measurement to the left of the equal sign or colon indicates a paper measurement, and the number to the right indicates a CAD drawing and real-world measurement. In other words, the architectural scale 1=8 1:0 means "⅛ inch on the plotted drawing corresponds to 1 foot – 0 inches in the CAD drawing and in the real world," assuming that the plot was made at the proper scale.

✔ *Drawing scale factor* is a single number that represents a multiplier, such as 96, 20, or 0.5. The drawing scale factor for a drawing is the conversion factor between a measurement on the plot and a measurement in a CAD drawing and the real world.

Those of you who did your math homework in junior high will realize that drawing scale and drawing scale factor are two interchangeable ways of describing the same relationship. The drawing scale factor is the multiplier that changes the first number in the drawing scale into the second number.

Figuring out a drawing's scale

Before you can plot a drawing to scale, you have to determine what the drawing's scale is. In some cases, making the determination is trivial, while in other cases it's tricky indeed. Here are some methods you can use:

✔ Ask the creator of the drawing.

This is usually the most direct way to determine the plot scale, unless of course the person who created the drawing doesn't return your phone calls, or you don't know who that person is!

✔ Look for text or a scale bar on the drawing that indicates the scale.

Many drawings contain a piece of text or a graphical symbol that indicates the drawing's proper scale.

Some possibility exists that the drawing shows the wrong scale. Perhaps the drawing's creator changed the scale, but not the text or symbol, during the drawing process. Or maybe someone created a new, differently scaled drawing from an older one and forgot to update the scale text. Use the other methods here to double-check the scale if you're not sure.

✔ Use a scale to measure distances on the plotted drawing.

If you were lucky enough to receive a hard-copy version of the drawing, and you suspect that it was plotted at the proper scale, then lay your scale down on an object whose size you know. By trying different sides of the scale, you'll often come up with a match.

✔ Check the DIMSCALE system variable setting.

For reasons that we explain in Chapters 9 and 13, the DIMSCALE system variable often is set to the drawing scale factor. You can inspect the DIM-SCALE setting by typing **DIMSCALE** and then pressing Enter at the AutoCAD LT command prompt. You'll see the current setting displayed in angled brackets like so:

```
Enter new value for DIMSCALE <96>:
```

Don't change the value; just make a note of it and press Esc to leave the setting as it is.

The DIMSCALE method isn't infallible. For various reasons, it isn't always set to the drawing scale factor. But it might confirm or call into question a hypothesis based on the other methods.

If you're going to plot a paper space layout, as we describe in "Plotting the Layout of the Land," earlier in this chapter, we have good news: You don't need to know the drawing scale or drawing scale factor! One of the big advantages of paper space is that it's normally used to create a plot layout whose plot scale is 1:1 — hence the name *paper* space. (The drawing in model space still has a normal drawing scale factor, such as 10 or 96, but the paper space layout gets set up with a drawing scale factor of 1.) Nonetheless, it's useful to know how to determine the model space drawing scale factor, because you need it when you draw certain kinds of objects, such as text, dimensions, and hatching (see Chapters 12, 13, and 14).

The 12-step plotting-to-scale program

Okay, so you understand all about drawing scales and drawing scale factors, and you've done enough sleuthing to determine the intended plot scale of the drawing you want to plot. The following steps show you how to plot to scale. Refer to "The 18 steps to plotting success" and "Five more steps to (paper space) plotting success," earlier in this chapter, if you need help with the details.

1. **Open the drawing in AutoCAD LT.**

2. **Click the tab that you want to plot — the Model tab or the desired paper space layout tab.**

   If you're plotting a paper space layout, make sure that the MODEL / PAPER button is set to PAPER.

3. **If you're plotting the model space tab, zoom to the drawing's current extents (choose View⇨Zoom⇨Extents) so you can verify the area that you're going to plot.**

4. **To display the Plot dialog box, click the Plot button on the Standard toolbar.**

5. **In the Plotter Configuration area on the Plot Device tab, select a device that's capable of plotting on the paper size you need.**

6. **In the Paper Size and Paper Units area on the Plot Settings tab, select the appropriate paper size.**

   Of course, you must make sure that the paper size is large enough to fit the drawing at its proper scale. For example, if you want to plot a D-size drawing, but you have only a B-size printer, you're out of luck — unless you resort to multiple pieces of paper and lots of tape.

7. **In the Plot Area section, choose Extents if you're plotting the model space tab, or Layout if you're plotting a paper space layout tab.**

   For plotting model space, the Limits or Window setting sometimes is a better choice than Extents. See "The Plot Settings tab" section, later in this chapter, for more information.

8. **In the Drawing Orientation area, choose either Portrait or Landscape.**

9. **In the Plot Scale area, choose the appropriate setting from the Scale list.**

   If you're plotting model space, choose a common scale from the list, as shown in Figure 4-9, or choose Custom and type a custom plot scale in the two edit boxes below the Scale list. If you're plotting paper space, choose 1:1 from the Scale list.

10. **View a partial preview and then a full preview, as described in the section "Preview one, two," earlier in this chapter.**

11. **If the plot previews turn up any problems, adjust the plot settings and repeat the previews until the plot looks right.**

12. **Click OK to create the plot.**

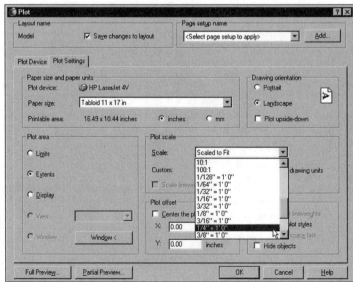

Figure 4-9:
Plotting to scale.

If you select the appropriate plot scale and then find out that the plot is too big for your plotter's largest paper size, you can revert to scaled to fit, instead. But if you're plotting paper space and have specified Layout as the plot area, you probably won't get the results that you expect. The person who sets up a paper space layout chooses a specific paper size (see Chapter 9 for details). If you later change to a different paper size in the Plot dialog box, Scaled to Fit refers to the original paper size, not to the new size that you chose. You can work around the problem by changing Plot Area from Layout to Extents. Alternatively, you can fix the problem if you want to have a paper space layout that permanently reflects a new paper size. Use the Page Setup dialog box to modify the layout settings, or copy the layout and modify the new layout.

It's common in many industries to create half-size plots for some purposes. To plot a paper space layout half-size, specify a plot scale of 1:2. For model space, double the drawing scale factor. For example, a ⅛ inch = 1 foot – 0 inch drawing has a drawing scale factor of 96, which is equivalent to a plot scale of 1=96. To make a half-size model space plot of it, specify a plot scale of 1=192.

Plotting with style

Plot styles are a brand-new AutoCAD LT 2000 feature, and they come in two exciting flavors: color-based plot styles and named plot styles. Plot styles provide a way to override object properties with alternative plot properties. (See Chapter 10 for information about object properties.) The properties include plotted lineweight, plotted color, and screening (plotting shades of gray). Figure 4-10 shows the full range of options. Color-based plot styles are based on the standard way of plotting in previous versions of AutoCAD and AutoCAD LT, while named plot styles provide a new way.

The good news is that, in some cases, you won't need to bother with plot styles. If the drawings you want to plot have layer and object properties (especially lineweight) that reflect how you want objects to plot, you can dispense with plot styles. The bad news is that most drawings created with previous versions of AutoCAD and AutoCAD LT will require plot styles in order to plot correctly. Also, most experienced users who upgrade to AutoCAD 2000 or AutoCAD LT 2000 are likely to use plot styles. Thus, unless you work completely alone and don't exchange drawings with other people, you'll have to deal with plot styles at some point.

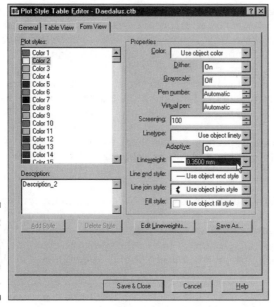

Figure 4-10:
Editing a
color-based
plot style
table.

The most common reason for using plot styles is to map screen colors to plotted lineweights. If this idea seems completely loony to you, try to suspend judgment until you've read the "Plotting through thick and thin" section, a bit later in this chapter.

The second-most common reason for using plot styles is to create *screened* lines on monochrome plots. Lines that are screened display in various shades of gray, rather than in black. Drafters sometimes use screened lines to de-emphasize secondary objects that otherwise would overwhelm the main objects in the drawing. Screening is expressed as a percentage, with 100% being completely black and 0% being invisible.

Using plot styles

If you want objects in your drawing to plot with properties that differ from their display properties, you need plot styles. For example, you might want to plot with different lineweights or colors from the ones you're using for display purposes. Or, as we mention in the preceding section, you might need to map display colors to plotted lineweights. AutoCAD LT 2000 groups plot styles into plot style tables, each of which is stored in a separate file.

Color-based plot style tables live in Color TaBle (CTB) files and they map the 255 AutoCAD LT display colors to 255 plot styles. AutoCAD LT 2000 automatically attaches the color-based plot styles to every object, based on — you guessed it — the object's color. (Are those AutoCAD LT programmers brilliant, or what?) Color-based plot style tables are especially handy for mimicking the old color-mapped-to-lineweight plotting approach of earlier AutoCAD LT releases.

Named plot style tables live in Style TaBle (STB) files. After you've created a named plot style table, you create one or more plot styles and give them any names you like. Then you can assign the named plot styles to layers or to individual objects. (See Chapter 10 for more information about object and layer properties.)

Named refers to the plot styles, not to the tables. Both color-based plot style *tables* and named plot style *tables* have names, but color-based plot *styles* don't have names and named plot *styles* do have names.

To use a plot style table, and its included plot styles (whether they're color-based or named), you must attach it to model space or a paper space layout. The plot style table then affects plotting only for that tab. This approach lets you plot the same drawing in different ways by attaching different plot styles to different tabs. (This is one of the many ways in which AutoCAD LT gives you great flexibility at some expense in additional complexity.)

You can attach a plot style to model space or a paper space layout by selecting its tab at the bottom of the drawing area, opening the Plot dialog box, and choosing the plot style table name in the Plot Style Table (Pen Assignments) area on the Plot Device tab. See "Controlling plotted lineweights with screen colors," later in this chapter, for an example.

The Plotting tab on the Options dialog box contains a setting called Default Plot Style Behavior for New Drawings. When you start a new drawing, the current value of this setting (Use Color Dependent Plot Styles or Use Named Plot Styles) determines whether you can choose CTB or STB files. The AutoCAD LT 2000 default setting is Use Color-Dependent Plot Styles. Unfortunately, changing this setting in the Options dialog box does *not* change the setting for the current drawing. If you want to change from color-based plot styles to named plot styles (or vice versa), use the CONVERTPSTYLES command.

Creating plot styles

If you're really lucky, you won't need to use plot styles. If you're somewhat lucky, you'll need to use plot styles, but someone will provide the plot style table files for you. If that's the case, you must put the CTB or STB files in the \Program Files\AutoCAD LT 2000\Plot Styles folder in order for AutoCAD LT to recognize them.

If you're not lucky at all, you'll get to create your own plot style table files. Here's how:

1. **Choose File➪Plot Style Manager.**

   The \Program Files\AutoCAD LT 2000\Plot Styles folder opens in a separate window.

2. **Double-click the Add-A-Plot Style Table Wizard program shortcut.**

3. **Read the opening screen and then click Next.**

4. **Choose the Start from Scratch option, or one of the other three options if you want to start with settings from another file. Then click Next.**

   The remaining steps in this procedure assume that you chose Start from Scratch. If you chose another option, simply follow the wizard's prompts.

   If the creator of a drawing provides you with an AutoCAD R14/LT 98 PC2 (version 2) or AutoCAD R12/LT 95 PCP (version 1) file, choose the Use a PCP or PC2 File option. With this option, the wizard will import color-to-plotted-lineweight settings automatically.

5. **Choose whether you want to create a color-based plot style table (CTB file) or a named plot style table (STB file). Then click Next.**

   Choose Color-Dependent Plot Style Table if you need to map screen colors to plotted lineweights.

6. **Type a name for the new CTB or STB file and then click Next.**

7. **Click the Plot Style Table Editor button.**

   The Plot Style Table Editor dialog box opens (refer to Figure 4-10).

8. **If you created a color-based plot style table, assign Lineweight, Screening, or other plot properties to each color that's used in the drawing. If you created a named plot style table, click the Add Style button and then assign plot properties to each of the named styles that you create.**

   To determine which colors are used in a drawing, switch to the AutoCAD window and open the Layer Properties Manager dialog box by clicking the Layers button located on the Object Properties toolbar.

   To change a setting for all colors or named styles, select all of them first by clicking the first color or named style, holding down the Shift key, and then clicking the last color or named style. Any subsequent changes you make get applied to all of the selected colors or named styles.

9. **Click the Save & Close button to close the Plot Style Table Editor dialog box. Then click Finish to complete the steps for the wizard.**

   The \Program Files\AutoCAD LT 2000\Plot Styles folder now displays your new CTB or STB file.

10. **Close the \Program Files\AutoCAD LT 2000\Plot Styles folder by clicking the X in its title bar.**

Creating your first plot style table can be a harrowing experience, because you have so many options. Just remember that your most likely reason for creating one is to map screen colors to plotted lineweights (as described in greater detail in the next section). Also remember that you might be able to minimize your effort by getting a PCP, PC2, or even CTB file from the person who created the drawing that you want to plot.

Plotting through thick and thin

Long ago, manual drafters developed the practice of drawing lines of different thicknesses, or *lineweights,* in order to distinguish different kinds of objects. Manual drafters did it with different technical ink pen nib diameters or with different hardnesses of pencil lead and varying degrees of pressure on the pencil. Since a computer mouse usually doesn't come with different diameters of mouse balls or a pressure-sensitive button, AutoCAD and AutoCAD LT's developers had to figure out how to let users indicate lineweights onscreen and on a plot. They came up with two different ways to indicate lineweight: mapping on-screen colors to plotted lineweights, and, new in AutoCAD LT 2000, displaying lineweights on-screen to match what the user can expect to see on the plot.

About colors and lineweights

AutoCAD drafters have traditionally achieved different printed lineweights by mapping the on-screen display colors of drawing objects to plotted lineweights. For example, a particular AutoCAD-using company might decide that red lines are to be plotted thin, green lines are to be plotted thicker, and so on. This indirect approach sounds pretty strange, but until AutoCAD 2000, it was the only practical way to plot from AutoCAD or AutoCAD LT with a variety of lineweights. Also, not many people plotted in color until recently, so few folks minded the fact that color was used to serve a different master.

AutoCAD LT 2000 offers lineweight as an inherent property of objects and the layers that they live on. (Or see Chapter 5 for an introduction to layers.) Thus, object display color can revert to being used for — surprise! — color. You can use display colors to control plot colors, of course. But even if you make monochrome plots, you can use color to help you distinguish different kinds of objects when you view them on-screen, or to make compelling on-screen presentations of drawings for others.

Although AutoCAD LT 2000 lineweights may have been assigned to objects in a drawing that you open, you won't necessarily see them on the screen. You must turn on the Show/Hide Lineweight button on the AutoCAD status bar (the button labeled LWT). Also, you may need to zoom in on a portion of the drawing before the differing lineweights become apparent.

Plotting with plodders

Color-as-color and lineweight-as-lineweight seem like great ideas, but Autodesk recognized that long-time users of AutoCAD and AutoCAD LT aren't going to abandon the old colors-mapped-to-lineweights approach overnight. Thus, you can still control plotted lineweight by display color in AutoCAD LT 2000.

Companies that have been using AutoCAD forever — at least, it seems like forever to some of us! — may choose to stick with their Old Way for some time to come. Or, they may be forced to stick with the Old Way by third-party applications that don't fully support lineweights and by the need to exchange drawings with clients and

subcontractors who haven't upgraded. In summary, the ripple effect of those who need to or want to continue using colors-mapped-to-lineweights is likely to last a long time. Don't be surprised if you find yourself going with the flow for awhile.

The default setting in AutoCAD LT 2000 is to plot object lineweights, so that's the easiest method if you don't have to consider the historical practices or predilections of other people with whom you exchange drawings. Mapping screen colors to lineweights requires some initial work on your part, but after you've set up the mapping scheme, the additional effort is minimal.

Controlling plotted lineweights with object lineweights

Plotting object lineweights is trivial, assuming that the person who created the drawing took the trouble to assign lineweights to layers or objects (see Chapter 10 for details). Just make sure that the Plot Object Lineweights setting in the Plot Options area is turned on, as shown in Figure 4-11. You might also want to turn off the Plot With Plot Styles setting, because plot styles can override the object lineweights with different plotted lineweights.

As long as you turn on the Plot Object Lineweights setting, you'll find that (those who hate cheap puns, read no further!) "the plot thickens!"

 If you *don't* want to plot the lineweights assigned to objects, you must turn off both the Plot Object Lineweights and Plot with Plot Styles settings in the Plot Options area of the Plot dialog box. Turning on Plot with Plot Styles turns on Plot Object Lineweights as well.

Controlling plotted lineweights with screen colors

To map screen colors to plotted lineweights, you need a color-base plot style table (CTB file), as we describe in the section "Plotting with style," earlier in this chapter. If you're plotting a drawing created by someone else, that someone else might be able to supply you with the appropriate CTB file, or at least with a PCP or PC2 file from which you can create the CTB file quickly. At the very least, the creator of the drawing should be able to give you a printed chart showing which plotted lineweight you should assign to each AutoCAD screen color. Use the instructions in the "Plotting with style" section to copy or create the required CTB file.

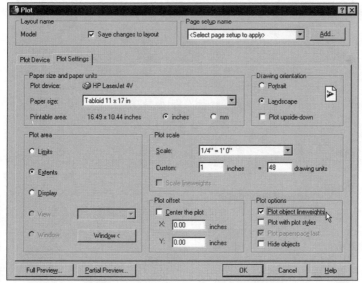

Figure 4-11:
Plotting
object
lineweights.

Unfortunately, no industry-wide standards exist for mapping screen colors to plotted lineweights. Different offices do it differently. That's why it's so useful to receive a CTB, PCP, or PC2 file with drawings that someone sends you.

After you have the appropriate CTB file stored in the \Program Files\ AutoCAD LT 2000\Plot Styles folder, follow these steps to use it:

1. **Click the tab that you want to plot — the Model tab or the desired paper space layout tab.**

2. **Open the Plot dialog box by clicking the Plot button on the Standard toolbar.**

3. **In the Plot Style Table (Pen Assignments) area on the Plot Device tab, select the CTB file from the Name list, as shown in Figure 4-12.**

   This action "attaches" the plot style table (CTB file) to the tab that you selected in Step 1. Assuming that you save the drawing after plotting, AutoCAD LT will use the CTB that you selected as the default plot style when you plot that tab in the future.

4. **Jump to Step 5 in the section "The 12-step plotting-to-scale program," earlier in this chapter and complete the plotting steps listed there.**

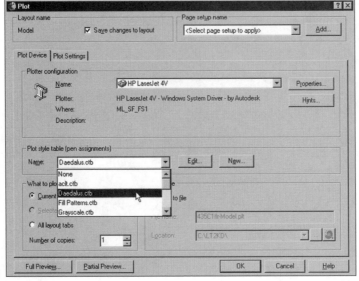

Figure 4-12:
Selecting a
plot style
table that
maps
screen
colors to
plotted
lineweights.

Plotting in color

There's no special trick to plotting the colors that you see on the screen. In
the absence of a plot style table (that is, if you set Plot Style Table (Pen
Assignments) to None in the Plot dialog box), AutoCAD LT sends color information as it appears on the screen to the plotter. As long as your output
device can plot in color, what you see should be what you get.

If you attach a plot style table to the tab that you're plotting (as described in
the previous section), you can — if you really want to — map screen colors
to different plotted colors. Mapping colors to other colors sounds even
loonier than mapping colors to lineweights. Do yourself a favor: If you use
plot style tables, leave the Color property set to Use Object Color.

If your goal is *not* to plot color, you may need to turn off an AutoCAD LT 2000
plotting option called *dithering*. If you try to plot colors on a monochrome
device, you may find that objects appear in various shades of gray, like in a
newspaper photograph, with lighter colors mapped to lighter shades of gray
and darker colors to darker shades of gray. (We assume that you read one of
those buttoned-down, respectable newspapers like the *Wall Street Journal*
that doesn't pander to the masses with color photos and ads. See, we told
you that we'd give equal time to conservatives!) This process of mapping
colors to shades of gray is called *monochrome dithering*, and it usually is *not*
what you want in a CAD drawing. To override it, use the Plot Style Table
Editor, as we describe in the section "Creating plot styles," earlier in this

chapter, to set the <u>D</u>ither option for all colors to Off. (The default setting is On.) If you don't already have a plot style table that you want to use, choose Monochrome.CTB, which comes with AutoCAD LT.

To see the full range of AutoCAD colors available on your plotter, or to see how a particular plot style table affects plotting, plot \Program Files\ AutoCAD LT 2000\Sample\Chroma.DWG. Chroma.DWG contains color swatches for all 255 AutoCAD colors.

When in doubt, send it out

Whether you plot to scale or not, with different lineweights or not, in color or not, you should consider using a service bureau for some of your plotting. In-house plotting on your office's output devices is great for small check plots on faster laser or inkjet printers. Large format plotting, on the other hand, can be slow and time-consuming. If you need to plot lots of drawings, you might find yourself spending an afternoon loading paper, replenishing ink cartridges, and trimming sheets.

Good plotting service bureaus have big, fast, expensive plotters that you can only dream about owning. Also, *they're* responsible for babysitting those fancy devices, feeding them, and fixing them. As a bonus, service bureaus can make blueline prints from your plots, if you need to distribute hard-copy sets to other people.

The only downside is that you need to coordinate with a service bureau to make sure it gets what it needs from you and can deliver the kinds of plots you need. Some service bureaus plot directly from your DWG files, while others ask you to make PLT (plot) files. Some service bureaus specialize in color plotting, while others are more comfortable with monochrome plotting and making blueline copies.

When you're choosing a service bureau, look for one that traditionally has served drafters, architects, and engineers. These service bureaus tend to be more knowledgeable about AutoCAD, and they should have more plotting expertise than the desktop publishing, printing, and copying shops.

Whomever you choose, do some test plots well before the day when that important set of drawings is due. Talk to the plotting people and get a copy of their plotting instructions. Have the service bureau create some plots of a couple of your typical drawings and make sure they look the way you want them to.

If you do lots of plotting with a service bureau, look into whether you can charge it to your clients as an expense (just like bluelines or copying).

And the Plot Goes On

In previous sections of this chapter, we cover most of the important options in the Plot dialog box. However, we still need to tell you about a few more fine points that will make your plotting life easier.

Use the Plot dialog box's "quick help" to find out more about any part of the dialog box: Click the double arrow next to the Help button to display a help panel to the right of the Plot dialog box. Then point to the part of the dialog box that's confusing you. If the pop-up help isn't enough, click the Help button at the bottom of the dialog box.

If your display resolution is 800 x 600 (as in the figures in this chapter), then the Plot dialog doesn't display the quick help double arrow. Instead, you can click the question mark in the Plot dialog box's title bar and then click the part of the dialog box that's confusing you.

Getting up close and personal with the Plot dialog box

The Plot dialog box segregates the many plotting choices into four groups (see Figure 4-13):

- ✔ Choices that concern the device you're plotting to (Plot Device)
- ✔ Choices that concern the paper you want to plot on and how to transfer the drawing onto that piece of paper (Plot Settings)
- ✔ Two choices for previewing a plot before you take the final, fateful step of sending it to the printer (Full Preview and Partial Preview)
- ✔ Choices that enable you to save your other plot choices (Layout Name for saving your choices as the default for the current layout, and Page Setup Name for saving your choices to a specific name that you can retrieve later)

In the following sections, we take you on a guided tour of three of these groups. (We discuss the Full and Partial Preview options in the section "Preview one, two," earlier in this chapter.) We don't cover every minute, obscure, useful-only-at-cocktail-party-discussions detail. We point out what's important, steer you away from what's less important, and guide you over the bumpy spots.

The Plot Device tab

In Hollywood, a *plot device* is a way to move the story forward. In AutoCAD LT, a *plot device* is a way to move your drawing closer to its happy conclusion on paper, vellum, or mylar.

The Plot Device tab choices are supposed to concern the device you're plotting to, but in fact they're a grab bag of things that didn't fit on the Plot Settings tab. When you click the Plot Device tab in the Plot dialog box, you see the following options, as shown in Figure 4-13:

- ✔ **Plotter Configuration:** As we describe in the section "Configure it out," earlier in this chapter, you use the Name list to select the Windows system printer or nonsystem driver configuration that you want to use for plotting.

  Use the Properties button to change media (type of paper) and other properties that are unique to the currently selected plotter or printer. In particular, you can define custom paper sizes.

- ✔ **Plot Style Table (Pen Assignments):** Choose a plot style table file. (See the section "Plotting with style" earlier in this chapter for details.)

- ✔ **What to Plot:** Specify whether to plot only the currently selected tab (Model or a paper space layout) or all drawing editor tabs. Also specify the number of copies.

- ✔ **Plot to File:** If you need to plot to a file rather than directly to your plotter or network printer queue, turn on this option and specify the file name and folder (Location).

  This option is especially useful when you want to use the ePlot feature to publish a DWF file on a Web site. (See Chapter 8 for details about using DWF files.) You also might need to create files to send to a plotting service bureau.

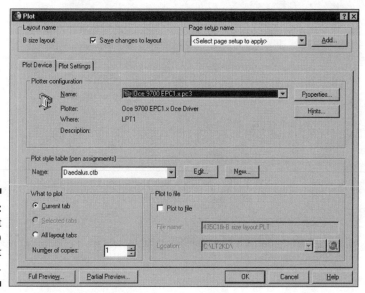

Figure 4-13:
The Plot Device tab in the Plot dialog box.

The Plot Settings tab

When you click the Plot Settings tab in the Plot dialog box, you see the following options, as shown in Figure 4-14:

- ✔ **Paper Size and Paper Units:** Specify a paper size, based on the choices provided by the device you selected on the Plot Device tab.

  AutoCAD LT displays the Printable area, which is a bit smaller than the actual paper size because most plotters and printers can't plot all the way to the edge of the paper; they need a small margin.

- ✔ **Drawing Orientation:** Specify whether AutoCAD LT should put the drawing on the paper in portrait or landscape orientation. Turn on Plot Upside-Down if you want to rotate the plot 180 degrees on the paper (a handy option for plotting in the southern hemisphere, or for avoiding having to cock your head at an uncomfortable angle as you watch plots come out of the plotter).

  If you're confused about whether Portrait or Landscape is the right choice, a quick detour through Full Preview will un-confuse you fast.

- ✔ **Plot Area:** Specify the area of the drawing to plot. Your choices include Extents, Display, View, and Window, regardless of whether you're plotting a paper space layout or the model space tab. In addition, your first choice is Layout for a paper space layout tab, or Limits for the model space tab.

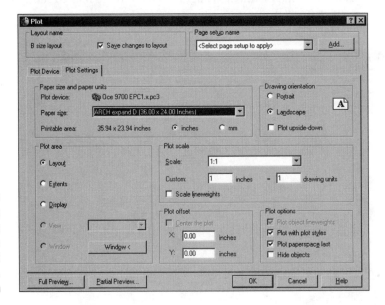

Figure 4-14:
The Plot Settings tab in the Plot dialog box.

Extents means the rectangular area containing all the objects in the drawing. *Display* means the drawing as it's currently displayed in the drawing window (including any white space around the drawing objects). *View* means a named view, which you select from the drop-down list. *Window* means a rectangular area that you specify by clicking the Window button.

Usually, you'll choose to plot layout in paper space. For model space, the choice depends on whether the drawing was set up properly and what you want to plot. If you set limits properly, as we suggest in Chapter 9, then plot limits in order to get the whole drawing area. If you're trying to plot a drawing in which the limits weren't set properly, try Extents instead. Use Window or View if you want to plot just a portion of model space.

✔ **Plot Scale:** As we describe in the section "The 12-step plotting-to-scale program," earlier in this chapter, select a plot scale from the drop-down list, or specify a Custom scale in the Inches (or millimeters) = Drawing Units text boxes.

When plotting a paper space layout onto the paper size for which the layout was created, 1:1 is the usual plot scale. Use smaller scales to do check plots on smaller sheets of paper (for example, 1:2 to create a half-size plot). Scaled to Fit is handy for squeezing a model space plot onto a piece of paper of any size. To plot model space at a specific scale, enter that scale in the Custom text boxes.

If you're plotting a paper space layout at a scale other than 1:1, you might want to turn on the Scale Lineweights option. For example, if you do a half-size check plot (plot scale = 1:2), turning on Scale Lineweights reduces the lineweights by 50 percent.

✔ **Plot Offset:** A plot offset of X=0 and Y=0 positions the plot at the lower-left corner of the plottable area. Enter nonzero numbers or turn on the Center the Plot option if you want to move the plot from this default position on the paper.

✔ **Plot Options:** The Plot Object Lineweights option and the Plot with Plot Styles option control whether AutoCAD LT uses the features that we describe in the "Plotting with style" and "Plotting through thick and thin" sections earlier in this chapter.

It's a (page) setup!

Page setups specify the plotter, paper size, and other plot settings that you use to plot a particular drawing. AutoCAD LT 2000 maintains separate page setups for model space and for each paper space model layout (that is, for each tab you see in the drawing area). AutoCAD LT 2000 remembers the last page setup settings you used to plot each tab, and it also lets you save page setups so you can re-use them later. Page setups are stored with each drawing, but you can copy them from one drawing to another.

If your plotting needs are simple, you don't need to do anything special with page setups. Just make sure the Save Changes to Layout setting at the top of the Plot dialog box is left on, so any plotting changes you make are saved with the tab you're plotting.

If you want to get fancier, you can create named page setups in order to plot the same layout (or the model tab) in different ways, or to copy plot settings from one drawing to another. Use the Add button to create a named page setup from the current plot settings.

You can use the PAGESETUP command to modify the current plot settings without plotting. PAGESETUP opens the Page Setup dialog box, which is really just the Plot dialog box in disguise; it just omits the What to Plot and Plot to File areas on the Plot Device tab (see Figure 4-15). Changes you make become the default plot settings for the current drawing tab.

The easiest way to run PAGESETUP is to right-click a paper space layout or model space tab and choose Page Setup from the cursor menu that appears.

The Page Setup dialog box, unlike the Plot dialog box, lets you save plot settings changes without plotting and without having to create a page setup name.

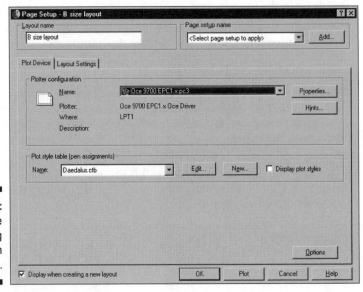

Figure 4-15: The Page Setup dialog box: Plot in disguise.

The Grand Unified Plot Procedure Integration

Physicists have — or would like to have — their Grand Unified Theory (GUT). We lowly CADicists will have to make do with a Grand Unified Plot Procedure Integration (GUPPI). The following set of steps summarizes all the material in this chapter. Refer to the individual sections earlier in the chapter for more details about each step:

1. **Open the drawing in AutoCAD LT.**

2. **Click the tab that you want to plot — the Model tab or the desired paper space layout tab.**

    If you're plotting a paper space layout, make sure that the MODEL / PAPER button is set to PAPER.

3. **Open the Plot dialog box by clicking the Plot button on the Standard toolbar.**

4. **In the Plotter Configuration area on the Plot Device tab, select a device that's capable of plotting on the paper size that you need.**

5. **If you want to use plot styles, select a plot style table name from the Name list in the Plot Style Table (Pen Assignments) area on the Plot Device tab. Otherwise, choose None.**

    Choose a CTB plot style table if you need to map screen colors to plotted lineweights.

6. **In the Paper Size and Paper Units area on the Plot Settings tab, select the appropriate paper size.**

7. **In the Plot Area section, choose the area that you want to plot.**

    Layout is the usual choice when plotting paper space. Limits, Extents, or Window are common choices when plotting model space.

8. **In the Drawing Orientation area, choose either Portrait or Landscape.**

9. **In the Plot Scale area, choose the appropriate setting from the plot Scale list.**

    When plotting paper space, 1:1 is the official, approved choice. Determine the appropriate model space plot scale using the guidelines in the "Scaling: To fit or not to fit?" section, earlier in this chapter. If you're confused, try Scaled to Fit.

10. **View a partial preview and then a full preview.**

11. **If the plot previews turned up any problems, adjust the Plot Settings and repeat the previews until the plot looks right.**

12. **Click OK to create the plot.**

Troubles with Plotting

No matter how many times you read this chapter or how carefully you study the AutoCAD LT documentation, you'll occasionally run into plotting problems. You're especially likely to encounter problems when trying to plot other people's drawings, because you don't always know what plotting conventions they had in mind. Table 4-1 describes some of the more common plotting problems and solutions.

Table 4-1	Plotting Problems and Solutions
Problem	*Possible Solution*
Nothing comes out of the plotter (system printer driver).	Check whether you can print to the device from other Windows applications. If not, then it's not an AutoCAD problem — try the Windows Print Troubleshooter (Start⇨Help⇨Contents⇨Troubleshooting).
Nothing comes out of the plotter (nonsystem printer driver).	Choose File⇨Plotter Manager, double-click the plotter configuration, and check the settings.
Objects don't plot the way they appear on-screen.	Check for a plot style table with weird settings, or try plotting without a plot style table.
Objects appear ghosted or with washed-out colors.	In the plot style table, set Dither to Off for all colors.
Scaled to Fit doesn't work right in paper space.	Change the plot area from Layout to Extents.

Chapter 5

Drawing 101: Mark-Up Methods

● ●

In This Chapter

▶ Zooming and panning in a drawing

▶ Making your own layer for mark-up comments

▶ Adding notes to a drawing

▶ Modifying your notes

▶ Drawing leaders with attached notes

▶ Highlighting areas with a cloud

▶ Doing simple line drawings

▶ Drawing with precision

● ●

Drawing objects with a CAD program is a complicated business — much more so than with a drawing program or an illustration program. The complexity comes from the nature of drafting, which usually requires the placement of objects using precise locations and distances. If you use an illustration program to draw a house for a brochure, as long as your sketch looks pretty much like a house, you've succeeded. If you use a CAD program to draw the plans for building a house, you need to be much more finicky about the placement and appearance of every line, arc, and squiggle.

Why is this? In an illustration, you're trying to evoke an image in the viewer's mind — tapping into existing knowledge with carefully chosen indications of what's present. Cartoonists who can represent a famous person with a few squiggles depend on this effect. But in CAD, you are trying to communicate precisely a specific plan for a part, building, or other object. If the viewer guesses anything, problems result. So, CAD requires a much higher level of care.

Most AutoCAD books introduce you to drawing by first covering all the tools and techniques for precision drafting: typing coordinates and distances, picking points with object snaps, manipulating object properties, and more. These topics are essential if you need to do full-blown drafting — and we cover them in Chapter 10. But many AutoCAD LT users aren't trying to become drafters — or not at first, anyway. Some people want to start by adding comments and simple, cartoon-like sketching to drawings created by others, as shown in Figure 5-1. After looking at these additions, a drafter can make the necessary changes to the drawing so that it communicates precisely what's needed. This process is called *marking up* a drawing, and it's traditionally been done on hard-copy plots with a red pencil or felt-tip pen.

In this chapter, we explain just enough so that you'll be able to mark up drawings in AutoCAD LT. (One of the authors wanted the next chapter to cover *budding up* a drawing, but we worried what might happen if hasty readers tried pouring beer on their plotters.)

Computer people who've never done a day of drafting in their lives usually refer to marking up a drawing as "red-lining." Those of you who were — or are — teenage car nuts know that *red-lining* describes the dangerous, irresponsible, and thoroughly delicious practice of pushing your car's engine so hard that the tachometer needle approaches the red zone. Far be it from us to co-opt such a descriptive term and apply it to drawing little red lines.

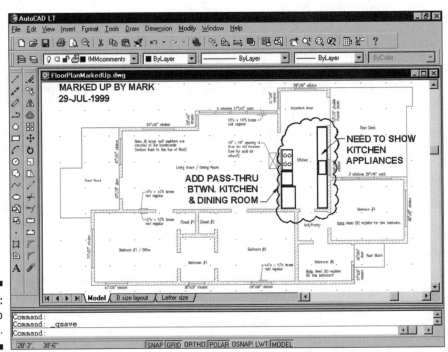

Figure 5-1:
A marked up drawing.

If you're a manager in a company that employs full-time drafters, markups may be all the CAD drawing that you need to do. If you're an engineer or architect, you might mark up drawings created by the more experienced CAD staff and occasionally get dragged into making last-minute additions and changes at crunch-time. Or, as CEO, project manager, staff engineer, drafter, secretary, and errand boy or girl for MegaHomeOffice Industries, you might be eager to get right to precision drafting. Whatever your station or inclination, this chapter serves as your gentle introduction to AutoCAD LT drawing tools and techniques. When you're ready for the detailed tour, Chapter 10 awaits you.

How to Zoom-Zoom-Zoom on Your Room-Room-Room

Unfortunately, computer monitors are smaller than the large D-size or E-size sheets on which many CAD drawings are plotted. To compensate for this discrepancy, AutoCAD LT includes a way to zoom in or out on the drawing and pan around it. Although zooming came about as the answer to limited monitor sizes, in some situations, it also can provide a big advantage over manual drafting. You can do detailed work on tiny little objects and then zoom out and move around rooms, houses, or neighborhoods from an Olympian perspective.

If you've ever used a video camera or watched one those oh-so-artsy films in which camera technique takes precedence over the story, then you'll be familiar with zooming and panning. Moving your viewpoint in to get a closer look at part of your drawing data is called *zooming in;* moving your viewpoint back to get a more expansive view is called *zooming out.* If you zoom in enough that some of your drawing no longer shows up on-screen, you're going to want to *pan* around — move left, right, up, and down in your drawing — without zooming in and out.

AutoCAD LT offers several approaches to zooming and panning, but the easiest and most flexible one is called *real-time* zooming and panning. The following steps demonstrate how to zoom and pan for the purposes of inspecting a drawing or in anticipation of marking up parts of it:

1. **Open a drawing that you want to inspect. Click the Model tab at the bottom of the drawing area to ensure that you're zooming and panning the model space contents.**

   If you don't have a drawing of your own handy, you can use the Foundation Plan.DWG sample drawing that comes with AutoCAD LT 2000. (Look in the \Program Files\AutoCAD LT 2000\Sample folder.)

After you have the hang of zooming in model space, you can zoom in paper space, if you like. To zoom in paper space, make sure that the MODEL / PAPER button on the status bar says PAPER. If it says MODEL, click it to change it to PAPER.

2. **Click the Zoom Realtime button on the Standard toolbar (the button showing the magnifying glass with the plus-and-minus sign next to it).**

   The cursor pointer icon changes to the Zoom Realtime magnifying glass icon. The command line helpfully points out that you can Press ESC or ENTER to exit, or right-click to display shortcut menu. It does not, however, tell you how to zoom!

3. **Move your cursor near the center of the drawing, press and hold down the left mouse button, and then drag the cursor toward the top of the screen.**

   You appear to fly in toward the center of the drawing. Figure 5-2 shows zooming in progress. Compare it with the zoomed-out view in Figure 5-1, earlier in this chapter.

4. **While pressing and holding down the left mouse button, drag the cursor toward the bottom of the screen.**

   You appear to fly out from the drawing's center.

5. **Right-click and choose Exit from the shortcut menu.**

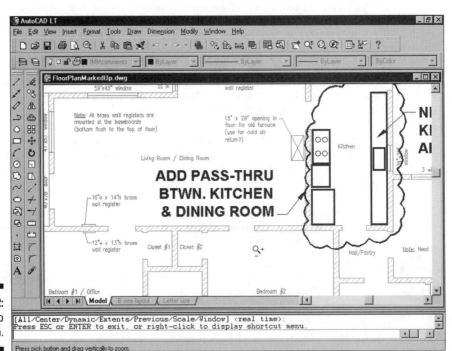

Figure 5-2:
Zoom into
your room.

6. **Click the Pan Realtime button on the Standard toolbar (the button showing the open hand).**

   The cursor pointer icon changes to the Pan Realtime open hand icon.

7. **Move your cursor near the center of the drawing, press and hold down the left mouse button, and then drag the cursor in any direction.**

   Your drawing slides around as though you were pushing it with the hand. The zoom magnification remains unchanged.

8. **Right-click to display the cursor menu shown in Figure 5-3.**

   Realtime Pan and Zoom use the same cursor menu. In fact, they're simply different entry points into the same combined pan and zoom functionality.

9. **Choose Zoom from the cursor menu to change to Realtime Zoom mode, then zoom as described in Step 3.**

10. **Right-click and choose Zoom Extents from the cursor menu.**

    AutoCAD LT automatically zooms out until the entire drawing displays. (As we explain in Chapter 4, a drawing's *extents* are the lower-left and upper-right corners of an imaginary rectangle that just surrounds all the objects in the drawing.)

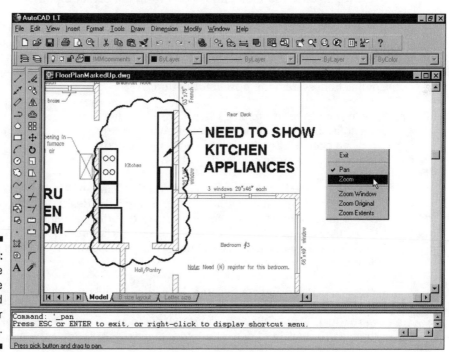

Figure 5-3:
The Realtime Pan and Zoom cursor menu.

11. **Right-click and choose Zoom Window from the cursor menu.**

The cursor changes to an arrow-with-window icon. By clicking and dragging this Zoom Window cursor, you can "draw" an imaginary rectangle around the part of the drawing area where you want to zoom.

12. **Pick a point at one corner of an imaginary rectangle representing the area you want to zoom into, hold down the mouse button, drag the cursor diagonally to the opposite corner of the rectangular area, and then release the mouse button.**

The area of the drawing inside the rectangle whose diagonal you specified fills the AutoCAD LT drawing area.

You must click and drag when specifying the two corners of the zoom window. For example, point to the lower-left corner of the desired zoom area, click and hold the left mouse button, drag the mouse to the upper-right corner of the zoom area, and then release the mouse button.

13. **Right-click and choose Zoom Original from the cursor menu.**

AutoCAD LT restores the view that was displayed when you initiated the current Realtime Pan and Zoom sequence (that is, at the beginning of Step 6, which was the most recent time that you clicked either the Pan Realtime or Zoom Realtime button).

14. **Right-click and then choose Exit from the cursor menu.**

The preceding steps demonstrate all the zoom and pan operations that you need to know in order to move around in a drawing. AutoCAD LT includes quite a few other zoom options, which you can see and experiment with by opening the View⇨Zoom submenu. Look up *zooming* in the AutoCAD LT online help system for more information.

If you want to return to an earlier view, as we demonstrate in Step 13 of the previous sequence, click the Zoom Previous button on the Standard toolbar. You can click the Zoom Previous button repeatedly in order "undo" previous zoom or pan sequences one step at a time.

You can use the Zoom Window button on the Standard toolbar to initiate a zoom window operation without going through the Realtime Pan and Zoom cursor menu. But if you do, you'll discover that the click-and-drag sequence for picking two points (described in Step 12, earlier in this section) doesn't work. Instead, you must pick the first point, release the mouse button, and pick the second point.

You also can pan and zoom using the mouse wheel on a Microsoft Intellimouse. To zoom in and out, roll the mouse wheel forward (in) or backward (out). Double-click the mouse wheel to zoom to the extents of your drawing. To pan, hold down the mouse wheel as you move the mouse.

The Layered Look

As we describe in Chapter 16, your motto when marking up a CAD drawing should be "First, do no harm." One of the principles of drawing mark-up is that you're not drawing Mark down. We mean, one of the principles is that you're simply pointing out to the creator of the drawing what needs to be changed or looked at; you're not making those changes yourself. If you do try to make the changes, you're taking responsibility for doing them right. And besides, what kind of a manager, editor, commentator, or advisor would you be if you let yourself get sucked into doing real work?

In deference to the creator of the drawing, you should make sure that anything you draw is well-separated from the rest of the objects in the drawing, easy to locate, and easy to undo. By working on a layer of your own, you can achieve all these goals, and thereby impress everyone with your excellent CAD organizational skills.

About layers

In AutoCAD LT, drawing objects reside on one or more *layers*. Layers are similar to those clear sheets of mylar (not plastic, *The Graduate* notwithstanding) that you draw on, then place on top of one another to build up a complete drawing. (You may remember something like this from a textbook about human anatomy, with the skeleton on one sheet, the muscles on the next sheet that you laid over the skeleton, and so on until you built up a complete picture of the human body. That is, if your mom didn't remove some of the more grown-up sections.)

Organizing objects on layers is an essential part of drafting with AutoCAD. The fundamental purpose of layers is to group related objects. For example, in a building plan, walls go on one layer, door symbols on another layer, bathroom fixtures on still another layer, and so on. By grouping objects logically on layers, the drafter can choose what to show on the screen or on the plot, because turning off a layer makes all objects on that layer invisible.

A secondary, but equally important, purpose of layers is controlling other object properties such as color, linetype, and lineweight. We tell you more about these properties in Chapter 10. For now, all you need to know is that you can assign each layer in a drawing a color, linetype, and lineweight. When you draw objects on a layer, they inherit these properties, unless you give AutoCAD LT instructions to the contrary. This inheritance is called assigning properties *by layer*.

Mayor of your own layer

In the following example, you create a layer of your own for storing all your drawing markups. You create the layer, assign it the color red for eye-popping visibility, and then make it the *current* layer so that AutoCAD LT places any objects you draw subsequently on the new layer.

1. **Click the Layers button (the one with the stack of white sheets of paper) on the Object Properties toolbar.**

    The Layer Properties Manager dialog box appears, as shown in Figure 5-4. A new drawing has only one layer, Layer 0. This layer is special — don't draw ordinary content on it. (We explain the special purpose of Layer 0 in Chapter 15.) Most drawings will contain a bunch of additional layers that the creator of the drawing added.

2. **Click the New button to create a new layer.**

    A new layer appears. It starts out with the name Layer1, but the name is selected so that you can easily type a new name to replace it.

3. **Type a name for your mark-up layer, such as !MMcomments, and press Enter.**

    It's a good idea to include your initials or name in a markup layer name, especially if other people might add their comments to the same drawing. If you put an exclamation point at the beginning of the layer name, your layer will appear at or near the top of the list when AutoCAD LT sorts it (after you close and re-open the Layer Properties Manager dialog box).

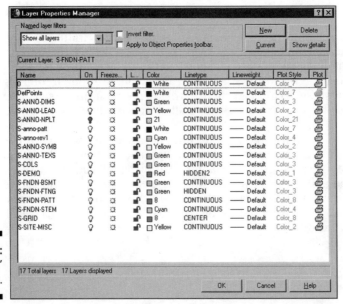

Figure 5-4:
Lots o'
layers.

4. **On the same line as the new layer, in the Color column, click the color block or color name, White, of the new layer.**

The Select Color dialog box appears, as shown in Figure 5-5.

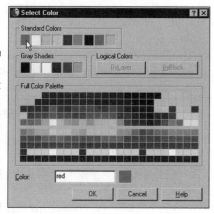

Figure 5-5:
The Select Color dialog box with the color red selected in the Standard Colors list.

AutoCAD LT provides you with 255 colors and refers to them by number (1 through 255). The first seven color numbers also have standard names in LT: red, yellow, green, cyan, blue, magenta, and white. Figure 4-10 in the previous chapter shows the colors that correspond to the first 15 color numbers.

Although the standard LT color name for color number 7 is White, the color swatch appears black if the background color of the AutoCAD LT drawing area is white. The reason for this confusion is that AutoCAD comes with a default background color of black, so white objects really do appear white. Autodesk decided to make the default model space background color in AutoCAD LT white, but didn't want to cause compatibility and usability problems for longtime AutoCAD users by changing the standard name assigned to color #7.

If you want "white" objects to appear white, change the model space background color to black on the Display tab in the Options dialog box. (Choose Tools⇨Options to display the dialog box.) An added bonus is that AutoCAD users will respect you more — most people find that the range of AutoCAD colors appears more clearly against a black background, and they expect you to figure this out at some point and join the crowd.

5. **Click a color to assign to this layer, as shown in Figure 5-5.**

We recommend that you choose one of the swatches in the Standard Colors area that stands out well. Red (the first swatch) is good for markups.

Avoid yellow, which doesn't show up well on a white background, and blue, which can be hard to read against a black background. Dark and light gray aren't very good choices if you want your markups to stand out.

6. **Click OK to exit the Select Color dialog box.**

   The Layer Properties Manager dialog box reappears, with the new color assigned to your layer. You should leave the remaining layer properties — Linetype, Lineweight, Plot Style, and Plot — set to their default values: `Continuous`, `Default`, `Color_1`, and `On`.

7. **Make sure that your new layer is selected, and then choose the <u>C</u>urrent button to make it the current layer.**

   The current layer is the one on which AutoCAD places new objects that you draw.

8. **Click OK to accept the new layer settings.**

   Notice that the Layer drop-down list on the Object Properties toolbar now displays the name of your new layer as the current layer.

Your office might have its own standards for mark-up layers, names, and colors. If so, find out what they are. Then use what they tell you to, not what we tell you to.

Please Note. . .

After you've gone to the trouble to create your own layer (see the preceding section), you'll no doubt want to draw something on it. Text is a good place to start, because many markups are of the "this is wrong; fix it!" variety. Before you can create text in AutoCAD LT, though, you need to figure out the height to make it.

Scaling the heights

In the "Figuring out a drawing's scale" section of Chapter 4, we give you some tips on how to determine the drawing scale and drawing scale factor of a drawing created by someone else. We also warn you that you need to know the drawing scale factor for tasks described in other chapters of this book. This is one of those chapters, and we're about to explain one of those tasks!

As a brief review, *drawing scale* is the traditional way of describing a scale with an equal sign or colon; for example 1=4 = 1:0, 1=20, or 2:1. The *drawing scale factor* represents the same relationship with a single number such as 48, 20, or 0.5. The drawing scale factor is the multiplier that converts the first number in the drawing scale into the second number.

One of the things that distinguishes knowledgeable CAD users is that they *always* know the drawing scale factor of any drawing they're working on. Make it a point to determine the drawing scale factor of a drawing before you add text or do any other drawing or editing in it.

Attack of the giant text strings

"Why do I need to know the drawing scale factor in order to draw text?" you might ask — especially if you've spent time *on the boards,* as we grizzled old-timers like to call manual drafting. You need to know the drawing scale factor because you handle scaling of objects and text in CAD exactly the opposite from the way you do in manual drafting.

In manual drafting, you squeeze real-world objects (the building, widget, or whatever) down by a specific scale factor, like 10 or 48, so that they fit nicely on a sheet of paper. Naturally, you always draw text the size that you want it to appear on the paper (for example, ⅛ inch or 3 mm high), regardless of the scale of the drawing.

In CAD drafting, on the other hand, you draw objects as if they were at their actual size. Then, when you plot, you shrink — or, if you make drawings of tiny things such as microprocessor circuitry, expand — the entire drawing by that same scale factor (for example, 10 or 48) to fit on the paper. But when you shrink the whole drawing to fit on the paper, text shrinks, too. In order to avoid indecipherably small text, you must create text at a size that's scaled up by the drawing scale factor. (If you're an architect, imagine that your text is neon lettering on the side of the building. If you're a mechanical designer, think of a brand name stamped on the side of a screw.)

For example, assume that someone has drawn a widget at a scale of 1=20 mm (corresponding to a drawing scale factor of 20), and you want your notes to appear 3 mm high when the drawing is plotted to scale. You need to create text that's 20 times 3 mm, or 60 mm, high. In a building plan drawn at a scale of ¼ = 1'-0" (drawing scale factor equals 48), text that will appear ⅛ inch when plotted needs to be ⅛ inch times 48, or 6 inches, high.

This tiny text / enormous text approach seems peculiar at first, especially if you were schooled in manual drafting. But it's a consequence of CAD's ability to let you draw and measure the geometry in real-world units. And after all, the geometry of what you're representing, rather than the ancillary notes, usually is the main point of the drawing.

Calculating text height

To calculate AutoCAD text height, you need to know the drawing scale factor, the desired plotted text height, and the location of the multiplication button on your calculator. Use the following steps to figure out text height:

1. **Determine the drawing's drawing scale factor.**

   Use the suggestions in the "Figuring out a drawing's scale" section of Chapter 4.

   Drafters in most industries restrict themselves to a limited, standard set of drawing scales from the theoretical infinitude of possible scales. See Chapter 9 for more information about choosing workable drawing scales.

2. **Determine the height that your notes should appear when you plot the drawing to scale.**

   Most industries have plotted text height standards. A plotted text height of ⅛ inch or 3 mm is common for notes. Some companies use slightly smaller heights (for example, 3⁄32 inch or 2.5 mm) in order to squeeze more text into small spaces. Ask the drafting experts in your office — or in another office that practices your profession — what they recommend.

   Manual CAD drafting standards often specify a minimum text height of ⅛ inch or 3 mm, because hand-lettered text smaller than that becomes difficult to read, especially on half-size prints. Plotted 3⁄32 inch or 2.5 mm CAD text is quite legible, but half-size plots with these smaller text heights can result in text that's on the margin of legibility. Text legibility on half-size — or smaller — plots depends on the plotter resolution, the lineweight assigned to the text, and the condition of your eyes! Test before you commit to using smaller text heights, or use ⅛ inch or 3 mm as a minimum.

3. **Multiply the numbers that you figured out in Steps 1 and 2.**

Table 5-1 lists some common drawing scales and text heights for drawings in imperial and metric units. You should know how to calculate the drawing scale factors and text heights, but you're allowed to use the table to check your work. (**Hint:** Multiply the number in the second column by the number in the third column in order to get the number in the fourth column!) The Cheat Sheet tables include some additional drawing scales and text heights.

Table 5-1	Common Drawing Scales and Text Heights		
Drawing Scale	**Drawing Scale Factor**	**Plotted Text Height**	**AutoCAD Text Height**
⅛"=1'–0"	96	⅛"	12"
¼"=1'–0"	48	⅛"	6"
¾"=1'–0"	16	⅛"	2"
1"=1'–0"	12	⅛"	1½"

Drawing Scale	Drawing Scale Factor	Plotted Text Height	AutoCAD Text Height
1=100 mm	100	3 mm	300 mm
1=50 mm	50	3 mm	150 mm
1=20 mm	20	3 mm	60 mm
1=10 mm	10	3 mm	30 mm

Making multiline text

After you calculated a text height (see the preceding section in this chapter), you can add notes to the drawing. AutoCAD LT calls the type of text object that you create *multiline text* (or *mtext*) in order to distinguish it from its more simple-minded cousin, single line text. Chapter 12 describes both kinds of text in greater detail. In the following example, you use the MTEXT command to create a comment.

MTEXT is one of those annoying AutoCAD LT commands that prompts you for some information on the command line and some in a dialog box. Be sure to read the command-line prompts during Steps 3 and 4 of this example:

1. **Make sure that you've created a mark-up layer and made it the current layer, as described in the section "Mayor of your own layer," earlier in this chapter.**

2. **Turn off running osnap (object snap) mode by clicking the OSNAP button on the status bar until the button appears to be pushed out and the words <Osnap off> appear on the command line.**

   Running object snap helps you pick precise locations in the drawing efficiently, but until you know how to use running object snap, it'll just make things unpredictable. See Chapter 10 for more information.

3. **Click the Multiline Text button (the one with the uppercase letter A on it) on the Draw toolbar.**

   The command line displays the current text style and height settings and prompts you to select the first corner of an imaginary rectangle that will determine the word-wrapping width for the text object:

   ```
   Current text style:  "!MMcomments"  Text height:  100.0
   Specify first corner:
   ```

4. **Pick a point in the drawing.**

   The command line prompts you for the opposite corner of the text rectangle that will determine the word wrapping width:

   ```
   Specify opposite corner or [Height/Justify/Line
         spacing/Rotation/Style/Width]:
   ```

5. **Pick another point in the drawing.**

   The width of the rectangle is all that matters. AutoCAD LT adjusts the height of the text rectangle to accommodate the number of lines of word-wrapped text. Don't worry too much about the width, either — you can adjust it later.

   The Multiline Text Editor dialog box appears. Figure 5-6 shows what the dialog box looks like after you enter text.

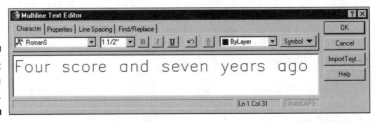

Figure 5-6:
Adding a
note.

6. **From the Font drop-down list (the first drop-down list in the toolbar above the text editing area), choose RomanS.**

   The AutoCAD LT font RomanS (Roman Simplex) is the best general-purpose font for drafting and adding comments. Stay away from Windows TrueType fonts, which will cause drawing performance to suffer.

7. **In the Font Height edit box and drop-down list (the second drop-down list in the toolbar above the text editing area), type the text height that you figured out in the "Calculating text height" section of this chapter.**

   Remember to use the scaled AutoCAD LT text height, not the plotted text height.

8. **Enter your comment into the text area of the dialog box, as shown in Figure 5-6.**

   AutoCAD LT word wraps multiline text automatically. If you want to force a line break at a particular location, press Enter.

   If your comment takes on Tolstoyan length, you can view more text lines by enlarging the Multiline Text Editor dialog box. Just grab and drag one of the corners of the dialog box.

9. **Click OK.**

   The Multiline Text Editor dialog box closes and adds your comment to the drawing.

The Multiline Text Editor dialog box provides a small but useful set of editing and formatting options. It's certainly no match for a full-fledged word processor, though. For example, you can't easily create a numbered list with hanging indents, such as the one that we used to format the steps in the preceding example. However, you're usually better off not creating such complex text within a drawing anyway.

If you discover that the rectangle you specified in Steps 4 and 5 of the preceding example is too wide or not wide enough, you can adjust it easily, as we describe in the next section.

Modifying multiline text

After you've added a note, you'll undoubtedly think of something to add to it (or a more clever or cutting way to express it). You might also want to adjust the word-wrapping width. You can perform both tasks by selecting a multiline text object, as the following example demonstrates:

1. **Make sure that the command line displays** Command: **and that no objects are selected.**

   If you're in doubt, press the Esc key twice to cancel any currently running command and unselect any selected objects.

2. **Select one of your comments by pointing to the text and clicking with the left mouse button.**

   AutoCAD LT displays the text ghosted to indicate that it's selected, and also displays small blue squares called *grips* at the corners of the text rectangle. (Chapter 6 contains more information about selecting objects and editing them with their grips.)

   If only one line of text in a paragraph appears ghosted, then you've selected a line text object rather than a multiline text object. The editing options for line text are more limited, and you won't be able to adjust word wrapping. See Chapter 12 for details.

3. **Right-click and choose Mtext Edit from the cursor menu.**

   The Multiline Text Editor appears and displays the text that you selected.

4. **Make editing or formatting changes to the text.**

   If you want to change the formatting — for example, text height — assigned to existing text, you must select all of the text to which you want to apply the change before making the formatting change.

5. **Click OK.**

   The Multiline Text Editor dialog box closes and applies your changes to the text. The text is no longer selected (to confirm this, note that the ghosting is gone) and no longer displays the blue grips.

6. **Reselect the text by pointing to it and clicking.**

   The text ghosts and displays the blue grips again.

7. **Click one of the blue grips.**

   It turns red to indicate that it's *hot,* or active.

8. **Move the cursor left or right, as shown in Figure 5-7, and then choose a new point.**

   AutoCAD LT rewraps the text lines based on the new width.

9. **Repeat Steps 7 and 8 until you're satisfied with the word wrapping.**

10. **Press Esc twice.**

    The first Esc unselects the object (that is, removes the ghosting). The second Esc removes the grips.

Figure 5-7:
Changing the word-wrapping width for a multiline text object.

Pointy-Headed Leaders

No, we're not talking about your boss (or about you, if you happen to be the boss). We're talking about arrows that point from your comment to the object or area about which you're commenting. AutoCAD LT makes it easy to draw leaders and text at the same time using the QLEADER (Quick Leader) command, as the following example demonstrates.

QLEADER is another one of those annoying AutoCAD LT commands that prompts you for some information on the command line and some in a dialog box. Pay close attention to the command-line prompts throughout this example:

1. **Make sure that you've created a mark-up layer and made it the current layer, as we describe in the section "Mayor of your own layer," earlier in this chapter.**

2. **Choose Dimension⇨Leader.**

   The command line prompts you to select the first leader point — that is, the arrowhead point — and gives you the option of changing leader settings first:

   ```
   Specify first leader point, or [Settings]<Settings>:
   ```

   If you want to draw curved instead of straight leader lines or choose a different leader arrowhead style, type S and press Enter to open the Leader Settings dialog box.

3. **Pick a point that you want to point to.**

   The command line prompts you for the next point — AutoCAD LT will draw a shaft from the arrowhead to this point:

   ```
   Specify next point:
   ```

4. **Pick a second point.**

   If you pick a second point that's too close to the arrowhead point, AutoCAD LT won't have enough room to draw the arrowhead, and thus will omit it.

   AutoCAD LT repeats the next point prompt, so that you can draw a multisegment shaft if you want to:

   ```
   Specify next point:
   ```

   This is yet another example of AutoCAD LT offering power (the ability to draw multisegment shafts) at the expense of simplicity (just ending the arrow after you draw the first shaft segment).

5. **Pick one more point if you want to, or press Enter if you want a leader with a single shaft.**

Enter tells the QLEADER command that you're finished selecting the points that define the leader shaft. By default, the QLEADER command lets you pick up to three points (the arrowhead point and two more points).

The command line prompts you to specify the width for word wrapping the text that you'll attach to the leader:

```
Specify text width <0.0>:
```

The default text width, 0.0, turns off word wrapping and displays your text on a single line. You can type a width or point using the cursor.

Turning off word wrapping works fine for short notes that fit on one line. If you think your note might be longer, specify a width instead of accepting the default value of 0.0.

6. **Press Enter to suppress word wrapping, or move the cursor to the right or left in order to specify a width for word wrapping and then click.**

The command line prompts you to type a short note directly at the command line, or press Enter to type your note in the Multiline Text Editor dialog box:

```
Enter first line of annotation text <Mtext>:
```

7. **Press Enter to open the Multiline Text Editor dialog box.**

8. **Enter your comment, just as we describe in the section "Making multiline text," earlier in this chapter.**

9. **Click OK.**

The Multiline Text Editor dialog box closes and adds your comment to the drawing, next to the leader.

Figure 5-8 shows several different leaders with notes.

If both the leader arrowhead and the text are the wrong size or appear to be missing entirely, then the dimension scale isn't set correctly in the drawing. (Believe it or not, AutoCAD LT treats leaders as a special kind of dimension object — see Chapter 13 for more about dimensions.) See the "Setting linetype and dimension scales" section of Chapter 9 for detailed instructions on how to set the dimension scale. After you've set the dimension scale properly, erase and re-create the leader and text.

If you add a comment to a drawing and later decide that the comment merits a leader, you can use the QLEADER command to draw the leader so that the end of the shaft ends up in the vicinity of the existing text object. Then, when the Multiline Text Editor dialog box appears (Step 7 in the previous example), click OK without entering any new text.

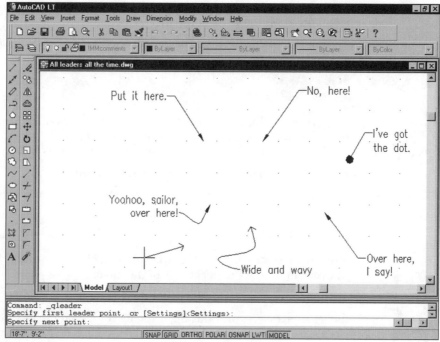

Cloud Cover

Leaders provide one way to call attention to an object. Clouds are another. The AutoCAD LT REVCLOUD (Revision Cloud) command is a good way to call attention to a particular area in a drawing. Not only is it quick, but it's also fun to use.

In some industries, clouds indicate revised areas, and some offices may prefer to limit the use of the REVCLOUD command to revision clouds. Check around in your office if you're unsure of how to use clouds. Then, if anyone questions what you're doing, you'll have cloud cover (as in covering your assets).

Here's how you create a revision cloud:

1. **Make sure that you've created a mark-up layer and made it the current layer, as we describe in the section "Mayor of your own layer," earlier in this chapter.**

2. **Click the Revcloud button (the one with — what else? — a white cloud on it) on the Draw toolbar.**

   The command line displays the default length of the arcs or *lobes* that will make up the cloud you draw:

   ```
   Current arc length: 1.0
   Specify start point or [Arc length]:
   ```

If you discover during Step 4 that the lobes of the cloud are too large or too small, repeat the REVCLOUD command, type **A** and press Enter to modify the arc length, and type a new length and press Enter.

3. **Pick a point where you want to begin the cloud.**

   The command line prompts you to move the cursor along a path where you want to draw the cloud:

   ```
   Guide crosshairs along cloud path...
   ```

4. **Move the cursor counter-clockwise along a circular or elliptical path in order to define the perimeter of the cloud.**

   You don't need to pick again; just move the mouse around.

As described in the previous tip, if you discover that the lobes of the cloud are too large or too small, cancel the command now by pressing Esc, and then restart the REVCLOUD command and change the arc length.

5. **Complete the circular or elliptical path by moving the cursor back to the point that you picked in Step 3.**

   The command line tells you when the REVCLOUD command locates the beginning point and is able to close the cloud:

   ```
   Revision cloud finished.
   ```

   Figure 5-9 shows an example of the finished product.

You'll often want to combine a cloud with a leader in order to indicate an area and then write a comment about it.

Line It Up

"A picture is worth a thousand words," as they say, and sometimes a few well-placed lines can convey your drawing comments better than many paragraphs of text. This section shows you how to sketch lines for the purposes of communicating a correction, suggestion, or graphical "comment."

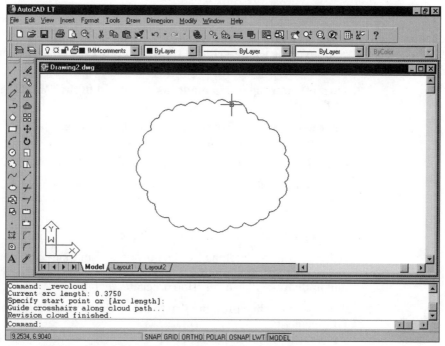

Figure 5-9:
Stormy
weather.

Our objective in this chapter is to show you how to mark up drawings, and this section demonstrates how to draw cartoon-like sketches using the LINE and PLINE (polyline) commands. Chapter 10 describes more drawing tools and additional precision drawing techniques. For mark-up purposes, you might draw a sketch in a blank area off to the side of the objects that you're commenting on. Your sketch would suggest to the drawing's creator how to fix the problematic objects, but you would leave the actual fixing to the creator. And don't make your sketches too suggestive, unless you want to get slapped.

The LINE king

The simplest drawing tool in AutoCAD LT's toolbox is the LINE command. There's no big secret to drawing lines in AutoCAD LT, as the following example demonstrates.

Like most object drawing commands, LINE prompts you at the command line. Read the command-line prompts during every step of the command.

Here's how you draw the line:

1. **Make sure that you've created a mark-up layer and made it the current layer, as we describe in the section "Mayor of your own layer," earlier in this chapter.**

2. **Turn off running osnap mode, as described in the "Making multiline text" example.**

   Later in this section, we show you how to use objects snaps to pick precise locations in the drawing.

3. **Click the Line button (the first button) on the Draw toolbar.**

   The command line prompts you to select the first endpoint of the line:

   ```
   Specify first point:
   ```

4. **Pick a point anywhere in the drawing area.**

   Because you're sketching for the purposes of markup, you don't need to worry about picking precise points in the drawing. Later in this section and in Chapter 10, we describe precision techniques.

   The command line prompts you to select the other endpoint of the first line segment:

   ```
   Specify next point or [Undo]:
   ```

5. **Pick another point anywhere in the drawing area.**

   AutoCAD LT draws the first line segment. The command line continues to prompt you for additional points, each of which will define a new line segment starting from the end of the previous segment:

   ```
   Specify next point or [Undo]:
   ```

   If you want to draw a single segment, right-click anywhere in the drawing area and choose Enter from the cursor menu. In this example, continue to draw segments.

6. **Pick additional points anywhere in the drawing area.**

   After you pick the third point — that is, after you've drawn two segments — the command line includes a Close option, in case you want to form a closed polygon:

   ```
   Specify next point or [Close/Undo]:
   ```

7. **Right-click anywhere in the drawing area and choose Enter from the cursor menu, as shown in Figure 5-10.**

   AutoCAD LT draws the final segment and returns to the Command prompt, indicating that the LINE command is finished.

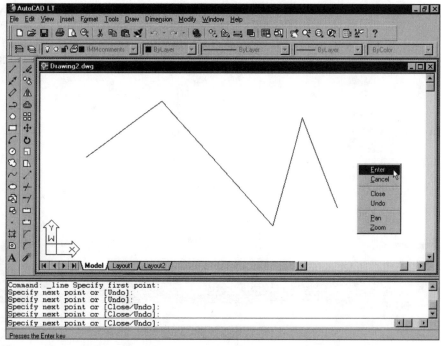

Figure 5-10:
Drawing line segments with the LINE command.

A polyline is a many-lined thing

The LINE command is fine for some mark-up tasks, but the PLINE command is a better, more flexible choice in many situations. The PLINE command draws a special kind of object called a *polyline* (sometimes referred to as a *pline* because of the command name). The most important differences between the LINE and PLINE commands are these:

✔ The PLINE command can draw curved segments as well as straight ones.

✔ The LINE command draws a series of single line segment objects. Even though they appear on the screen to be linked, each segment is a separate object. If you move one line segment, the other segments that you drew at the same time don't move with it. The PLINE command, on the other hand, draws a single, connected, multisegment object. If you select any segment for editing, your changes affect the entire polyline. Figure 5-11 shows how the same sketch drawn with the LINE and the PLINE commands responds when you select one of the objects.

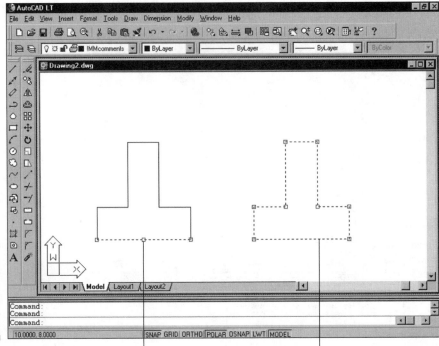

Figure 5-11:
Results of
the LINE
and PLINE
commands.

Line (each segment is a separate object)   Polyline (all segments form one object)

The following example demonstrates how to draw a polyline that includes an arc segment.

The PLINE command, like the LINE command, prompts you at the command line. Pay attention to the prompts at each step:

1. **Make sure that your mark-up layer is the current layer, and that running osnap mode is turned off, as we describe at the beginning of the example in the preceding section of this chapter.**

2. **Click the Polyline button (the button that looks like a fishhook) on the Draw toolbar.**

    The command line prompts you to select the first endpoint of the polyline's starting segment:

    ```
    Specify start point:
    ```

3. **Pick a point anywhere in the drawing area.**

    The command line prompts you to select the other endpoint of the first line segment, and also provides a half-dozen other options (see Chapter 10 for details):

```
Specify next point or
        [Arc/Close/Halfwidth/Length/Undo/Width]:
```

4. **Pick another point anywhere in the drawing area.**

   AutoCAD LT draws the first (straight) segment of the polyline. The command line continues to prompt you for additional points:

```
Specify next point or
        [Arc/Close/Halfwidth/Length/Undo/Width]:
```

   In this example, you'll draw a curved segment (or *arc*) next.

5. **Right-click anywhere in the drawing area and choose Arc from the cursor menu.**

   The command-line prompt changes to reflect arc segment options.

```
Specify endpoint of arc or
        [Angle/CEnter/CLose/Direction/Halfwidth/Line/Radi
        us/Second pt/Undo/Width]:
```

6. **Pick a point anywhere in the drawing area.**

   AutoCAD LT draws the second segment of the polyline, which is curved. The command line continues to prompt you with arc options:

```
Specify endpoint of arc or
        [Angle/CEnter/CLose/Direction/Halfwidth/Line/Radi
        us/Second pt/Undo/Width]:
```

   You've thrown enough curves. Return to drawing straight polyline segments.

7. **Right-click anywhere in the drawing area and choose Line from the cursor menu.**

   The command line returns to the original straight segment prompt:

```
Specify next point or
        [Arc/Close/Halfwidth/Length/Undo/Width]:
```

8. **Pick additional points to create additional straight segments.**

9. **Right-click anywhere in the drawing area and choose Enter from the cursor menu.**

   AutoCAD LT draws the final polyline segment.

 You also can end the PLINE or LINE command by choosing the Close option instead of the Enter option from the cursor menu. The Close option draws a final line segment connecting back to the first point that you picked after you started the PLINE or LINE command, thus forming a closed polygon.

Figure 5-12 shows various polylines, which give you some sense of the flexibility of the PLINE command.

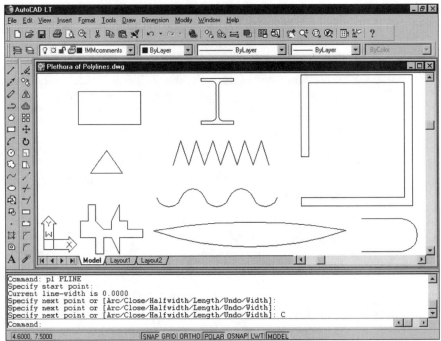

Figure 5-12:
A plethora
of polylines.

Neatness Counts

All the preceding examples in this chapter show you how to draw things as though you were using an illustration or drawing program — without specifying points or distances precisely. Although this approach often is adequate for markups, we'd be remiss if we didn't introduce precision drawing techniques alongside the drawing commands that you'll normally use them with. You don't want to get into the habit of specifying approximate points or distances all the time and then have to unlearn that habit later.

AutoCAD LT provides a range of tools for ensuring precision, including snap, object snaps, ortho mode, tracking, and typed coordinates and distances. We cover all these techniques in Chapter 10; in this chapter, we introduce object snaps and a special type of typed distance called direct distance entry. These two precision techniques are flexible and relatively easy to understand, so they'll serve you well for the mark-up and editing procedures described in this chapter and the next one.

As soon as you graduate from doing markups to doing real drawing and editing work, you *must* use precision techniques to specify most points and distances. Use the techniques described in this chapter and Chapter 6 as a starting point, and refer to Chapters 10 and 11 for in-depth information.

Precision is especially important when you're drawing or editing *geometry* — the lines, arcs, and so on that make up whatever you're representing in the CAD drawing. Precision placement usually is less important with notes, leaders, and other *annotations* that describe rather than show. Thus, in the context of this chapter, you should consider using precision techniques with the LINE and PLINE commands. You often don't need to use precision techniques with the MTEXT, QLEADER, and REVCLOUD commands.

Pick a point, and make it snappy

In many situations, the easiest way to draw a new object precisely is to attach it to a particular point on an existing object (assuming, of course, that someone drew the existing object precisely — Chapter 10 tells how). AutoCAD LT calls this technique *object snapping,* because you instruct the program to pull, or *snap,* the cursor to a point on an existing *object.* The object snapping feature in general and object snap points in particular often are referred to as *osnaps.*

AutoCAD LT provides two kinds of object snapping modes: *single point* (or *override*) object snaps and *running* object snaps. This section introduces single point object snaps; Chapter 10 covers running object snaps. The following example demonstrates how to use single point object snaps with the LINE command. The same procedure applies to using PLINE or any other drawing command.

CAD precision versus accuracy

Don't confuse precision with accuracy. When we use the word *precision*, we mean controlling the placement of objects so they lie exactly where you want them to lie in the drawing. For example, lines whose endpoints meet must meet exactly, and a circle that's supposed to be centered on the coordinates 0,0 must be drawn with its center exactly at 0,0. We use *accuracy* to refer to the degree to which your drawing matches its real-world counterpart. An accurate floor plan is one in which the dimensions of the CAD objects equal exactly the dimensions of the as-built house.

CAD precision usually helps produce accurate drawings, but that's not always the case. You can produce a very precise CAD drawing that's inaccurate because you started from inaccurate information (for example, the contractor gave you a wrong field measurement). Or, you might deliberately exaggerate certain distances in order to convey the relationship between objects more clearly on the plotted drawing.

In summary, CAD drawings always should be drawn precisely, but they may or may not be drawn accurately.

Until you know how to use running object snaps, make sure you turn off running osnap mode before you draw or edit. Turn off running osnap mode by clicking the OSNAP button on the status bar until the button appears to be pushed out and the words `<Osnap off>` appear on the command line.

Here's how you draw lines using single point object snaps to maintain precision:

1. **Open a drawing containing some geometry.**

2. **Start the LINE command by clicking the Line button on the Draw toolbar.**

   The command line prompts you to select the first endpoint of the line:

   ```
   Specify first point:
   ```

3. **Hold down the Shift key, right-click anywhere in the drawing area, and release the Shift key.**

   The object snap cursor menu appears, as shown in Figure 5-13.

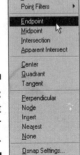

Figure 5-13:
The object snap cursor menu.

4. **Choose Endpoint from the object snap cursor menu.**

   The object snap cursor menu disappears, and the command line displays an additional prompt indicating that you've directed AutoCAD LT to seek out endpoints of existing objects:

   ```
   _endp of:
   ```

5. **Move the cursor slowly around the drawing, pausing over various lines and other objects.**

   When you move the cursor near an object with an endpoint, a colored square icon appears at the endpoint, indicating that AutoCAD LT can snap to that point. If you stop moving the cursor for a moment, a yellow ToolTip displaying the word Endpoint appears to reinforce the idea.

6. **Click after you've moved the cursor so the endpoint object snap square appears on the endpoint that you want to snap to, click.**

   AutoCAD LT snaps to the endpoint, which becomes the first point of the new line segment that you're about to draw. The command line prompts you to select the other endpoint of the new line segment:

   ```
   Specify next point or [Undo]:
   ```

   As you move the cursor around the drawing now, AutoCAD LT no longer seeks out endpoints, because single point object snaps last only for a single pick. Use the object snap cursor menu again to snap the other end of your new line segment to the midpoint of an existing object.

7. **Use the "press Shift, right-click, release Shift" sequence described in Step 3 to display the object snap cursor menu, and then choose Midpoint from the object snap cursor menu.**

   The command line displays an additional prompt indicating that you've directed AutoCAD LT to seek out midpoints of existing objects:

   ```
   _mid of:
   ```

   When you move the cursor near the midpoint of an object, a colored triangle appears at the snap point. Each object snap type (endpoint, midpoint, intersection, and so on) displays a different icon. If you stop moving the cursor for a moment, the ToolTip text reminds you what the icon means. Figure 5-14 shows what the screen looks like during this step.

8. **Draw additional line segments by picking additional points. Use the object snap cursor menu to specify a single object snap type before you pick each point.**

   Try the Intersection, Perpendicular, and Nearest object snaps. If your drawing contains arcs or circles, try Center and Quadrant.

9. **When you're finished experimenting with single point object snaps, right-click anywhere in the drawing area and choose Enter from the cursor menu.**

   Notice the difference between right-clicking and Shift+right-clicking in the drawing area. Right-click displays a menu with options that are tailored to the current command. Shift+right-click always displays the same object snap cursor menu.

Use object snaps to enforce precision by making sure that new points you pick coincide *exactly* with points on existing objects. In CAD, it's not good enough for points to almost coincide or to look like they coincide. AutoCAD LT knows the difference between "looks the same" and "*is* the same," and will cause you untold amounts of grief if you try to make due with "looks the same." You lose points, both figuratively and literally, if you don't use object snaps or one of the other precision techniques covered in Chapter 10 to enforce precision.

Already object-snapped to Endpoint ⌐About to object-snap to Midpoint

New line segment

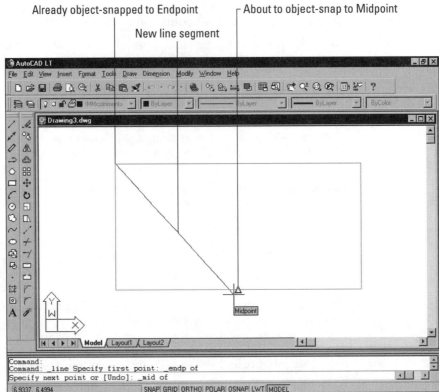

Figure 5-14:
A snappy
line.

And one further point . . .

The one other precision technique that you should understand early in your AutoCAD LT drawing and editing career is *direct distance entry*. This technique simply involves pointing the cursor in a particular direction, typing a distance at the command line, and pressing Enter. AutoCAD LT calls it direct distance entry because it avoids the older, indirect AutoCAD methods of specifying a distance at the command line. (We tell you about the indirect methods in Chapter 10, because they sometimes are useful.)

You can use direct distance entry any time the crosshair cursor is anchored to a point and the command line prompts you for another point or a distance. You'll usually use direct distance entry with *ortho mode,* in order to specify a distance in an orthogonal direction (0, 90, 180, or 270 degrees). The following example demonstrates how to use direct distance entry with the LINE command to draw line segments of a particular length:

1. **Open an existing drawing or create a new one.**

2. **Start the LINE command by clicking the Line button on the Draw toolbar.**

   The command line prompts you to select the first endpoint of the line:

   ```
   Specify first point:
   ```

   Don't use direct distance entry yet — the crosshair cursor isn't yet anchored to a point, because you haven't yet picked the line's first endpoint.

3. **Choose a starting point for the line.**

   You can use a single object snap, as we describe in the previous section, to place the first endpoint of the line precisely. The command line then prompts you to select the other endpoint of the new line segment:

   ```
   Specify next point or [Undo]:
   ```

4. **Turn on ortho (orthogonal) mode by clicking the ORTHO button on the status bar until the button appears to be pushed in and the words** `<Ortho on>` **appear on the command line.**

   With ortho mode on, AutoCAD LT constrains your cursor to moving at an angle of 0, 90, 180, or 270 degrees from the point that you picked in the previous step. Now that the crosshair cursor is anchored to a point, you can use direct distance entry.

5. **Move the cursor to the right (at an angle of 0 degrees from the point that you picked in Step 3).**

6. **Type a distance, such as 6, at the command line and press Enter.**

   AutoCAD LT draws a horizontal line segment six units long.

   If your drawing uses feet-and-inches units, the number you type represents inches, not feet. See Chapters 9 and 10 for information about units and how to type distances in different kind of units.

7. **Move the cursor up (at an angle of 90 degrees) from the point to which the crosshair cursor is anchored.**

8. **Type another distance, such as 3, at the command line and press Enter.**

   AutoCAD LT draws a vertical line segment three units long.

9. **Move the cursor left (at an angle of 180 degrees) from the point to which the crosshair cursor is anchored.**

10. **Type the same distance that you typed in Step 6 at the command line and then press Enter.**

    AutoCAD LT draws a horizontal line segment six units long, but this time to the left.

11. **Right-click anywhere in the drawing area and choose Close from the cursor menu.**

   AutoCAD LT completes the rectangle, as shown in Figure 5-15.

In this example, you drew a rectangle that was *precisely* six units long by three units high — not more-or-less, not looks-pretty-much-like-it, but spot on. If you used an object snap in Step 3 to pick the first corner of the rectangle, then you further made sure that the rectangle has its lower-left corner located *precisely* at the object snap point. That's the kind of precision that you want to get in the habit of imposing as you build your CAD drawing skills.

Because you used the LINE command in this example, the rectangle is composed of four separate line segments. If you repeat the exercise using the PLINE command, you'll create a single object, which is preferable in many situations. AutoCAD LT also has a RECTANG command for drawing rectangles by picking two corners, and you find out about it in Chapter 10.

As Chapter 6 demonstrates, direct distance entry is especially useful for editing operations such as moving, copying, and stretching objects.

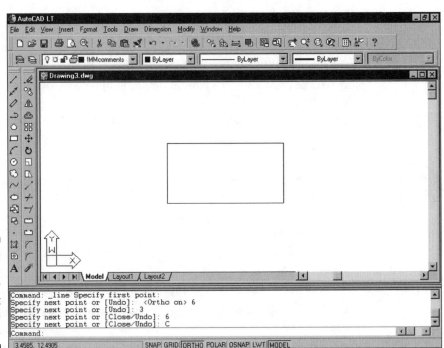

Figure 5-15: Drawing precisely with direct distance entry.

Chapter 6

Editing 101: Making a Change

● ●

In This Chapter

▶ Choosing an editing style

▶ Selecting objects

▶ Erasing objects

▶ Undeleting objects and undoing or redoing steps

▶ Using grips to move, copy, and stretch objects

▶ Editing with precision

● ●

*I*n Chapter 5, we warn you that you should limit drawing markup to pointing out things that need changes or another look. Leave the messy, hard work of making the changes to the person who created the drawing.

That's an excellent theory, but the world is an untidy place, and you might be called upon early in your LT-using career to make modest editing changes to existing drawings. This procedure is called "picking up red-marks" in some industries, because the drafter traditionally works from a hardcopy that's been marked up with a red pencil. Whatever it's called, there tends to be a lot of it at the end of a project, as everyone races around trying to incorporate all the last-minute changes in the drawings. The project manager may grab anyone who knows AutoCAD, or used AutoCAD 10 years ago in school, or can at least find the AutoCAD LT icon on the Windows desktop, to help out in the last-minute crunch.

What if you're working on your own drawings and are new to AutoCAD? Editing isn't just what you do at the end of a project; it's very much a part of the initial drawing creation process. In manual drafting, you try to spend most of your drawing creation time drawing and avoid editing as much as possible, because making changes on paper is messy and slow. In CAD, on the other hand, you switch back and forth frequently between drawing objects and editing them throughout the drawing creation and revision process. That's because editing is much easier and cleaner in CAD. Also, in many situations, the most efficient method of drawing new objects is copying and then modifying existing objects.

In this chapter, we tell you just enough about editing so that you can make modest changes to existing drawings and to the objects that you create in new drawings. As Chapter 5 does for drawing, this chapter serves as a gentle introduction into the big, wide world of AutoCAD LT editing. Chapter 11 picks up where this chapter leaves off and explores more of editing-land.

The motto of those who work on other people's drawings — or one's own, after some work has gone into them — should be, "First, do no harm." Before you make changes to someone else's drawing, stop to ask yourself, "Would she mind? (And if so, does she have any input on the size of my bonus?)" When in doubt, make a copy of the drawing and edit your copy.

Which Came First: The Command or the Selection?

AutoCAD LT inherits from AutoCAD a panoply of ways to accomplish the same editing result. Some of these ways differ somewhat from techniques you might know from using a drawing or diagramming program. Some of the differences are the result of *backward compatibility* — AutoCAD has always done it that way, and lots of loyal users would raise Cain if Autodesk changed it. But many of the differences come from the exacting demands of CAD. Many CAD drawings contain lots of closely spaced, overlapping, and squeezed-together objects. CAD programs have to provide flexible but precise ways of selecting and editing objects.

AutoCAD LT offers two main styles of editing: *command-first editing* and *selection-first editing*. Within the selection-first editing style, you have an additional choice of editing that uses actual, named commands and *direct manipulation* of objects without named commands. We don't know about you, but we need a review of how these editing styles work.

Editing styles

With *command-first editing*, you enter a command and then click the objects on which the command works. You're unlikely to be familiar with this style of editing for graphics work unless you're a long-time user of AutoCAD or LT. But command-first editing is common in nongraphical environments such as the old MS-DOS. When you typed **DEL *.*** in DOS, you were issuing a command — **DEL**, for *del*ete — and then choosing the objects on which the command works — *.*, meaning all the files in the current directory. Command-first editing is the oldest, most venerable style of editing in AutoCAD.

In *selection-first editing*, you perform the same steps — in the same order — as you do in most Windows-based applications (such as a typical word processor or drawing program) and on the Macintosh: You select the object first and then choose the command. To delete a line of text in a word processor, for example, you highlight (select) the line and then press the Delete key. The text you highlight is the object you select, and pressing the Delete key is the command. Notice that whether you want to delete, underline, or copy the text, the first act is the same: You highlight the text to select it.

Direct manipulation is a refinement of selection-first editing in which you perform common editing operations by using the mouse to grab the selected object and perform an action on it, such as moving all or part of it to a different place in the drawing. No named command is involved; the act of moving the mouse around and clicking the mouse buttons in certain ways causes the editing changes to happen.

AutoCAD LT supports direct manipulation through a powerful but somewhat complicated technique called *grip editing*. *Grips* are little square handles that appear on an object when you select it; you can use the grips to stretch, move, copy, rotate, or otherwise edit the object. The complications arise from the fact that you can do so many things with an object after you select it.

This chapter uses selection-first editing exclusively, and the direct manipulation refinement (that is, grip editing) whenever possible. Chapter 11 covers command-first editing.

Some AutoCAD LT commands can be used only with the command-first editing style — when you start these commands, they ignore any already selected objects and prompt you to select objects. We tell you more about some of these malefactors in Chapter 11.

Selection defaults

AutoCAD LT provides not only the three editing styles — command-first, selection-first, and direct manipulation — but also ways of tinkering with how they work. Figure 6-1 shows the AutoCAD LT 2000 selection settings, which are located on the Selection tab of the Options dialog box, and their default values. Choose Tools⇨Options to display the dialog box.

We could write volumes about the various settings and the pros and cons of each. (In fact, in previous books we did — aren't you glad you're reading this book instead?) To keep things as consistent as possible in AutoCAD LT, we recommend that you stick with the default settings. If you're the kind of person who can't leave well enough alone, at least work through this chapter using the default settings. Then come back to the Options dialog box and use the "What's This" help to learn about the settings: Click the question mark on the dialog box's title bar and then click the setting that you want to know more about. Use the experience you gain in this chapter and what you learn from the Help system to make intelligent choices about how to set the selection options.

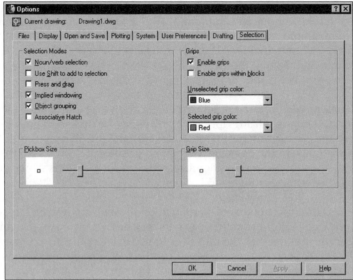

Figure 6-1:
The
selection
defaults.

Grab It

Part of AutoCAD LT's editing flexibility comes from its object selection flexibility. For example, command-first editing offers 16 different selection modes! (You meet the most useful ones in Chapter 11.) Selection-first editing, including grip editing, reduces this horde to a manageable three: selecting a single object, enclosing objects completely in a window, and including part or all of objects in a window.

Each of the things that you draw in AutoCAD LT — lines, circles, arcs, text strings — is called an *object*. It didn't used to be that way, though. You'll hear AutoCAD old-timers refer to objects as *entities*, because older versions of AutoCAD used that term. Some AutoCAD customization terms even use the shortened form *ent*, which gives rise to all kinds of horrible puns, such as "capturing a swarm of ents is no picnic."

The ent (itie)s go marching one by one

The most obvious way to select objects is to pick (by clicking) them one at a time. Assuming that you leave the Use Shift to Add to Selection option turned off, as shown earlier in Figure 6-1, you can build up a selection set cumulatively with this "pick one object at a time" selection mode. This cumulative convention might be different from what you're used to. In most Windows programs, if you select one object and then another, the first object is deselected and the second one selected. Only the object you select last remains selected. But in AutoCAD LT, *all* the objects you select, one at a time, remain selected and are added to the set, no matter how many objects you pick. Most editing commands affect the entire group of selected objects.

Why the label "Use Shift to Add to Selection," you ask? With this option turned off (the default setting), you can use the Shift key to *remove* already selected objects from the selection set. This feature turns out to be extremely useful when you're building a selection set in a crowded drawing (which is one reason why we suggest that you stick with the default setting). If you turn on this option, single object selection works pretty much like in other Windows programs — selecting an object deselects any already selected objects, unless you hold down the Shift key while selecting. You gain consistency with other Windows programs, but you lose the ability to use Shift to remove objects, which can be critical in some editing situations. As we suggest earlier in the chapter, try the default AutoCAD LT way for awhile, and if it drives you nuts, then go back and change it.

How much is that object in the window?

Selecting objects one at a time works great when you want to edit a small number of objects, but many CAD editing tasks involve editing lots of objects. Would you like to pick 132 lines, arcs, and circles one at a time? Do you really want to stress-test your mouse's pick button, not to mention the susceptibility of your finger to repetitive strain injury? We thought not.

Like most Windows graphics programs, AutoCAD LT provides a *selection window* feature for grabbing a bunch of objects in a rectangular area. As you might guess by now, the AutoCAD LT version of this feature is a bit more powerful than the analogous feature in other Windows graphics programs, and therefore slightly confusing at first. AutoCAD LT calls its version *implied windowing*.

If you click a blank area of the drawing — that is, not on an object — you're *implying* to AutoCAD LT that you want to specify a selection window or box. If you move the cursor to the right before picking the other corner of the selection box, you're further implying that you want to select all objects that reside completely within the selection box. If you instead move the cursor to the left before picking the other corner of the selection box, you're implying that you want to select all objects that reside completely *or partially* within the selection box.

The AutoCAD LT terminology for these two kinds of selection boxes gets a little confusing. The move-to-the-right, only-select-objects-completely-within-the-box mode is called *window* object selection. The move-to-the-left, select-objects-completely-or-partially-within-the-box mode is called *crossing* object selection. You might think of these modes as *bounding box* (to the right) and *crossing box* (to the left). Fortunately, AutoCAD LT gives you a visual cue that there's a difference. As you move to the right, the bounding box appears as a solid rectangle. As you move to the left, the crossing box appears as a ghosted, or dashed, rectangle.

The Implied Windowing setting in the Options dialog box shown in Figure 6-1 earlier in this chapter must be turned on — which it is by default — in order for window and crossing object selection to work. The Press and Drag setting determines whether you specify window and crossing boxes using the default AutoCAD LT convention (click one corner, move the mouse, click the other corner) or the Windows convention (pick one corner and hold down the mouse button, drag to the other corner, release the button).

Figures 6-2 and 6-3 show a bounding box and a crossing box, respectively, in action.

To sum up: To create a *bounding box* for selecting objects that are fully within the window, click and then move the mouse *from the left side* of the objects *to the right*. To create a *crossing box* for selecting objects that are fully or partially within the window, click and then move the mouse *from the right side* of the objects *to the left*. These two types of selection windows are distinguished *only* by the direction in which you move the cursor on-screen.

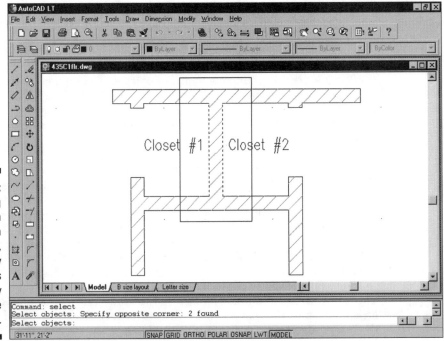

Figure 6-2:
A bounding selection box, drawn left to right, selects only objects completely within the window.

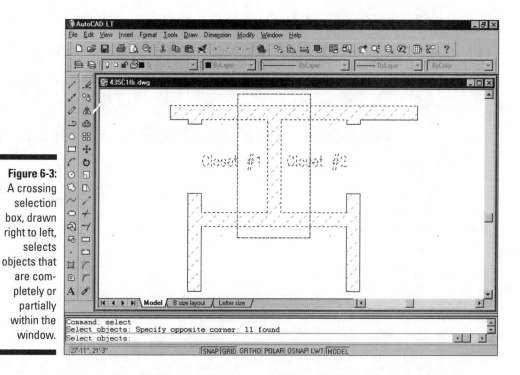

Figure 6-3:
A crossing
selection
box, drawn
right to left,
selects
objects that
are com-
pletely or
partially
within the
window.

You can mix and match selecting individual objects, specifying a bounding box, and specifying a crossing box. Each selection adds to the current selection set, enabling you to build up just the right selection of objects and then operate on them with one or more editing commands. For example, on a crowded archi-tectural floor plan, you might select all of the objects representing furniture in one office in order to copy them to other, similar offices. AutoCAD LT's selec-tion flexibility makes it relatively easy to grab the furniture objects without also getting walls, text, and other nearby or even overlapping objects.

Ghosts and grips

The most confusing difference between selected objects in AutoCAD LT and those in other programs involves *grips* (which we describe in detail in the section "Get a Grip," later in this chapter). In most other programs, only selected objects display grips, or *handles*, at certain key points on the objects. In AutoCAD LT, however, a selected object retains its grips even *after* you deselect it. To the new user, the object probably looks as though it's still selected. In AutoCAD LT, the only visual cue you can trust to indicate that an object is selected and therefore subject to editing is the *ghosted* (or dashed) appearance that the object takes on. The currently selected object in Figure 6-4, for example, appears ghosted to indicate that it's still selected.

Previously selected object (retains grips)

Unselected object (no grips)   Currently selected object (has grips and is ghosted)

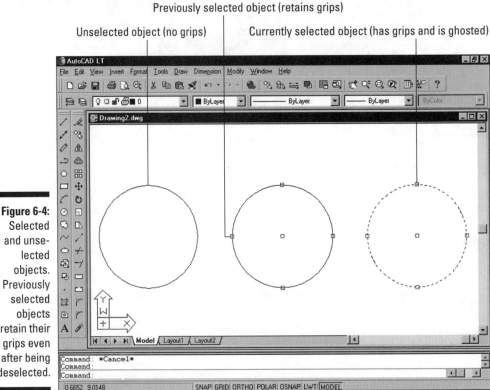

Figure 6-4:
Selected
and unse-
lected
objects.
Previously
selected
objects
retain their
grips even
after being
deselected.

We use the term ghosted to describe selected objects in order to avoid confusion with the AutoCAD LT dashed and dotted linetypes. Some objects in drawings appear dashed or dotted all the time — even when they're not selected — because the objects or the layer that they reside on has been assigned a special dash-dot linetype. Fortunately, the dashes in most dashed linetypes are longer than the ghosting dashes and the dots are much smaller, so you usually won't mistake a legitimately dashed or dotted object for a selected object.

To unselect all currently selected objects, but leave their grips turned on, press the Esc key. To remove grips from all objects, press the Esc key once more. As we explain in the section "Get a Grip" later in this chapter, there's a reason for this "gripped-but-not-selected" object state that at first seems so confusing.

Erase and Leave No Trace

Enough selection and grip theory — let's kill some objects! After you know how to select objects, erasing objects is as simple as pressing the Delete key. The following example demonstrates the three object selection modes and using them to erase objects.

If you have the slightest doubt about whether you should be erasing objects in someone else's drawing, make a copy and do your erasing in the copy. Especially in an example like this one, where you're going to annihilate vast armies of objects for the mere pleasure of it, you should work on a copy.

1. **Open a drawing containing objects that you want to erase.**

2. **Select an individual object, such as a line or arc, by moving the little square at the center of your crosshairs over the object and clicking.**

   The object highlights to indicate that it's selected. It also displays grips.

   If you don't click right on the object — that is, if you miss — AutoCAD LT assumes that you want to draw a bounding or crossing selection box. Just press the Esc key to cancel and try again.

3. **Press the Delete key.**

   The object disappears.

4. **Select two or three individual objects by clicking each one.**

   AutoCAD LT adds each object to the selection set — all the objects you select remain ghosted and with grips.

5. **Specify a bounding selection box that completely encloses several objects. You can use Figure 6-2, earlier in this chapter, as a guide.**

   Move the cursor to a point below and to the left of the objects, click, release the mouse button, move the cursor above and to the right of the objects, and click again.

   Notice that the selection box displays as a solid rectangle, indicating that you moved the cursor to the right and thus created a bounding box. After you pick the second corner of the rectangle, all the objects that are completely within the bounding box ghost and display grips.

6. **Specify a crossing selection box that encloses a few objects and cuts through several others. You can use Figure 6-3, earlier in this chapter, as a guide.**

   Move the cursor to a point below and to the right of some of the objects, click, release the mouse button, move the cursor above and to the left of some of the objects, and click and release again.

This time, the selection box displayed as a ghosted rectangle, indicating that you moved the cursor to the left and thus created a crossing box. After you pick the second corner of the rectangle, all the objects that are completely or partially within the bounding box ghost and display grips.

7. Press the Delete key.

All the objects that you selected in Steps 4 through 6 disappear.

8. Select a few more objects, using any of the three object selection modes.

The objects ghost and display grips.

9. Press the Esc key once.

The objects are no longer ghosted (indicating that they're not selected), but still display grips.

10. Select some more objects.

The objects that you selected in this step ghost and display grips. The objects that you selected in Step 8 continue to display grips.

11. Press the Delete key.

The objects that you selected in Step 10 disappear. The objects that you selected in Step 8 remain, but lose their grips.

12. Continue selecting objects and erasing objects until you have the hang of the three object selection modes: clicking an object, bounding boxes, and crossing boxes.

You might think that the Delete key, by its very nature, deletes objects. In AutoCAD LT, it's not that simple. In fact, pressing the Delete key runs the AutoCAD LT ERASE command, as you'll notice if you look at the command line after you delete an object using the Delete key. You don't have to memorize this cocktail party fact, but as you'll discover in Chapter 11, most toolbar buttons and some keyboard keys work by feeding command names to the AutoCAD LT command line.

Oops!

So what do you do after you press the Delete key when you didn't mean to? If you notice the error right away, you can correct it by clicking the Undo button (the backward-pointing arrow) on the Standard toolbar once. Each click of the Undo button undoes one step, so if you erased some objects, then zoomed in to find out what had disappeared, you'd need to click Undo twice — once to undo the zoom and once to undo the erasure.

If you undo too many steps, click the Redo button (the forward-pointing arrow) until you return to where you want to be. At this point, you can gloat over the AutoCAD users in your office — AutoCAD LT 2000 offers multiple levels of redo, while AutoCAD 2000 can redo only the last undo step!

Undo and redo work for all editing operations — not just erasing. AutoCAD LT 2000 has a special "undelete" command for those tricky circumstances when you erase some objects and then perform some additional, useful commands before realizing that you didn't want to erase the objects after all. For example, imagine that you erase some objects, add some text comments explaining to the drawing's creator why the objects shouldn't be there, and then realize that you should let the drawing's creator make the final decision about whether the objects live or die. You could click the Undo button until the objects reappear, but then your text comments would be gone. Not to worry — the OOPS command comes to the rescue. OOPS undeletes the last group of erased objects, no matter what other commands you might have run since the erasure. The following example demonstrates how to use OOPS.

Autodesk inexplicably excluded the OOPS command from the toolbars and menus. You have to type it at the command line:

1. **Erase some objects, as described in the previous example.**

2. **Click the Undo button on the Standard toolbar.**

   The objects reappear.

3. **Erase some more objects.**

4. **Click the Zoom Realtime button on the Standard toolbar and zoom in to where the objects used to be.**

   If you need help with this procedure, refer to Chapter 5.

5. **Add a text comment, or any other object that you know how to draw.**

   If you need help adding text, see Chapter 5.

6. **Type** OOPS **at the command line and then press the Enter key.**

   The objects reappear, the view remains zoomed in, and the text remains.

Get a Grip

You might have encountered *grip editing* when using other kinds of graphics programs, or even when doing something as simple as resizing a graphic that you placed in a word processing document. Even if you're an experienced user of other graphics programs, though, you've never seen grips used in quite the way that AutoCAD LT uses them.

About grips

Grips, as we explain earlier in this chapter, are little handles that appear on an object after you select it. You employ these handles in many programs for direct manipulation of the object. *Direct manipulation,* as used in most other Windows programs, involves the following common operations: To move an object, you grab the object's middle grip and drag that grip; to stretch an object, you grab a corner, or edge grip, and drag that grip; to move a copy of the object, you hold down the Shift key while dragging the middle of the object. Even the little frames around the graphics you import into a word processing document are likely to work this way.

In their simplest guise, AutoCAD LT grips work similarly. Instead of clicking and dragging a grip, though, in AutoCAD LT, you must click, release the mouse button, move the cursor, and click again at the new location.

AutoCAD LT grips are, for sophisticated users, better than the grips found in most other programs, because you can do so much more with them. For example, you can use AutoCAD LT grips to move, stretch, or copy an object. You also can use them to rotate an object, scale it to a different size, or *mirror* an object — that is, create one or more "backwards" copies. Grips also act as *visible object snaps*, or little magnets that draw the cursor to themselves. That's why grips remain on an object even after it's deselected — you may want to edit a selected object by connecting it to a "leftover" grip on an unselected object.

As we describe earlier in this chapter, an object that displays grips isn't necessarily a selected object, but by default a selected object always displays grips. A selected object, in addition to displaying grips, appears ghosted.

AutoCAD LT grips are also better — but correspondingly more complicated — than grips in other programs because AutoCAD grips come in three varieties: hot, warm, and cold, as shown in Figure 6-5. (We could compare these types to the grip a person may have on a significant other, but that would just be causing trouble.) A *hot grip* is the grip you use to perform an action, such as stretching an object. A *warm grip* is any grip on a selected object that isn't a hot grip (nothing's happening to its object at the moment). A *cold grip* is a grip on an unselected object that acts only as an object snap target. Cold grips and warm grips both appear as empty, not-filled-in squares; their default color on-screen is blue. Hot grips, on the other hand, appear on-screen as red, filled-in squares.

What all these grip capabilities really mean to the beginning user, however, is that using grips effectively in AutoCAD LT requires some practice. If you make a habit of using them regularly for doing editing changes to drawings, the little buggers slowly — but surely — yield their secrets to you.

Object with warm grips (object selected)

Object with cold grips (object not selected)   A hot grip (object selected and grip picked)

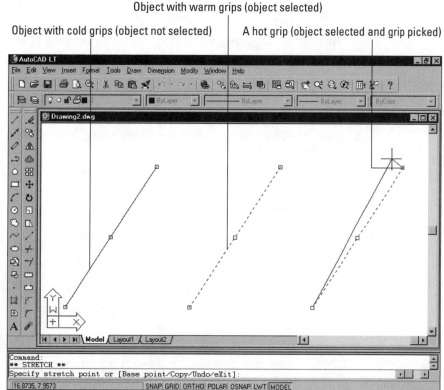

Figure 6-5:
All-weather
grips.

Can't get a grip? If you don't see grips when you select objects, then someone turned off the grips feature on your computer. Turn on the Enable Grips setting in the Options dialog box, as shown in Figure 6-1, earlier in this chapter.

A gripping example

Before you delve into the details of grip editing, take a look at the three kinds of grips and the five grip editing modes. Use the following steps to get a grip:

1. **Click an object on-screen to select it and display its grips.**

   Warm grips — empty blue squares on the selected object — appear at various points on the object.

2. **Press the Esc key.**

   The grips are now cold, because they reside on an unselected object. There's no visual difference between warm and cold grips — only between the objects on which they appear.

3. **Click another object.**

The newly selected object displays warm grips, while the deselected object continues to display cold grips.

4. **Click one of the grips on the object that you selected in Step 3.**

    The blue, empty square turns to a red, filled-in square. This grip is now hot.

    Grip editing options now appear on the command line. The first option to appear is STRETCH.

5. **Press the spacebar to cycle through the five grip editing options on the command line:**

```
** STRETCH **
Specify stretch point or [Base point/Copy/Undo/eXit]:
** MOVE **
Specify move point or [Base point/Copy/Undo/eXit]:
** ROTATE **
Specify rotation angle or [Base
        point/Copy/Undo/Reference/eXit]:
** SCALE **
Specify scale factor or [Base
        point/Copy/Undo/Reference/eXit]:
** MIRROR **
Specify second point or [Base point/Copy/Undo/eXit]:
```

The grip editing option displayed on the command line changes as you press the spacebar. The options that appear are, in order, STRETCH, MOVE, ROTATE, SCALE, and MIRROR. If you move the cursor around (without picking) in between each press of the spacebar, you'll notice that the appearance of your selected object changes as you display each option. Choosing STRETCH, for example, causes a stretched version of the object to appear on-screen.

Pressing the spacebar a bunch of times is a good way to become familiar with the grip editing modes, but there's a more direct way to choose a particular mode. After you've clicked a grip to make it hot, right-click to display the grip editing menu. This cursor menu contains all the grip editing options plus some other choices, as shown in Figure 6-6.

Figure 6-6: The grip editing cursor menu.

6. **Keep pressing the spacebar until** STRETCH **(or the option you want) reappears as the grip editing option.**

7. **Move the hot grip in the direction in which you want to stretch (or otherwise manipulate) your object.**

   AutoCAD LT dynamically updates the image of the object in order to show you what the modified object will look like before you click the final location.

8. **Click again to finish the grip editing operation.**

   The selected object with the hot grip updates. The object with the cold grips doesn't change.

9. **Click the same grip that you chose in Step 4 (now in a different location) to make it hot.**

10. **This time, move the cursor near one of the cold grips on the unselected object. When you feel the magnetic pull of the cold grip, click again to connect the hot grip with the cold grip.**

    The object points represented by the hot grip and the cold grip now coincide exactly.

11. **Press Esc twice to deselect all objects and remove all grips.**

Figure 6-7 shows a hot endpoint grip of a line being connected to the cold endpoint grip of another line. The ghosted line shows the original position of the line being edited, and the continuous line shows the new position. Using a grip in this way as a visible object snap offers the same advantage as using single point object snaps, as described in Chapter 5: It ensures precision by making sure that objects meet exactly.

You can experiment with all the grip editing options to find out exactly how they affect a selected object, including using all the options that are available while holding down the Shift key (see the following tip).

If you want to see what a grip editing option does to your object without actually changing it, press and hold the Shift key while dragging the object's grip. Holding down the Shift key during grip editing causes the grip editing action to affect a *copy* of the object rather than the original; the original object remains in place, unchanged. (You can consider this one a Grip Tip.)

The two most useful grip editing modes are MOVE and STRETCH, so we'll demonstrate how to use them for making editing changes.

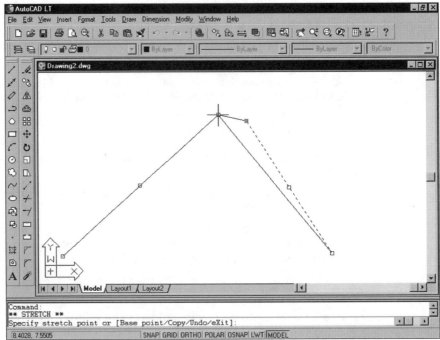

Figure 6-7:
Using grips
to connect
two objects.

Move it!

Back in the days of manual drafting, moving objects was a big pain in the
eraser. You had to erase the stuff you wanted to move and redraw the objects
in their new location. In the process, you usually ended up erasing parts of
other stuff that you didn't want to move and left smudged lines and piles of
eraser dust everywhere. CAD does away with all the fuss and muss of moving
objects, and AutoCAD LT grip editing is a great way to make it happen. The
following steps show you how:

1. **Select one or more objects.**

   Use any combination of the three editing modes — single object, bounding box, or crossing box — that we cover in the section, "Grab It," earlier
   in this chapter.

2. **Click any one of the warm grips to make it hot.**

   At this point in your editing career, it doesn't matter which grip you
   click. As you become more familiar with grip editing, you'll discover that
   certain grips serve as better reference points than others for particular
   editing operations.

3. **Right-click anywhere in the drawing area and choose Move from the cursor menu.**

4. **Move the cursor to a different location and click.**

   As you move the cursor around, AutoCAD LT displays the tentative new positions for all the objects, as shown in Figure 6-8. After you click, the objects assume their new position.

5. **Press Esc twice to deselect all objects and remove all grips.**

Copy — a kinder, gentler Move

If you were paying attention during "A gripping example," earlier in the chapter, you might have noticed while pressing the spacebar that COPY was not among the five grip editing modes. Why not? Because every grip mode includes a copy option! In other words, you can STRETCH with copy, MOVE with copy, ROTATE with copy, SCALE with copy, and MIRROR with copy.

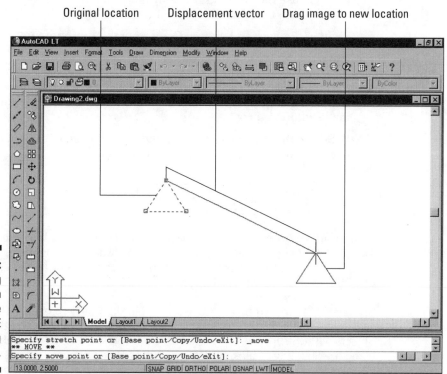

Original location   Displacement vector   Drag image to new location

Figure 6-8:
Dragging objects in the middle of the MOVE grip editing operation.

As a previous tip points out, the copy option leaves the selected objects in place and does the editing operation on a new copy of the objects. You can activate the copy option by pressing the Shift key while clicking the new location for the hot grip. Alternatively, you can type **C** at the command prompt and press the Enter key, as the grip editing command-line prompts indicate:

```
Specify move point or [Base point/Copy/Undo/eXit]:
```

By far the most common use for the copy option is with the MOVE grip editing mode. If you think about "MOVE with copy" for about two seconds, you'll realize that it's just a complicated way of saying "copy." The following example shows you how to copy objects quickly using grip editing:

1. **Select one or more objects.**

2. **Click any one of the warm grips to make it hot.**

3. **Right-click anywhere in the drawing area and choose <u>M</u>ove from the cursor menu.**

   If you want to copy objects in the normal sense of the word "copy," you must choose the MOVE grip editing mode first. Otherwise, you'll be copying with the STRETCH grip editing mode.

4. **Right-click again and choose <u>C</u>opy from the cursor menu.**

5. **Move the cursor to a different location and click.**

   After you click, new objects appear in the new location.

6. **Move the cursor to additional locations and click there if you want to make additional copies.**

7. **Press Esc three times — once to end the copying operation, once to deselect all objects, and once to remove all grips.**

A warm-up Stretch

In AutoCAD LT, stretching is the process of making objects longer *or* shorter. The STRETCH grip editing operation is really a combination of stretching and compressing, but the programmers probably realized that STRETCHAND-COMPRESS didn't exactly roll off the tongue.

The STRETCH grip editing mode works a bit differently than the other modes. By default, it affects only the object with the hot grip on it, rather than all objects with warm grips on them. You can override this default behavior by using the Shift key to pick multiple hot grips. The following set of steps shows you how to use the STRETCH grip editing mode to stretch one or more objects:

1. **Turn off ortho (orthogonal) mode by clicking the ORTHO button on the status bar until the button appears to be pushed out and the words `<Ortho off>` appear on the command line.**

   Ortho mode forces stretch displacements to be *orthogonal* — that is, parallel to lines running at 0 and 90 degrees. During real editing tasks, you'll often want to turn on ortho mode, but for this stretching example, leaving ortho mode off makes things clearer.

2. **Select several objects, including at least one line.**

3. **On one of the lines, click one of the endpoint grips to make it hot.**

   All the objects remain selected, but as you move the cursor, only the line with the hot grip changes. Figure 6-9 shows an example.

4. **Click a new point for the hot endpoint grip.**

   The line stretches to accommodate the new endpoint location.

5. **On the same line, click the midpoint grip to make it hot.**

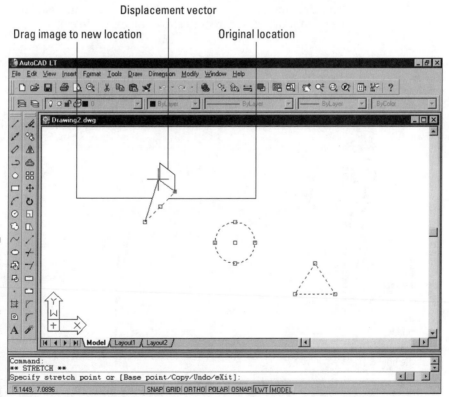

Figure 6-9:
Dragging a line's endpoint in the middle of the STRETCH grip editing operation.

As you move the cursor, the entire line moves. Using the STRETCH grip editing mode with a line's midpoint "stretches" the entire line to a new location.

6. Click a new point for the hot midpoint grip.

The line moves to the new midpoint location.

7. Hold down the Shift key and then click one of the endpoint grips on one of the lines to make it hot.

8. As you continue holding down the Shift key, click one of the endpoint grips on a different line to make it hot.

Two grips on two different lines are now hot, because you held down the Shift key while clicking both grips.

You can create more hot grips by continuing to hold down the Shift key and clicking more grips.

9. Release the Shift key and repick any one of the hot grips.

Releasing the Shift key signals that you're finished making grips hot. Repicking one of the hot grips establishes it as the base point for the stretch operation. Figure 6-10 shows an example.

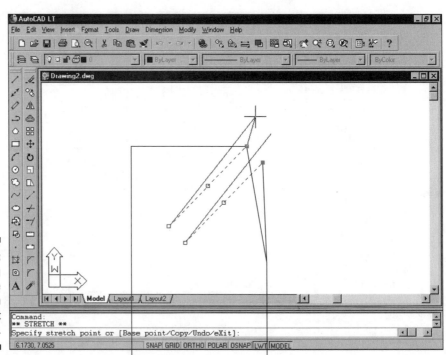

Figure 6-10:
Stretching multiple objects with multiple hot grips.

The hot grip used as a base point   Multiple hot grips

10. **Click a new point for the grip.**

    All the objects with hot grips stretch based on the displacement of the grip that you clicked in Step 9.

11. **Turn on ortho mode by clicking the ORTHO button on the status bar until the button appears to be pushed in and the words <Ortho on> appear on the command line. Then repeat Steps 2 through 10 in order to see the effect of ortho mode on stretching.**

For most real-world editing situations, you'll want to turn on ortho mode before stretching (not that we want to contradict your yoga instructor's advice or anything). In fact, ortho mode is good for all kinds of drawing and editing tasks, because it enforces a nice, rectilinear orderliness on your drawing. Chapter 5 describes how to use ortho mode to draw orthogonal lines.

The STRETCH grip editing mode takes some practice, but it's worth the effort. In Chapter 11, we explain the STRETCH command, which is like a supercharged version of the STRETCH grip editing mode.

Other grip editing modes

The remaining grip editing modes are MIRROR, ROTATE, and SCALE. These probably will be less useful to you than the MOVE and STRETCH modes. In addition, each of these modes has a counterpart AutoCAD LT *command* that you can use command-first style or selection-first style and which you may find a bit easier to use than the grip editing versions. See Chapter 11 for more information.

Precision Editing

In most of the previous exercises in this chapter, you edit loosey-goosey fashion — shoving objects around carelessly and positioning them by eye. If you read our warnings about maintaining precision in the "Neatness Counts" section of Chapter 5, you probably realize that this lackadaisical approach to editing is *not* a good way to modify real drawings. It is, however, a good way to become comfortable with the grip editing operations, and that's why we don't hassle you about precision when we introduce the basic grip editing techniques. This section explains the *right* way to do grip editing — with precision — and shows you one way to do it.

So sit up and pay attention. Here's the rule: When you move, copy, or stretch objects in real drawings, *don't* just eyeball the distances. *Do* use one of the AutoCAD LT precision techniques to specify a precise distance or destination point for the editing operation. In Chapter 5, we show you how to use direct distance entry and single point object snaps. Earlier in this chapter, we explain how to use grips as object snaps to ensure precision. Those three techniques will take you a long way with move, copy, and stretch. (We show you other techniques in Chapters 10 and 11.)

Direct distance entry is an especially useful and efficient technique, because you frequently need to move, copy, or stretch objects a specific distance in an orthogonal direction. (If you need to review direct distance entry, see the section "And one further point. . .," in Chapter 5.) The following example demonstrates how to use direct distance entry:

1. **Select several objects.**

2. **Click any one of the warm grips to make it hot.**

3. **Right-click anywhere in the drawing area and choose** <u>M</u>**ove from the cursor menu.**

4. **Use the ORTHO button on the status bar to turn on ortho mode.**

5. **Move the cursor to the right (at an angle of 0 degrees from the grip that you picked in Step 2).**

6. **Type a distance, such as 4, at the command line, and press Enter.**

   The objects move four units to the right.

7. **Hold down the Shift key, click any one of the warm grips to make it hot, and click grips on a couple of other objects in order to make them hot as well.**

   You now should have multiple objects with hot grips, in preparation for stretching multiple objects.

8. **Release the Shift key and repick any one of the hot grips.**

9. **Move the cursor up (at an angle of 90 degrees from the grip that you picked in the previous step).**

10. **Type a distance, such as 1.5, at the command line, and press Enter.**

    The objects move 1.5 units up.

Chapter 7

Swapping Stuff with Other Programs

*I*n many companies that use AutoCAD, drafting runs on its own track — apart from the other project activities and from documentation work. As a result, AutoCAD users often are fairly isolated, software-wise. They make drawings in AutoCAD all day long, plot them out from AutoCAD (sometimes all night long!), and usually don't spend lots of time worrying about how to exchange data with other programs. In many cases, a CAD drafter's Windows taskbar displays buttons for nothing more than AutoCAD and maybe Windows Explorer most of the day.

AutoCAD LT users like yourself, on the other hand, tend to be more widely traveled in the software world. In all likelihood, you use a variety of software and routinely work on types of documents other than AutoCAD DWG. Your Windows taskbar, like your work schedule, is crowded and ever-changing.

At various times, you probably need to transfer information from one kind of document to another. You might even have taken the AutoCAD LT plunge because you want to import AutoCAD drawing data into your word processing or other documents, as shown in Figure 7-1. If so, then this chapter is for you. It covers exchanging AutoCAD drawing data with other programs — what works, what doesn't, and how to do it. We provide step-by-step instructions for the most common exchange scenarios and tell you what kinds of techniques and formats to try in other scenarios. We also tell you when to give up and reach for the scissors and glue stick.

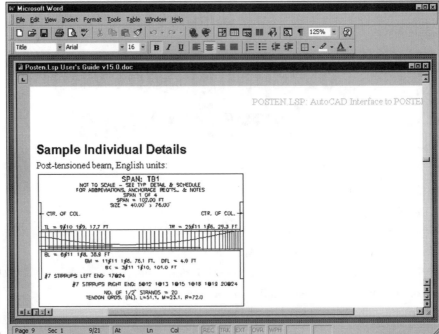

Figure 7-1:
LT finds the
Word.

Why Swap . . . and Why Not?

People such as CAD drafters who spend most of their computing day in one program often try to use that one tool for everything. Before the days of What-You-See-Is-What-You-Get word processors, it wasn't too uncommon to see AutoCAD users' group newsletters produced completely in AutoCAD! This one-tool-fits-all-jobs approach isn't necessarily completely stupid. In some cases, using a program that you know really well is more efficient than spending the time learning another program that's a little better at the task you're performing. However, producing a newsletter in AutoCAD is over-doing it.

AutoCAD LT supports the one-tool-fits-all-jobs approach up to a point, at least for the types of things that most people want to put in technical drawings. But LT isn't a very efficient tool for entering or editing large amounts of text, and it isn't very good for creating raster images. At some point, you'll want to grab some of the other tools in your software toolbox and use them to create a more handsome piece of handiwork than you can with AutoCAD LT alone.

If you need a refresher course on the difference between vector and raster graphics, see Chapter 1. Briefly, a *vector format* stores graphics as collections of geometrical objects (such as lines, polygons, and text), while a *raster format* stores graphics as a series of little dots, or *pixels*. Vector graphics are good for high geometrical precision and for stretching or squeezing images to different sizes. These two characteristics make vector formats especially suitable for CAD. Raster graphics are good for depicting photographic detail and lots of colors.

The basic idea behind swapping data is pretty obvious. Different programs are better at different jobs. Ideally, you'd like to use each program for what it's good at — for example, AutoCAD for drawing technical graphics, Word for creating and formatting text, and Excel for arranging tables of numbers and text. Then, you'd like to transfer or translate stuff from one program to another in order to create a compound document that displays the cumulative results of all your hard work in all those complicated programs.

In practice, this approach sometimes works great, especially if you're familiar with each of the programs and with their data exchange strengths and quirks. Sometimes, you have to try a bunch of different techniques or exchange formats to get all the data to transfer in an acceptable way. Occasionally, no practical exchange method exists for preserving formatting or other properties that are important to you.

Where your exchange efforts will fall in this spectrum depends on the kind of drawings you make, the other programs you work with, and the output devices or formats that you use. We provide recommendations in this chapter, but be prepared to spend time experimenting.

When you do stumble upon that magical combination of exchange steps that gives you just what you're looking for, write the steps down! It's tempting to think that you'll remember how to do it the next time around, but too often you'll forget where that sub-sub-sub-dialog box setting or menu choice was.

In general, AutoCAD LT is better at transferring stuff to other programs than it is at receiving stuff from them. If you want to create a compound document that contains drawing and other objects, such as lots of text or spreadsheet tables, you'll usually be better off transferring the drawing objects to the other program, rather than vice versa.

Why not just shout, "OLE!"?

The Microsoft Windows family of operating systems includes a data transfer feature called Object Linking and Embedding, or OLE. (By the way, you pronounce OLE like the Spanish bullfight cheer, not like the cockney way of saying hole.) Microsoft touts OLE as an all-purpose solution to the data exchange problem. If the two programs that you want to share data between are OLE-aware (and most Windows applications are), then creating an embedded or linked document isn't much more complicated than using the Windows cut and paste features. That's the theory, anyway.

First, here's how it works. In OLE lingo, the program that you're taking the data from is called the *source*. The program that you're sending the data to is called the *container*. For example, if you want to place a spreadsheet table from Excel into an AutoCAD LT drawing, Excel is the source, and AutoCAD LT is the container.

In Excel, you select the range of spreadsheet cells that you want to put in the AutoCAD LT drawing and choose Edit⇨Copy to copy them to the Windows Clipboard. Then, you switch to AutoCAD LT and choose Edit⇨Paste Special. The Paste Special choice displays a dialog box containing the choices Paste and Paste Link, as shown in the accompanying figure. The Paste option creates a copy of the object from the source document and *embeds* the copied object into the container document. The Paste Link option *links* the new object in the container document to its source document, so that any changes to the source document are automatically reflected in the container document. In other words, if you link a spreadsheet object to an AutoCAD LT drawing, changes that you make later in the Excel spreadsheet get propagated to the AutoCAD LT drawing automatically. If you embed the same spreadsheet object in an AutoCAD LT drawing, changes that you later make to the data in Excel aren't reflected in the AutoCAD drawing.

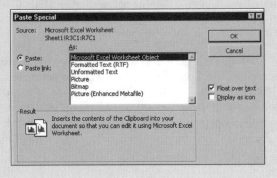

The OLE idea is a good one. You're not translating data from one application to another, with all the attendant problems of mistranslation and lost formatting. Instead, with OLE, you're placing an *object*, such as a group of spreadsheet cells or paragraphs of word processing text, that retains the appearance that it had in the source application.

Unfortunately, OLE is afflicted with numerous practical problems. First, compound OLE documents can slow down performance — sometimes a lot. Before you start experimenting with OLE, make sure that you have either a fast computer with lots of memory or lots of time on your hands. Second, supporting OLE well is a difficult programming job, and many applications — including AutoCAD LT — suffer from OLE design limitations and bugs. Third, getting consistent hard-copy output can be tricky, especially when you plot from AutoCAD LT. OLE objects that look fine on the screen often undergo amazingly creative but not necessarily desirable transformations when they come out on paper.

In our experience, the potential benefits of using OLE with AutoCAD LT just aren't worth all the pitfalls and limitations that you have to work around. So, use the alternative methods described in this chapter instead, and save OLE for your next trip to Spain.

Good Trades and Bad

Every program has its data exchange strengths and weaknesses, and AutoCAD LT is no exception. Before you start down the exchange path between AutoCAD LT and another program, get a feel for the lay of the land. Exchanges between certain kinds of programs and file formats tend to go more smoothly than with others. It's nice to know before setting out on a journey whether you're going to be out for a Sunday afternoon drive or a bushwhack through an impenetrable jungle.

Here are the most common kinds of file formats that you encounter when exchanging data with other programs:

✔ **AutoCAD DWG format (when exchanging with AutoCAD):** Both AutoCAD 2000 and AutoCAD LT 2000 use the same native DWG file format. That's probably one of the main reasons that you bought LT instead of a competing low-cost CAD program. Because the AutoCAD and LT program code for reading and writing the DWG format comes from the same company, AutoCAD and LT give you excellent compatibility. LT can't *create* every kind of object that AutoCAD can — raster attachments and most 3D objects, for example — but it can successfully *read* and *save* DWG files that contain these objects. Thus, you can easily and safely exchange DWG files between AutoCAD and LT — it's one of the more hassle-free exchange methods around.

✔ **Other CAD formats:** AutoCAD and AutoCAD LT aren't the only CAD programs in the world, and AutoCAD users often need to exchange files with users of other CAD programs. AutoCAD is, however, the King of the PC CAD Hill, so it expects other CAD programs' data to come to it, rather than vice versa. Autodesk publishes its DXF (Drawing eXchange Format) specification and recommends that all file exchanges between AutoCAD or AutoCAD LT and other CAD programs take place via DXF files. Autodesk does not document the native AutoCAD and AutoCAD LT DWG file format, but several companies have reverse engineered it, so that their CAD programs can read and sometimes write DWG files directly, with greater or lesser accuracy. Because the DWG format is complicated, isn't documented, and gets changed every couple of years, no one ever figures it out perfectly. Thus, exchanging DWG files with non-Autodesk programs always involves some compatibility risks.

Even "minor" compatibility problems between CAD programs can cause serious hassles to CAD users and to the users of the documents produced by the CAD program. Consider the consequences of errors in your drawings, then think twice, and test more than twice, before depending on DWG "compatibility."

✔ **Vector graphics:** Besides CAD programs, other applications, such as drawing and illustration programs, work with vector graphics. AutoCAD LT can exchange vector graphics with other programs using a variety of formats. The two most common are DXF and WMF (Windows MetaFile). DWF (Drawing Web Format) is a special Autodesk vector format just for displaying AutoCAD drawings on the Web, and we describe it in Chapter 8.

✔ **Raster (bitmap) graphics:** Paint and photo manipulation programs store their documents as a series of dots. These raster or bitmap images are fundamentally different from the vector graphics of a CAD program like AutoCAD LT. If you need a raster version of your drawing objects for another program, AutoCAD LT can convert all or part of a drawing to several raster file formats, most commonly the Windows BMP (BitMaP) format.

If you need to go the other direction — raster image into an AutoCAD drawing — then you need full AutoCAD. AutoCAD includes an excellent IMAGE command for importing raster files so that you can plot them together with your CAD vector data. Unfortunately, AutoCAD LT doesn't include this feature. LT will display raster images that an AutoCAD user has placed in a DWG file, but LT can't do the placing. Sometimes it's tough being the little brother . . . .

✔ **Text:** AutoCAD LT's text creation and editing features, as we describe in Chapters 5 and 12, are adequate for short, simple blocks of text. If you need to include larger amounts of text or fancier text formatting in drawings, you'll be tempted to import text from other applications. AutoCAD LT does a reasonable job of importing plain ASCII text files and RTF

(Rich Text Format) files, as long as you don't get too fancy with the formatting and aren't too fussy about the alignment of words and characters. Because no sane person would use AutoCAD LT to create text for another program, or for creating a text-heavy document such as a newsletter, LT doesn't provide any tools for exporting text.

In all of the preceding summaries, we've ignored the question of file format versions. Some file formats, such as ASCII TXT, are very stable — they don't change much or at all. Other formats, such as DWG and DXF, change with every major program upgrade. A few raster formats have several different "flavors" depending on the type of compression and other factors. In short, don't assume that, just because a program claims to support a particular format, exchanging with that format always will work. Other programs' DXF and DWG support, in particular, tend to lag behind AutoCAD and AutoCAD LT. It's not uncommon for other programs to be one or two AutoCAD versions behind in their support of DXF files, which means that your drawing or illustration program probably won't be able to read AutoCAD 2000 version DXF files. Fortunately, AutoCAD LT can read and write older DXF versions (though parts of your drawing that depend on newer parts of the file format will be lost on export).

AutoCAD LT and AutoCAD are *downwardly compatible*, which means AutoCAD LT 2000 and AutoCAD 2000 can read DWG files saved by earlier versions. In addition, LT 2000 and AutoCAD 2000 can save in the DWG formats of the previous two AutoCAD versions (AutoCAD R14/LT98/LT97 and R13/LT95). AutoCAD LT and AutoCAD are not *upwardly compatible*, which means that an older version of AutoCAD LT can't read DWG files saved by a later version in the later version's native DWG format. If you send DWG files to someone who uses AutoCAD R14 or AutoCAD LT 98, for example, you need to use File⇨Save As to save the files to the older format. When you do so, always save to a different folder or filename, so your original LT 2000 format DWG remains unaffected.

One way, frequent flyer, or round trip?

Before you start transferring stuff between programs, you should stop to think about whether it's going to be a one-time proposition or a regular commute. If you just need to get a drawing or image or chunk of text from program A into program B once, you don't need to worry about finding an elegant or easily repeatable way to do it.

If you envision later changing the drawing or image or chunk of text in program A, you may need to perform the same transfer operation to program B repeatedly. In that case, you want the transfer to be efficient and, above all, repeatable — you want to make sure that you get the same results every time. Thus, it's worth spending a bit of time experimenting with, refining, and documenting your transfer procedure.

Captured on the silver (or turquoise) screen

If your goal is to show the entire AutoCAD LT program window, and not just the drawing contained in it, then all you need to do is create a *screen capture*. Most of the figures in this book are screen captures. You might use similar figures to put together a training manual or to write a letter to your mom showing all the cool software you use.

Windows includes a no-frills screen capture capability. Press the Print Screen key to capture the entire Windows screen, including the desktop and taskbar. Hold down the Alt key and press the Print Screen key to capture just the current application's program window (for example, AutoCAD LT). When you press Print Screen or Alt+Print Screen, Windows copies a bitmap image of the screen to the Windows Clipboard. From there, you can paste the image into a paint program — for example, Paint, which comes with Windows — and then use that program to save the image to a raster file format such as BMP. Alternatively, you can paste the bitmap image directly into a document — for example, a Word document — without creating a separate raster file.

The Windows Print Screen method works okay for an occasional screen capture, but if you need to do lots of captures, a screen capture utility program makes the job much faster and gives you many more options. You can control the area of the screen that gets captured, save to different raster file formats with different monochrome, grayscale, and color options, and print screen captures. Two good screen capture utility programs are FullShot by Inbit, Inc., (www.inbit.com) and Collage Complete by Inner Media, Inc. (www.innermedia.com).

When you create screen captures, you need to pay attention to resolution and colors. High screen resolutions — for example, those above 800 x 600 — can make your captures unreadable when they get compressed onto an 8½-x-11-inch sheet of paper. Some colors don't show up when you print in monochrome, and a black AutoCAD LT drawing area is overwhelmingly dark. For the screen captures in this book we used 800 x 600 resolution, a white LT drawing area, and dark colors — mostly black — for all the objects in the drawing.

One of OLE's big advantages is that it can automatically update an object in program B after you change it in program A. But see the warnings about OLE earlier in this chapter.

The most demanding — and elusive — kind of data exchange is called round-trip transfer. *Round-trip* means that you create and save a drawing in one program, edit and save it in another program, and then edit and save it in the first program again. A perfect round-trip is one in which all the data survives and the users of both programs can happily edit whatever they want to. Unfortunately, the perfect round-trip, like the perfect vacation visit to your distant cousins, rarely happens.

In CAD, round-trip transfer becomes an issue when two people want to work on the same drawings with different CAD programs. In all likelihood, one of the reasons you bought AutoCAD LT is its excellent round-trip compatibility with AutoCAD. Expect a bumpier road if you're exchanging drawings with users of other CAD programs. Perform some test transfers before you assume that your drawings can get from here to there and back again unscathed.

Safe swapping

Now that you know something about different kinds of data exchange with AutoCAD LT, you can cut to the chase and find out how to swap information with specific programs. Table 7-1 lists common programs and recommended formats for exchanging between them and AutoCAD LT.

Table 7-1	Swapping Information Between AutoCAD LT and Other Programs
Swap	*Recommended Formats*
LT to AutoCAD	DWG
LT to other CAD program	DXF or DWG
LT to Word	WMF
LT to paint program	BMP
LT to draw program	WMF
LT to the Web	DWF (see Chapter 8)
AutoCAD to LT	DWG
Other CAD program to LT	DXF or DWG
Word to LT	RTF or TXT
Draw program to LT	WMF
Paint program to LT	Buy AutoCAD and use the IMAGE command
Excel to LT	Don't bother; printing may be unpredictable

The remainder of this chapter gives you specific procedures for making the exchanges recommended in this table.

Swap Meet

In this section, we describe the general-purpose graphics formats that AutoCAD LT can write, read, or both, and we show you how to export and import the formats. You can use these formats to swap information with lots of different programs. In particular, we demonstrate how to place AutoCAD drawing objects into Word.

Always consider the option of simply creating the document or data anew within AutoCAD rather than converting. It often takes less time to redraw than it does to convert, and the results are likely to be better and more reliable.

DXF for eXtra Fidelity

As we describe in the "Good Trades and Bad" section earlier in the chapter, DXF is the Autodesk-approved format for exchanging between different CAD programs. In addition, some other vector graphics applications, such as drawing and illustration programs, can read and write DXF files.

DXF is a documented version of the DWG format. Because DXF more-or-less exactly mimics the DWG file's contents, it's a faithful representation of AutoCAD and AutoCAD LT drawings.

How well DXF works for exchanging data depends largely on the other program that you're exchanging with. Some CAD and vector graphics programs do a good job of reading and writing DXF files, while others don't. In practice, geometry usually comes through well, but properties, formatting, and other nongeometrical information can be tricky. Test before you commit to large-scale exchange, and always check the results.

Exporting DXF

The following example shows how to create a DXF file from an AutoCAD or AutoCAD LT drawing:

1. **Open the DWG file.**

2. **Choose File⇨Save As.**

   The Save Drawing As dialog box appears.

3. **In the Save as Type drop-down list, choose one of the DXF version formats.**

AutoCAD LT 2000 DXF maintains the best fidelity to the AutoCAD LT 2000 DWG format, but isn't supported by all applications. AutoCAD R12/LT2 DXF is compatible with most other applications, but requires that LT "dumb-down" any of your drawing objects that use newer AutoCAD LT features. If you're in doubt about which DXF version to use, ask the intended recipients which version their programs support, or save to several different versions and have them try each one.

4. **Click the Options button and then click the DXF Options tab on the Save As Options dialog box.**

   The DXF Options tab on the Save As Options dialog box appears, as shown in Figure 7-2. The default options usually are fine. Use the dialog box help to learn more: Click the question mark in the dialog box title bar and then click the area of the dialog box about which you want information.

Figure 7-2:
Options for
creating
DXF files.

5. **If necessary, adjust the DXF options and then click OK.**

   If you want LT to include only some of the drawing objects in the DXF file, turn on the Select Objects setting.

6. **Type a name for the new DXF file and then click Save.**

   If you didn't turn on the Select Objects setting in the previous step, AutoCAD LT creates the new DXF file and you're finished. If you did turn on this setting, LT prompts you to select the objects that it should include in the DXF file.

7. **Select objects using the single object, bounding box, or crossing box selection techniques described in the "Grab It" section of Chapter 6.**

8. **When you're finished selecting objects, press Enter.**

   AutoCAD LT creates the new DXF file, containing the objects that you've selected.

Importing DXF

Importing a DXF file into AutoCAD LT is not much more complicated than opening a DWG file, as the following example demonstrates:

1. **Click the Open button on the Standard toolbar.**

   The Select File dialog box appears.

2. **In the Files of Type list, choose DXF.**

3. **Choose the DXF file that you want to import.**

4. Click the Open button.

LT opens the DXF file in a new drawing window. Notice that the name of the "drawing" in the title bar ends in DXF, because at this point, it's still a DXF file.

5. Click the Save button on the Standard toolbar.

Because this is a DXF file and AutoCAD LT prefers to use its native DWG format for working purposes, the Save Drawing As dialog box appears so that you're encouraged to create a DWG version of the DXF file.

6. Type a name for the new DWG file and then click Save.

You can use the same name as the DXF file (minus DXF), as long as that name doesn't conflict with any existing DWG files.

LT creates a new DWG file from the objects in the DXF file. Notice that the name of the drawing in the title bar now ends in DWG.

If you need to copy objects from a DXF file into an existing file, open the DXF file as described in the preceding example, open the existing DWG file, and then copy the objects between the two windows using the technique described in Chapter 11.

The subject of CAD file exchange is a big, complicated one. We demonstrate the mechanics of how to do it in the preceding two examples, but you also need to consider many drawing organization and standards issues. Different CAD programs represent objects in different ways, and those differences often impede — or at least complicate — exchange. If you plan to exchange drawings with users of other CAD programs, do some test exchanges at the beginning of the project and be prepared to spend some time working out kinks. If possible, get experts from your offices who know AutoCAD and the other CAD program well to help you.

DWG with care

Thanks to a lot of hard work reverse-engineering the undocumented DWG format, many CAD programs from other companies now can read and/or write DWG files. Visio's IntelliCAD even uses DWG as its native format. This DWG file support can be handy, but you should approach it with some wariness. Perfect fidelity to the AutoCAD and AutoCAD LT interpretation of DWG is impossible to achieve, so be prepared for possible translation glitches when you exchange DWG files with users of other CAD programs. In any case, test before you commit to using DWG as an exchange format, and always check the results.

Note also that it's not uncommon for other programs to be one DWG version behind, or to support the current DWG version only partially. If users of other CAD programs ask you for DWG files, make sure you know which version their programs support, and save your files — or copies of your files — accordingly.

If you have problems exchanging DWG files with users of non-Autodesk "DWG-compatible" CAD programs, tell them to get with the program and buy AutoCAD LT. No, what we meant to say was "try DXF instead."

Windows never meta WMF file it didn't like

There are lots of different vector and raster graphics file formats, but Microsoft has been pretty successful at making its WMF and BMP formats the *lingua franca* — or should that be *lingua bill-a*? — for exchanging graphical information in Windows. WMF and BMP aren't the best formats for every situation, but they're fairly reliable lowest common denominators among Windows programs, and AutoCAD LT supports them reasonably well.

WMF (Windows MetaFile) is a vector format, so it does a decent job of representing AutoCAD LT objects such as lines, arcs, and text. When you place a WMF into another document, you can stretch it without losing resolution — that is, the diagonal lines don't turn into staircases.

Exporting WMF files

The following example demonstrates how to create a WMF file from AutoCAD LT drawing objects.

Set your LT background color to white before you create WMF or BMP files. If you've changed the drawing area color to black, LT will create images that look like nighttime photos of glow-in-the-dark objects. To change the drawing area color, choose <u>T</u>ools⇨Optio<u>n</u>s to open the Options dialog box, click the Display tab, and click the <u>C</u>olors button.

Because most people don't use the file export and import commands as often as other commands, LT doesn't include all of them in the menus and doesn't have a dialog box interface for all of them. Be prepared to do some typing at the command line in the following example:

1. **Turn on lineweight display by clicking the LWT button on the status bar until the button appears to be pushed in and the words** <Lineweight On> **appear on the command line.**

If the objects and layers in your drawing aren't assigned lineweights, you can skip this step. If they are assigned lineweights, you must turn on lineweight display if you want LT to include the lineweight information in the WMF file. (See the section "About colors and lineweights," in Chapter 4, for more information about object lineweights.)

2. **Type** WMFBKGND **at the command line and press Enter.**

   LT prompts you to turn the WMF BacKGrouND system variable on or off:

   ```
   Enter new value for WMFBKGND <ON>:
   ```

   The ON setting tells LT to use the current drawing area color as the background color for the WMF file image. The OFF setting tells LT to make the background transparent. ON is like copying your drawing objects onto a place mat that's the same color as the drawing area. OFF is like copying your drawing objects onto a piece of glass.

3. **Type** ON **or** OFF **and press Enter.**

   The best setting for WMF files that you intend to place in a word processing document and then print on white paper is WMFBKGND ON (which is the default). If you're not sure which setting is best for your needs, create one WMF file using each setting, place each file in your document, and do a test print.

4. **Zoom and pan to locate the view you want to use for the new WMF file. If necessary, adjust the drawing window size to control the relative length and height of the WMF file.**

   The current drawing window view defines the physical size and shape of the WMF file. See Chapter 5 if you need help with zooming and panning.

5. **Type** WMFOUT **at the command line and press Enter.**

   The Create WMF File dialog box appears.

6. **Type a name for the new WMF file and then click Save.**

   LT prompts you to select the objects that it should include in the WMF file.

7. **Select objects using the single object, bounding box, or crossing box selection techniques described in the "Grab It" section of Chapter 6.**

   If you want to include all drawing objects in the WMF file, type **ALL** at the command line and press Enter.

8. **When you're finished selecting objects, press Enter.**

   AutoCAD LT creates the new WMF file, containing the objects that you've selected.

AutoCAD LT puts objects in the WMF file with the colors and display lineweights that you see in LT. If you want to create a WMF file that looks like a monochrome plot — that is, with varying lineweights and all objects black — you need to set layer and object properties in LT so the objects look that way on the screen before you create the WMF file. For example, you could change all layers to color White (which displays as Black on a white background) and assign a different lineweight to each layer in the Layer Properties Manager dialog box. See Chapter 10 for information about setting layer and object properties.

Placing WMF files in Word documents

One of the more common reasons to create WMF files from AutoCAD LT objects is to place them as figures in word processing documents. This example demonstrates how to place all or part of a drawing into a Word document as a WMF picture:

1. **Create a WMF file in AutoCAD LT, as described in the previous example.**

2. **Change to Microsoft Word and open the document in which you want to place the drawing objects as a figure.**

3. **Move the cursor to the place in the document where you want the figure to go.**

4. **Choose Insert⇨Picture⇨From File.**

   The Insert Picture dialog box appears, as shown in Figure 7-3.

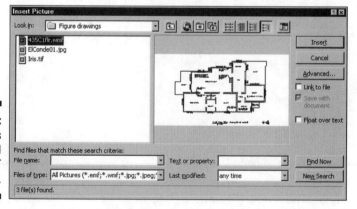

Figure 7-3: Word gets (W)MifFed with LT objects.

5. **Select the WMF file that you created in Step 1 and then click Insert.**

   Word places the WMF file into the document.

6. **If you need to modify the picture's size, click the picture and drag its handles. If you need to modify other properties, right-click the picture to display a menu of choices.**

Transferring WMF images via the Windows Clipboard

The preceding example uses an intermediate WMF file to transfer objects from AutoCAD LT to Word. If you need to transfer lots of figures, you can do it a bit more quickly with the Windows Clipboard, which bypasses the WMF file. The next example demonstrates how:

1. **In AutoCAD LT, select objects using the single object, bounding box, or crossing box selection techniques described in the "Grab It" section of Chapter 6.**

2. **Choose Edit⇨Copy.**

   This menu choice runs the COPYCLIP command, which copies objects to the Windows Clipboard in several formats, including WMF and BMP.

3. **Change to Microsoft Word, open the document in which you want to place the drawing objects as a figure, and move the cursor to the place in the document where you want the figure to go.**

4. **Choose Edit⇨Paste Special.**

   The Paste Special dialog box appears, as shown in Figure 7-4.

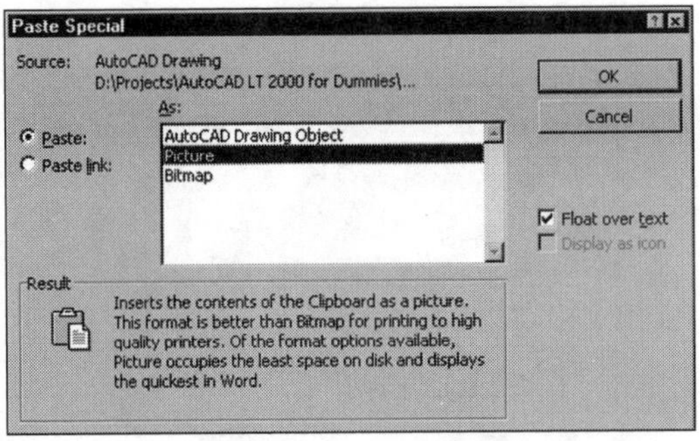

Figure 7-4:
Copying
objects via
the
Clipboard
using WMF
format.

5. **Choose Picture from the As list.**

   Picture corresponds to the WMF format. Bitmap corresponds to the BMP format. The AutoCAD Drawing Object choice uses OLE, as described in the "Why not just shout, 'OLE!'?" sidebar earlier in this chapter. Picture is the simplest and most robust choice for most purposes.

6. **Click OK.**

   Word places the object in the document as a new WMF picture.

Importing WMF

Importing a WMF file into an AutoCAD LT drawing is similar to inserting an AutoCAD block, which we tell you about in Chapter 15. The following example demonstrates how to import a WMF file, without dwelling on the finer points that we cover in Chapter 15:

1. **Turn off running osnap (object snap) mode by clicking the OSNAP button on the status bar until the button appears to be pushed out and the words** <Osnap off> **appear on the command line.**

2. **Choose Insert⇨Windows Metafile.**

   The Import WMF dialog box appears.

3. **Select a WMF file and then click Open.**

   LT displays the WMF file contents as you move the cursor around in the drawing area, and prompts you to specify an insertion point or an option to change:

   ```
   Specify insertion point or
           [Scale/X/Y/Z/Rotate/PScale/PX/PY/PZ/PRotate]:
   ```

4. **Pick a point where you want to place the WMF file.**

   After you've picked the insertion point for the WMF file, LT prompts you to specify the X scale factor:

   ```
   Enter X scale factor, specify opposite corner, or
           [Corner/XYZ] <1>:
   ```

5. **If the WMF file contents appeared to be the right size when you were dragging the image around the screen in Step 3, press Enter twice. Then jump to Step 7.**

   The first Enter responds to the X scale factor prompt, and the second Enter responds to the Y scale factor prompt:

   ```
   Enter Y scale factor <use X scale factor>:
   ```

6. **If the WMF file contents didn't appear to be the right size in Step 3, drag the cursor farther from or closer to the insertion point in order to change the insertion scale factor. Click when the size looks right.**

   LT prompts you to supply the rotation angle:

   ```
   Specify rotation angle <0>:
   ```

7. **Press Enter to accept the default rotation angle of zero.**

   LT places the WMF file.

The command-line prompts, for all their obtuseness, do provide several useful ways of scaling WMF files when you insert them. For example, if the contents of the WMF file look too small or too large, you can type **S** and press Enter during Step 3 to scale the contents before you place the file. See Chapter 15 for more information about the insertion options.

If you want to edit the line or other vectors in the inserted WMF image, you must explode it first. See Chapter 15 for details.

The other Windows way: Exporting BMP files

BMP (BitMaP) is the standard Windows raster format, and AutoCAD LT can export but not import it. When you export AutoCAD LT drawing objects to a BMP file, all the objects get converted to patterns of dots. Turning a line into a bunch of dots isn't such a swell idea if you ever want to work with the line as a line again. But it is a good idea — and a necessary step — if you want to bring a drawing into a paint program. You might perform this step in order to create a desktop publishing-friendly image for a company brochure.

One problem with BMP files is that they're BIG in file size. Unlike some other raster formats, BMP doesn't offer any kind of compression. Because CAD drawings usually are fairly large in area, they can turn into monstrously large BMP files — we're talking multiple megabytes. As an example, we opened a small 100KB DWG file showing a simple house plan and exported it to both WMF and BMP formats. The exported WMF file was about the same size as the DWG file, while the exported BMP file was over 2MB! Imagine what this implies for the BMP version of a 2MB DWG file. For this reason, AutoCAD LT to BMP transfers are best limited to small drawings or small parts of larger drawings.

The following example demonstrates how to create a BMP file from AutoCAD LT drawing objects:

1. **Turn on lineweight display, as described in Step 1 of the "Exporting WMF files" example, earlier in this chapter.**

2. **Zoom, pan, and adjust the drawing window size, as described in Step 4 of the "Exporting WMF files" example.**

   A smaller drawing window will result in a smaller BMP file, because LT doesn't have to create as many pixels.

3. **Type** BMPOUT **at the command line and press Enter.**

   The Create BMP File dialog box displays.

4. **Type a name for the new BMP file and then click Save.**

   LT prompts you to select the objects that it should include in the BMP file.

5. **Select objects using the single object, bounding box, or crossing box selection techniques described in the "Grab It" section of Chapter 6.**

   If you want to include all drawing objects in the BMP file, type **ALL** at the command line and press Enter.

6. **When you're finished selecting objects, press Enter.**

   AutoCAD LT creates the new BMP file, containing the objects that you've selected.

AutoCAD LT doesn't provide a way to import BMP files into drawings. For that you need AutoCAD.

Going abroad: Other output formats

DXF, WMF, BMP, and to a lesser extent, DWG, are the most reliable AutoCAD LT exchange formats. These formats don't serve all needs, though. If the other program that you're trying to exchange with requires or works better with other formats, you have a couple of options.

One option is to create one of the AutoCAD LT-friendly formats — for example, WMF — and then translate it to another graphics format using a translation program such as HiJaak Pro (www.quarterdeck.com) or VuePrint (www.hamrick.com).

If you need to convert drawings to a raster format other than BMP, the second option is to use the AutoCAD LT Raster File Format driver. This driver enables you to "plot" to a file using one of nine raster formats, including PCX, JPEG, and TIFF. Before you can use the Raster File Format driver, you must create a new plotter configuration: Choose File➪Plotter Manager and then run the Add-A-Plotter wizard. Figure 7-5 shows the driver that you need to choose, along with some of the raster formats from which you can choose.

After you create the Raster File Format driver configuration, you use the Plot dialog box as described in Chapter 4 to generate "plots" to raster files.

If you want to add drawings to your Web pages, consider using DWF, the AutoCAD Drawing Web Format. See Chapter 8 for details.

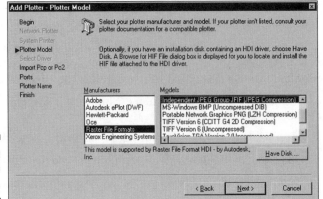

Figure 7-5:
Plot to
raster files.

Chapter 8

Drawing on the Internet

• •

In This Chapter

▶ Developing a CAD Internet strategy

▶ Using good drawing exchange etiquette

▶ Exchanging drawing files via e-mail

▶ Downloading drawings via FTP

▶ Viewing and plotting drawings on the Web

▶ Using ePlot

▶ Putting your own drawings on the Web

• •

*U*nless you've been living under a rock for the past five years, you know
that the Internet is causing major changes in the way that people work.
Most of us communicate differently, exchange files more rapidly, and fill out
express delivery forms less frequently.

AutoCAD users were among the online pioneers, well before the Internet
burst onto the public scene. Many early users gathered on the CompuServe
ACAD forum to trade tips, AutoLISP programs, and lame jokes. (One of the
authors of this book was a moderator on the forum and the source of some of
those lame jokes. He now brings his "talents," such as they are, to the print
world in this book.) The more savvy companies used CompuServe mail or
other pre-Internet e-mail services to exchange drawing files.

Despite this early adoption, the CAD world has been relatively slow to take
the full-immersion Internet plunge. Exchanging drawings via e-mail and using
the World Wide Web for CAD software research and support are pretty
common nowadays. But it's still uncommon to find drawings incorporated
into Web pages or Web-centric CAD applications. This scarcity is a result
more of CAD users' insularity from the general computing community than of
any lack of Web features in AutoCAD or AutoCAD LT. LT, along with some
additional free software from Autodesk, gives you the tools to weave your
CAD work into the Web. Figure 8-1 shows an example.

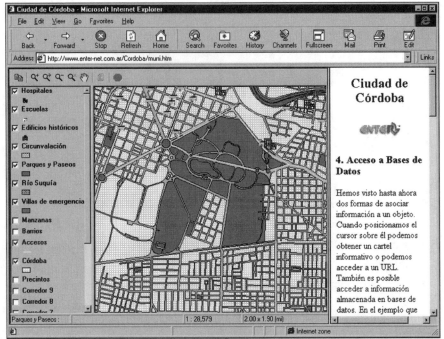

Figure 8-1:
Drawings
caught in
the Web.

This chapter shows you how — and when — to use e-mail, the Web, and FTP (File Transfer Protocol) in connection with AutoCAD LT or AutoCAD. As with the other chapters in this part of the book, we don't assume that you're an AutoCAD LT expert — yet! We show you how to get your drawings ready to publish on the Web and use all facets of the Internet to make existing drawings more widely available.

AutoCAD includes the same Web connectivity features as AutoCAD LT, but many hard-core AutoCAD users aren't very familiar with these features. If linking your company's CAD work with the Web seems like a good idea, you can use the information in this chapter to help lead the charge.

Casting Your Net

Amidst all the buzz about the Web, you can easily forget that the Internet comprises a range of useful features for CAD and general computer use:

- ✔ E-mail
- ✔ File Transfer Protocol (FTP)
- ✔ The World Wide Web
- ✔ Newsgroups

Your ticket to all these handy features is an account with an Internet service provider (ISP). You probably already have Internet access through work or a private ISP account — or both; but if not, now is the time to get connected. Other CAD users will expect to be able to send drawings to you and receive them from you via e-mail. Software companies, including Autodesk, expect you to have Web access in order to download software updates and support information.

The most common means of connecting to your ISP is through dial-up modem access, at speeds up to 56 Kbps (kilobits per second). Dial-up modem performance is adequate for many CAD users' needs now, but it probably won't stay that way for long. Internet access speed is like computer processor speed: What seems fast today becomes hopelessly slow two years from now. Thus, if you're shopping around for an ISP, consider one of the faster options, such as Digital Subscriber Line (DSL) or a cable modem. The many options, pricing schemes, and installation and configuration details are complicated. If you're not up to tangling with all these concerns yourself, hire a consultant to handle the messy details for you.

Browse me up, Billy Gates

The Web browser titans, Microsoft and Netscape, continue to battle it out, and zealous devotees of each browser continue to argue the choice between Internet Explorer and Navigator with religious fervor. Leaving aside questions about which company has the richer feature set (this month, anyway), the more worrisome security holes, or the more ruthless business practices, we suggest that you use Internet Explorer if your main concern is AutoCAD LT.

Both browsers work fine with the AutoCAD LT Web features, but the LT Help system requires Internet Explorer, so you need to have that 50MB gorilla loaded on your system anyway. Also, Internet Explorer makes installing the additional software component that's required for viewing drawings on the Web more automatic. But if you're wedded to Netscape, that's okay, too — just be prepared to maintain two browsers on your system: Internet Explorer for AutoCAD LT Help, and Netscape Navigator for Web browsing.

Surfing defensively

As you probably know, the Internet is not just a highly efficient way to exchange messages, files, and Web pages. It's also a highly efficient way to exchange viruses. Before you get too tangled up in the Web or e-mail, make sure that you've installed up-to-date virus protection software, and that you continue to update it regularly — every month is a reasonable schedule. Two of the more popular virus protection programs are Norton AntiVirus (www.symantec.com) and McAfee VirusScan (www.mcafee.com).

Configure your virus protection software to scan DOC and XLS files, and update the software regularly so that it catches the many new macro viruses that appear every month. The most common sources of viruses these days are Microsoft Word documents and Excel spreadsheets. So-called *macro viruses* can hide in documents and spreadsheets, and then infect your system when you open them. We even ran into virus problems in exchanging Word files during the writing of one of our books. Fortunately, there haven't yet been any reported viruses that infect DWG files.

One more quick but work-saving tip: Save your drawings before you start running any Internet access program or Web browser. The race between Microsoft and Netscape to lead Web browser development, and the simultaneous race among online services to provide fast access and the latest and greatest features, mean that plenty of buggy and crash-prone Internet software gets sent out. So save early and often if you're running AutoCAD LT and any kind of Internet connection at the same time.

Zip It on Over

In the good ol' days of pencil leads and eraser dust, the standard way of exchanging drawings was to make a bunch of blue-line prints from the mylar or vellum originals and then send them via overnight delivery service or local courier. When computers got in the act, everyone first added plotting on mylar or vellum to the front end of this paper drawing exchange procedure.

As more companies switched from manual drafting to CAD, people started sending DWG files on floppy disks, or higher-capacity media such as Zip disks, along with the blue-line prints. Thus, the recipients could try to re-use some of the stuff in the sender's CAD drawings to create their own drawings for the project.

A few years ago, some bean-counters realized, "Hey, most of the people we're sending blue-line prints to are AutoCAD users. Let them make their own *\^@~# plots!" Those bean-counters probably didn't realize how complicated it can be to plot someone else's drawing faithfully (if only they'd read Chapter 4 of this book!), but now we're stuck with their decision. As e-mail and Web access became more widespread, the bean-counters even got to save the costs of a high-capacity disk and overnight delivery.

Thus, e-mail and FTP have largely replaced blue-line prints, overnight delivery, floppies, and higher capacity disks as the standard means of exchanging drawings. Whether you're exchanging drawings in order to re-use CAD objects or simply to make hard-copy plots of someone else's drawings, you need to be comfortable sending and receiving by e-mail and FTP.

Sending and receiving DWG files doesn't differ much from sending and receiving other kinds of files, except that

- DWG files tend to be bigger than word processing documents and spreadsheets. Consequently, you may need to invest in a faster Internet connection, as described earlier in this chapter.

- You can easily forget to include all the dependent files. We tell you in the next section how to make sure that you send all the necessary files — and how to pester the people who don't send you all of *their* necessary files.

- It's often not completely obvious how to plot what you receive. Use the information in Chapter 4 and in the "Follow the Golden Exchange Rule" section of this chapter to solve plotting puzzles.

Package and go

Before you start exchanging drawings via e-mail or FTP, you should develop a procedure for packaging the drawings. Many AutoCAD DWG files depend on other files, and most sets of drawings benefit from an accompanying message that explains what they are and how to plot them.

If you're one of those people who backs up only selected files on your hard disk each day (you do create daily backups, don't you?), you should use the same procedure that you use for sending your files when you create the daily backups. Otherwise, you might not back up all the files that are connected with your main drawings. This is one of many reasons why it's easier and better to back up your entire hard disk onto tape or another high-capacity backup medium.

Each drawing file created in AutoCAD LT or CAD can contain references to three kinds of files, as described in Table 8-1. Later in this section, we present an example that shows how you handle references to these three types of files.

Table 8-1	Swapping Information Between AutoCAD LT and Other Programs		
Description	*File Types*	*Consequences if Missing*	*Notes*
Other drawings (*xrefs*)	DWG	Stuff in the main drawing disappears.	See the following example and Chapter 15.
Custom font files	SHX, TTF	LT substitutes another font.	See the following example.
Raster graphics files	JPG, PCX, TIF, and so on	Stuff in the drawing disappears.	See the following example. Raster graphics can be attached in AutoCAD only, not LT.

As you can see from the table, the consequences of not including a custom font aren't that dire: The recipient still will see your text, but the font will be different. If, on the other hand, you forget to send xrefs or raster graphics that are attached to your main drawing, the objects contained on those attached files simply will be gone when the recipient opens your drawing. Not good!

Like so much else in AutoCAD and AutoCAD LT, the tools and rules for mapping fonts are flexible but somewhat complicated. Look up the FONTALT and FONTMAP system variables in the AutoCAD LT online help system for detailed information.

The following procedure shows you how to determine all the additional files that your drawing depends on:

1. **Open the DWG file that you want to send to someone and write down the file's name.**

2. **Choose Insert⇨Xref Manager.**

   The Xref Manager dialog box appears, as shown in Figure 8-2.

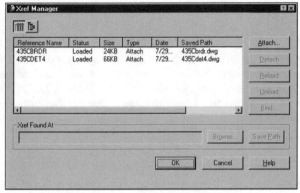

Figure 8-2:
Your draw-
ing has xref
vision.
(There's that
forum
moderator
humor
again . . .)

3. **Write down each name that appears in the Saved Path column.**

   Each of these names is an xref on which your drawing depends.

4. **Click Cancel.**

   The Xref Manager dialog box disappears.

   The next three steps are optional. If you don't care whether text fonts appear correctly when the recipient of your drawing opens it, then you don't have to send custom font files.

5. **Choose Format⇨Text Style.**

   The Text Style dialog box appears, as shown in Figure 8-3.

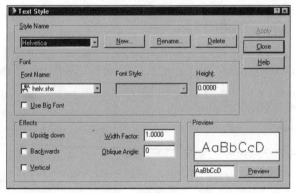

Figure 8-3:
Custom
fonts are in
style.

6. **In the Style Name drop-down list, select each style name in turn. For each style name, write down the corresponding Font name.**

   Your drawing uses all the fonts that correspond to one or more text styles — see Chapter 12 for details.

If the Use Big Font box is checked for any of the fonts, write down the name of the Big Font as well as the name of the main SHX font.

If the font is a standard AutoCAD or Windows font, you don't need to write down its name or send it. To see a list of the standard AutoCAD fonts, look in the \Aclt\Fonts folder on your AutoCAD LT 2000 CD. The standard Windows fonts include the Arial, Courier New, and Times New Roman families.

7. Click Cancel.

The Text Style dialog box disappears.

You can skip the next three steps if all work on your drawing has been done in AutoCAD LT. LT can't attach raster images — only AutoCAD can.

8. Type IMAGE **at the command line and press Enter.**

The Image Manager dialog box appears, as shown in Figure 8-4.

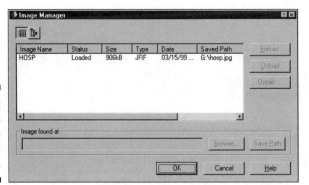

Figure 8-4:
LT worries
about the
AutoCAD
image.

9. Write down each name that appears in the Saved Path column.

Each of these names is a raster image that an AutoCAD user attached and on which your drawing depends.

10. Click Cancel.

The Image Manager dialog box disappears.

11. Choose File⇨Close to close the current drawing.

Save any changes, if necessary.

12. Repeat Steps 1 through 11 for each additional drawing that you want to send.

13. **Use Windows Explorer to create a new folder for the "packaged" drawings and referenced files.**

    It's always best to create a separate folder in which to assemble files that you want to send. That way, you can make sure that you don't forget a crucial file. You might want to name the new folder Send and create it underneath your project or main drawing folder.

14. **Copy the main and externally referenced DWG files, whose names you wrote down each time you performed Steps 1 and 3, to the new folder.**

15. **Copy the font files, whose names you wrote down each time you performed Step 6, to the new folder.**

    You find files whose names end in TTF in the Windows Fonts folder (for example, C:\Winnt\Fonts). Files whose names end in SHX could be in a variety of locations, including the AutoCAD LT Fonts folder (usually C:\Program Files\AutoCAD LT 2000\Fonts) and the main drawing's folder. You can use Tools⇨Find⇨Files and Folders in Windows Explorer to search for files.

    Many custom font files are licensed software, and sending them to others is just like sharing your AutoCAD LT program CD with others. No, we don't mean that it's easy and fun; we mean that it's illegal and unethical. Before you send a custom font file to someone else, find out what the licensing restrictions are on the font and be prepared to work within them.

16. **Copy the raster image files, whose names you wrote down each time you performed Step 9, to the new folder.**

As you can see, this is an exhaustive — that is, thorough — procedure, but also an exhausting one, especially if you have to perform it on many drawings. You can save yourself a lot of time if you keep track of the required references as you create the drawings. We remind you to do just that when we discuss text styles and xrefs in Chapters 12 and 15, respectively.

If you have access to a colleague's computer with full AutoCAD, this might be a good time to borrow it. AutoCAD includes an Express⇨Tools⇨Pack 'n Go program that automates the process of assembling a drawing's dependent files. Because LT doesn't support most programming interfaces, it doesn't support programs like Pack 'n Go.

Checking your package

After you copy all the main and dependent files to a separate folder, you can test for completeness by opening each main drawing in that folder. After you open each file, press the F2 key to view the command-line window, and look for missing font and xref error messages of the following sort:

```
Substituting [simplex.shx] for [helv.shx].
Resolve Xref "GRID": C:\Here\There\Nowhere\grid.dwg
Can't find C:\Here\There\Nowhere\grid.dwg
```

Press F2 again to return to the drawing window. Any missing raster files will appear as rectangular boxes with the names of the image files inside the rectangles. Close the drawing and then proceed to the next one.

This procedure also works well for testing whether a set of drawings that someone sent you is complete. Copy all the files to a separate folder and open each one in turn. Write down each missing file and then tell the sender to get on the ball and send you the missing pieces. While you're at it, tell that person to buy this book and read this chapter!

If you receive drawings with custom TrueType font files (that is, files whose extensions are TTF), you must install those files before Windows and AutoCAD LT will recognize them. Choose Start➪Settings➪Control Panel and then double-click the Fonts icon to open the Fonts window. Then choose File➪Install New Font.

Follow the Golden Exchange Rule

Many of the "rules" of exchanging files — CAD or otherwise — are simple consequences of exercising common courtesy. If you're one of those unfortunate souls whose mother didn't teach you to acknowledge a letter, write thank-you notes, and avoid slurping your soup, now is the time to learn.

The Golden Exchange Rule is "Send files unto others as you would have them sent unto you." If you think in terms of the kind of information *you* need for figuring what you've received, what to do with it, and how to plot it, then you won't go too far wrong.

Of course, basing your practices on your own needs doesn't always work. One of the authors remembers a science-fiction story wherein a planet of deranged psychopaths went a-conquering, making their new subjects completely subservient. Turns out that's how they liked to be treated, so they were just following the Golden Rule! So, also take the recipient's needs and AutoCAD knowledge level into account when putting your file exchange package together.

Here's a list of what you should include when sending drawings to someone else:

✔ A transmittal describing the project name, purpose of the files, how to get in touch with you if any problems occur, and all the other usual stuff that you put on your office transmittals.

You can create the transmittal in a text editor such as Notepad. Alternatively, if you know that your recipient has Microsoft Word, you might want to use Word to take advantage of fancier formatting options. In either case, give the file an easy-to-recognize name, such as Readme.TXT or CAD-DWG-Transmittal.DOC

✔ The main DWG files.

✔ All dependent drawing, custom font, and raster image files, as described in the previous section.

✔ Plotting instructions and plotting support files. If you normally plot the drawings with a plot style file, send the CTB or STB file, which is located in the Program Files\AutoCAD LT 2000\Plot Style folder. If you normally plot with a nonsystem device driver, it might be helpful to send the PC3 file for that plotter configuration. You find that file in the \Program Files\AutoCAD LT 2000\Plotters folder. See Chapter 4 for more information about CTB, STB, and PC3 files.

Many CAD drafters need help with drawing exchange etiquette. This is another area where you, the more Internet-savvy LT user, can help nudge your office or workgroup toward more effective, professional CAD practice.

ZIP is hip

After you have a long list of files assembled and ready to go, do everyone a favor and compress the files into a single *ZIP file* — a ZIP file being a file compressed to the ZIP standard. No one likes to receive an e-mail message carrying an endless cargo of attached files. A single ZIP file makes a nice, tidy package, and in some cases it speeds up transmission over the Internet. You can choose from several good ZIP/unZIP shareware utilities for Windows, including WinZip (www.winzip.com), which is shown in Figure 8-5.

Figure 8-5: ZIP compresses those unsightly DWG bulges.

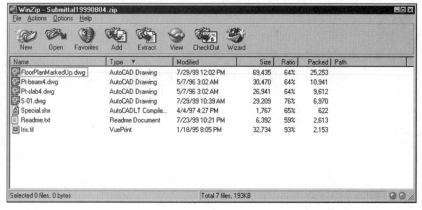

After you've created a ZIP file containing all the files in your Send folder, you can delete all the other Send files — assuming, of course that you *copied* all your drawings into the Send folder, like we told you to, and didn't *move* them there. The new ZIP file serves both for transmitting and as an archive of what you sent.

Don't confuse ZIP files with Zip disks. ZIP is a compression format that's been around since the MS-DOS days. Zip disks look like fat floppy disks, but they hold 100MB or more. Both ZIP and Zip fit more stuff in less space, but ZIP requires software to do the squeezing (a ZIP/unZIP utility) and Zip requires hardware (a Zip drive from Iomega).

All hail e-mail

E-mail is the easiest method of transferring files, as long you don't want to send anything that's too large — more than 1MB, say. Some ISPs enforce limitations on the size of e-mail attachments, and truncate or simply discard any attachments that exceed the limit. For example, AOL limits attachments to 2MB (unless the message is sent both from *and* to an AOL account). Even if your ISP doesn't enforce any file size limitations, some people don't appreciate being sent a 10MB e-mail attachment, because it ties up their modem and phone line for a long time, and they can't control when they do the downloading. If your file package exceeds file size limitations, you may need to use a Zip drive and overnight delivery rather than e-mail.

After you create a ZIP file containing your drawings, dependent files, transmittal document, and so on, you simply attach it to an e-mail message as you would any other file attachment. In the message body, type a description of what you're sending, so the recipient doesn't have to figure out what 990234BXREV1.ZIP is. Figure 8-6 shows a message with an attached ZIP file about to be sent from Microsoft Outlook.

Some older e-mail programs have problems dealing with attached files whose names don't fit the old MS-DOS 8.3 filename rule (maximum of eight characters, then a period, then a three-character extension; no spaces allowed anywhere in the filename). If a recipient reports problems receiving a file that you sent, try renaming it to an 8.3 name and then re-sending it. For example, you might rename 990234BXREV1.ZIP to 990234R1.ZIP.

One fast and effective way to compose the message text is to copy the text of your transmittal document into the message body.

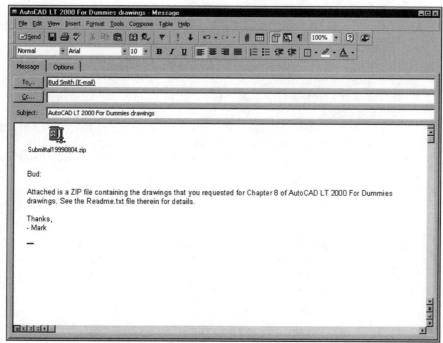

Figure 8-6:
Drawings on
the way.

When you receive a message containing drawings (ZIPped, we hope!), copy the ZIP file to a new folder on your hard disk or a network disk and unZIP the files. You may want to at least spot-check a few of the drawings for completeness, as we describe in the "Checking your package" section earlier in this chapter. After you verify that you have everything you need, you can proceed to plotting, copying objects into your own drawings, or whatever other plans you have in store for the drawings.

FTP for you and me

FTP, or *File Transfer Protocol,* is a simple but robust protocol for copying larger files over the Internet. A computer that's connected to the Internet can act as an FTP *server,* which means that part of its hard disk is accessible over the Internet. The person who configures the FTP server can place restrictions so that only people who enter a particular logon name and password can see and download files. FTP overcomes the e-mail file size limitations described in the previous section.

Because of all these FTP benefits, it's increasingly common for people at larger companies to place drawing files on their company's FTP site and tell you to go get them. This approach relieves them of having to e-mail you the files, and relieves you of waiting through that 10MB e-mail download when you least expected it.

In most cases, the person making the files available to you via FTP will send you a Uniform Resource Locator (URL) that looks like a Web page address, except that it starts with FTP:// instead of HTTP://. If you open your Web browser and enter the FTP URL into the address field, the browser should connect to the FTP site, ask you for a location and name to use for the file when it gets copied to your system, and begin downloading the file. If the FTP site uses password protection, you'll have to enter a logon name and password first.

If you want fancier FTP download options, you can use an FTP utility program such as WS_FTP (www.ipswitch.com).

Even if you work for a small company, you might be able to post files on your ISP's FTP server in order to make them available to others. Check with your ISP to find out whether you can do it and, if so, what the procedures are.

Drawings on the Web

In previous sections of this chapter, we explain how you can exchange drawings via e-mail and FTP. That's all the Internet connectivity that many AutoCAD and LT users need, but if you're curious about connecting drawings to the Web, then this section is for you.

The AutoCAD LT Web features are built on two pieces of technology: a special "lightweight" drawing format called DWF that Autodesk developed especially for putting drawings on the Web, and a driver called *WHIP!* that enables Web browsers to display and work with DWF files. This section describes DWF and *WHIP!* and shows you how to browse DWF files that others have put on Web pages. The final section of the chapter describes how to add drawings to your own Web pages.

WHIP! up a DWF

The AutoCAD DWG format works well for storing drawing information on local and network disks, but the high precision and large number of object properties that AutoCAD uses make for comparatively large files.

To overcome this size problem and encourage people to publish drawings on the Web, Autodesk developed an alternative "lightweight" vector format for representing AutoCAD drawings: DWF (Drawing Web Format). A DWF file is a more compact representation of a DWG file. DWF uses less space — and less transfer time over the Web — because it's less precise and doesn't have all the information that's in the DWG file.

The DWG drawing file format stores coordinates of points — such as the end-points of a line or the corners of a rectangle — in *double-precision* format, which assigns 64 bits of information to each number in the coordinate. This enables AutoCAD and LT to be very precise indeed in creating plots, scaling objects, and so on. DWF files, because they're only for display and printing purposes, not for additional work involving scaling and other complex operations, have their coordinates stored in single-precision format, which uses only half as many bits for each number. This makes the file size smaller and displaying the file somewhat faster.

The other big advantage of DWF files is that people who don't have AutoCAD can view them. All you need is either Microsoft Internet Explorer or Netscape Navigator and the *WHIP!* viewer, which is available for free on Autodesk's Web site (www.autodesk.com).

DWF files and *WHIP!* open up all kinds of interesting possibilities for sharing your drawings — or representations of your drawings that have been "plotted" to a file, anyway — with others. For example, you can present your work to prospective clients, post a current set of drawings on the Web for review by clients and subcontractors, or create a drawing library that coworkers can browse over the office intranet.

Plug in your WHIP!

To see AutoCAD DWF files from within your browser, you need the *WHIP!* ActiveX control (for Microsoft Internet Explorer) or plug-in (for Netscape Navigator).

Saying "the *WHIP!* ActiveX control or plug-in" all the time gets tiring, so Autodesk just calls it "the *WHIP!* viewer." We do the same thing in this chapter, unless we're emphasizing the distinction between installing the viewer for Internet Explorer and installing it for Netscape Navigator.

If you use Internet Explorer, you're in luck; the needed version of the ActiveX control is automatically downloaded to and installed on your machine the first time you access a Web page with a DWF file in it. If you don't like Microsoft, or you just prefer to use Netscape Navigator, point your Web browser to the *WHIP!* area of Autodesk's Web site (www.autodesk.com/products/whip/index.htm) and download and install the current version of the *WHIP!* plug-in.

Stop and think before you load up your Web site with a zillion DWF files. Only a minority of Web users are going to have the *WHIP* viewer installed. Although the *WHIP!* viewer is free from Autodesk, users still have to download it, which takes time. As of this writing, the download size is 1.3MB. If your Web site is intended primarily for AutoCAD and LT users, then you can reasonably expect them to have or get the *WHIP!* viewer. If, on the other hand, you're hoping to attract a wider audience to your Web site, you may not want to force them to download the *WHIP!* viewer. In any case, if you do publish DWF files on the Web, include instructions on how the user can get and install the *WHIP!* viewer.

If DWF isn't appropriate for your Web pages, you might be able to use the popular JPEG format instead. Any Web browser can display JPEG files without the need for a special plug-in. As we describe at the end of Chapter 7, you can use the Raster File Format driver to "plot" all or part of a drawing to a JPEG file.

Browsing DWFs

After you install the *WHIP!* viewer, you can view and plot DWF files, as well as zoom, pan, and change layer visibility in them. The following example demonstrates how. In the section "Making DWFs with ePlot" later in the chapter, we show you how to create DWF files from DWG files.

Here's how you use the *WHIP!* viewer:

1. **Make sure you have your Web browser and the *WHIP!* viewer installed, as we describe in the previous section.**

2. **Open a Web page that contains a DWF file or double-click a DWF file to open it in your Web browser.**

If you don't have any DWF files or DWF-ed Web pages handy, point your browser to Autodesk's *WHIP!* Gallery (www.autodesk.com/products/ whip/gallery.htm) or create a DWF file from one of your drawings using the instructions in the section "Making DWFs with ePlot" later in this chapter.

The *WHIP!* viewer displays the DWF file and changes the cursor to a "pan hand," indicating that you can pan by clicking and dragging.

3. **Right-click to display the *WHIP!* viewer menu, as shown in Figure 8-7. Choose Zoom.**

The pan hand changes to a zoom magnifying glass.

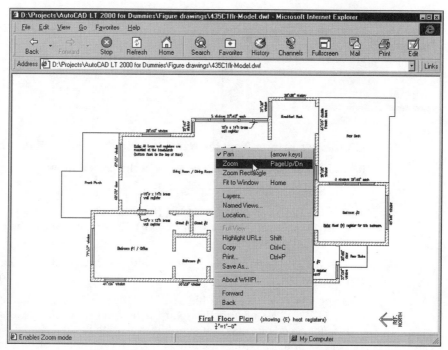

Figure 8-7:
Cracking the
WHIP!

4. Zoom by clicking and dragging the mouse either up or down.

Refer to the zoom and pan procedures in Chapter 5. The *WHIP!* viewer's
zoom and pan features are very similar to real-time zooming and panning in AutoCAD LT.

5. Right-click and choose Layers from the cursor menu.

A simple Layers dialog box appears and lists the layers in the DWF file
and their on/off settings, as shown in Figure 8-8.

**6. Turn a few layers off and then back on by clicking the light bulb icons
adjacent to their names.**

As you click each light bulb, the objects on the corresponding layer turn
off or on immediately.

7. Close the Layers dialog box by clicking the X in its title bar.

8. Right-click and choose Print from the cursor menu.

A simplified Windows Print dialog box appears, including check boxes
for forcing the printed background color to white and printed objects to
black.

Note that you don't have all the AutoCAD LT plotting options described
in Chapter 4. A DWF file is supposed to be like an electronic plot, so the
WHIP! viewer provides only simple options for paper plots.

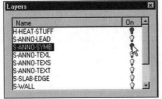

Figure 8-8:
The simplified *WHIP!* Layers dialog box.

9. **Choose a printer from the Name list and then click OK to print.**

10. **Right-click and choose Save As from the cursor menu.**

    The Save As dialog box appears.

11. **Change the Save as Type setting from Autodesk Drawing Web Format (*.dwf) to AutoCAD Drawing (*.dwg). Enter a name for the new DWG file and click Save.**

    The *WHIP!* viewer creates a new DWG file from the information in the DWF file.

Being able to save a DWF file to a DWG file is handy, but the newly created DWG file is no substitute for the original DWG. Remember that DWF is a *lightweight* format that simplifies the data in the original DWG file. For example, DWF files include only the model space or paper space layout tab that you plotted. When you save a DWF file back to DWG, none of the other tabs will contain any objects.

If you want others to be able to view and print your DWG files as well as DWF files, check out Autodesk's free Volo View Express program (www.autodesk.com/products/volo/index.htm). As of this writing, Volo View Express is available only for Internet Explorer.

ePlot, not replot

DWF files and the *WHIP!* viewer aren't just for the Web. Beginning with AutoCAD 2000, Autodesk is pushing DWF as an "electronic plotting" or *ePlotting* format. A DWF file captures a single, plotted view of your drawing, so, unlike a DWG file, it can provide a relatively unambiguous snapshot of what you want to see on paper. With a DWG file, on the other hand, you have to provide lots of information to other people — drawing view, scale, plot style settings, and so on — in order for them to get the same plotting results that you did.

Potential ePlotting scenarios include:

- ✔ Architects and other consultants on a building project periodically upload DWF files to the project Web site. CAD drafters from the various companies can save the DWF files as DWG in order to extract geometrical information. Architects and engineers with some minimal CAD knowledge can review the drawings on-screen and create their own hard-copy plots, if necessary. Principals and clients who don't want anything to do with CAD can have their secretaries or other employees create hard-copy plots for them to examine.

- ✔ When Internet-savvy people need hard-copy prints of your drawings, you e-mail a ZIP file containing DWF files, along with the URL for the *WHIP!* viewer and simple instructions for creating plots from the DWF files.

- ✔ A CAD plotting service bureau encourages its customers to send DWF files instead of DWG files for plotting. The DWF files are much smaller and require less intervention on the part of the service bureau's employees.

The ePlot concept is brand new, and some of the critical features, including creating a DWF file that can be plotted to scale, are new in AutoCAD 2000 and AutoCAD LT 2000. It remains to be seen whether ePlotting will become a popular way to generate hard-copy output. In particular, many people outside of CAD-using companies don't have access to large-format plotters. They're limited to 8½-x-11-inch — or, at best, 11-x-17-inch — reduced-size check plots. Consequently, many people won't be able to plot your DWF files to scale, and may not even be able to plot them large enough to read everything.

Don't be afraid to try ePlotting with colleagues inside or outside your company, but don't become too dependent on it until you see whether the rest of the CAD world shares your enthusiasm. Otherwise, you risk becoming the only one who's willing to use your DWF files for plotting — in which case the next version of the feature will be called mePlot.

Anyone who wants to ePlot your DWF files must install the *WHIP!* viewer along with Internet Explorer or Netscape Navigator.

Hand-y objects

No Web file format would be complete without hyperlinks, and DWF has those, too. In the case of DWF images, you can attach hyperlinks to any drawing *object*, rather than just to a text string. As you pass the cursor over an object with a hyperlink, the *WHIP!* viewer changes from the pan hand to a hand with a pointing finger, as shown in Figure 8-9.

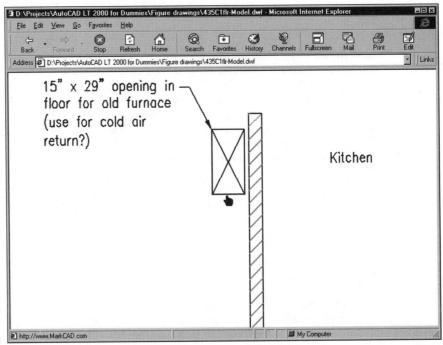

Figure 8-9:
WHIP!
points the
way to
hyperlinks.

Because of the density of objects in many CAD drawings, the *WHIP!* viewer also can make all objects with hyperlinks blink (until you get annoyed with the blinking and turn it off). The following example shows you how to locate and use a hyperlink. Later in the chapter, we show you how to add hyperlinks to objects in your drawings before you create DWF files from them.

1. Open a DWF-ed Web page or DWF file that contains hyperlinks.

If you don't have any suitable DWF files or Web pages handy, you can use the examples on `www.MarkCAD.com`.

2. Right-click and choose Highlight URLs.

Objects with hyperlinks start blinking.

If the Highlight URLs menu choice isn't available, the current DWF file doesn't have any objects with hyperlinks.

3. Point to one of the blinking objects.

The pan hand changes to the pointing finger, and the hyperlink's URL displays in your browser's status bar, as shown in Figure 8-9.

4. With the finger pointing at one of the blinking objects, click.

Your Web browser navigates to the location specified by the URL.

5. **Click your browser's back button.**

   You return to the DWF file or the Web page containing the DWF file. The blinking is gone.

6. **Move your cursor around and try other hyperlinks.**

   You can toggle the blinking on or off any time.

Web-Enabling Your Drawings

The previous section shows you how to work with other people's DWF files and Web pages containing them. This section tells you how to turn your own drawings into DWF files and Web pages.

Making DWFs with ePlot

As we describe in the previous section, AutoCAD LT 2000 treats DWF files like *electronic plots,* or ePlots. (Previous versions of AutoCAD and LT used a separate DWFOUT command that didn't provide enough options to make ePlotting possible.)

You create a DWF file from the current drawing just as if you were plotting it to a piece of paper, as we describe in Chapter 4. The only difference is that, on the Plot dialog box's Plot Device tab, you choose the plotter configuration named DWF ePlot.pc3, as shown in Figure 8-10. When you do so, AutoCAD automatically turns on the Plot to File setting, and you can specify a filename and location for the DWF file that gets created. The location can be a folder on a hard disk or a Web site.

Pay particular attention to the Scale setting on the Plot Settings tab. If you're creating a DWF simply for viewing in a browser, you can plot Scaled to Fit. If you want to enable others to ePlot your DWF file to scale, as described earlier in this chapter, you need to choose the desired plot scale factor.

AutoCAD LT 2000 includes two DWF plotter configurations: DWF ePlot.pc3 and DWF Classic.pc3. These two configurations give similar results, except that DWF ePlot is supposed to show a paper boundary similar to the one that AutoCAD LT shows in paper space layouts (it doesn't — that's saved for a future version of the *WHIP!* viewer). In addition, DWF ePlot forces the background color of the DWF to white, while DWF Classic uses the LT drawing area background color. You can change these and other settings by clicking the Properties button on the Plot Device tab.

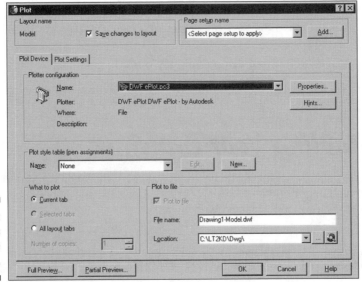

Putting hyperlinks in your drawings

If you want people to be able to navigate to other Web pages by clicking objects in your DWF files, you need to add hyperlinks to objects in the drawings before you ePlot them to DWF files. Each hyperlink stores a URL (Uniform Resource Locator), such as the Web address www.dummies.com.

You don't *have* to add hyperlinks to objects. For many purposes, a DWF file without hyperlinks is perfectly adequate. It also may be less confusing for people who view your Web pages — most people aren't used to being able to use lines and other objects as hyperlinks. Remember that you always can create traditional underlined text hyperlinks in the body of the Web page. Save AutoCAD object hyperlinks for situations when text hyperlinks won't do and when the audience for your Web pages is likely to be somewhat conversant with CAD or the *WHIP!* viewer.

In AutoCAD and LT 2000, hyperlinks are just another object property, similar to color or lineweight. (See Chapter 10 for detailed information about object properties.) You attach and edit hyperlinks with the HYPERLINK command, as shown in Figure 8-11. The following example demonstrates:

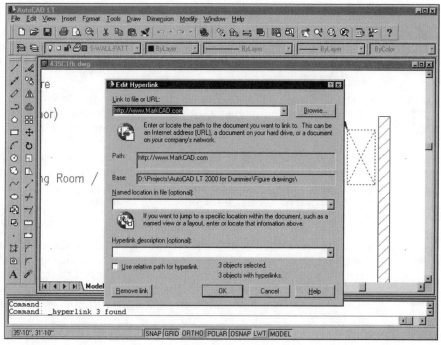

Figure 8-11:
Where does your object want to go today?

1. **Open a DWG file that contains objects to which you want to add hyperlinks.**

2. **Select one or more objects.**

   You can attach the same hyperlink to multiple objects. If you want to select multiple objects, refer to the "Grab It" section of Chapter 6.

3. **Click the Insert Hyperlink button on the Standard toolbar (the one that shows a globe and chain).**

   The Insert Hyperlink dialog box appears. With the exception of the title bar and the additional Remove Link button, this dialog box looks exactly like the Edit Hyperlink dialog box shown in Figure 8-11.

4. **Type a URL into the Link to File or URL edit box.**

   Use the drop-down list to choose a URL that you recently used in AutoCAD LT or your Web browser.

   The remaining fields are optional. You can use the dialog box help to learn more about them.

5. **Click OK.**

   The Insert Hyperlink dialog box closes, and LT adds the hyperlink as a property to the object.

6. Move your cursor over the object.

The cursor changes to the globe and chain icon to show that the object contains a hyperlink property. If you stop moving the cursor for a moment, a ToolTip displays the hyperlink URL that you entered, as shown in Figure 8-12.

If you select and then right-click an object with a hyperlink, the cursor menu displays a Hyperlink submenu with choices for opening the link in your Web browser, editing the URL, or copying the link to other objects.

That's all there is to adding hyperlinks to objects. You can change an existing hyperlink URL by selecting the object and clicking the Insert Hyperlink button again. When you're finished adding hyperlinks to objects, ePlot the drawing to a DWF file using the procedure we describe in the previous section.

Be sure to test each link that you create. Or, better yet, have someone else test each link. ePlot the DWF file, copy it to a network disk or Web server, open it in your browser, and turn on the Highlight URLs setting so that all objects with hyperlinks blink. Click each blinking object to make sure that the link works, and then click your browser's Back button to return to the DWF file.

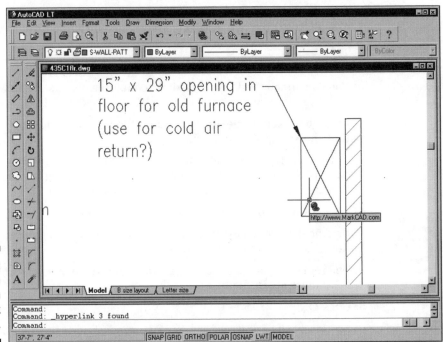

Figure 8-12:
The globe
and chain
hyperlink
icon.

We encourage you to put URLs in drawings that you publish on the Internet or an intranet. We are conservative enough, however, to discourage you from putting URLs in ordinary drawings that are viewed and modified by using AutoCAD. Why? Not everyone has a reliable connection to the Web at all times. If your drawing contains links to other drawings stored on your company intranet, those drawings become inaccessible when your drawing goes outside your organization. Or, if you store drawings on a public Web site, someone may move them without notifying you. Nothing is more frustrating than for you or others to be unable to print, build, or sell via your drawing file because a piece of it has become inaccessible. Be careful before putting URLs in your drawings.

Creating your own Web pages

The biggest single reason for the Web's popularity is that anyone — and that does mean anyone — can put up a Web page or a Web site. Here comes some self-serving self-promotion: As the co-author of *Creating Web Pages For Dummies,* 4th Edition (IDG Books Worldwide, Inc., 1999), one of the authors of this book (Bud) has discovered many free and easy ways to get a Web site up and running on the Web. If you want to try the most popular self-publishing site on the Web on your own, go to www.geocities.com and follow the instructions; you can probably get a simple, free Web site up and running within a couple of hours. For detailed instructions and descriptions of the best Web publishing options and tools, buy the book!

Adding DWFs to Web pages

DWF files alone are fine for ePlotting and e-mailing to others who want to view your work. The *raison d'être* of DWF files, though, is to be placed in Web pages. And you thought *raison d'être* was a French breakfast cereal . . . .

Unfortunately, the job of adding DWF files to Web pages is more complicated than creating the DWF files in the first place. You'll need to have some experience creating Web pages, so buy Bud's book! You'll also need either a Web page editing program — such as Microsoft FrontPage or the Netscape Navigator Gold HTML editor — or a tolerance for editing raw HTML code in a text editor. Once you're ready to go, Autodesk's "Publishing DWFs" document will show you how. As of this writing, the document is located at www.autodesk.com/products/whip/publish.htm.

If you just want a little taste of the subject, see the "Placing a Drawing Web Format File in a Web Page" Learning Assistance tutorial. (See the section "Fun with F1" in Chapter 1 for information about the AutoCAD LT Learning Assistance CD that comes in your LT package.) Once you have the Learning

Assistance program running, choose "Tutorials," then "Using Internet Access Tools to Share Drawings," and finally, "Placing a Drawing Web Format File in a Web Page."

Briefly, you have two options for placing a DWF file on a Web page. The simpler but less slick way is to create an ordinary text hyperlink such as `Click here to see my drawing` and use the HREF HTML tag to open the DWF file in a separate browser window. Figure 8-13 shows an example. The HREF tag will look something like this in your HTML file:

The cool but more complicated way is to display DWF files in windows that are embedded in the Web page. With this approach, you can place text and other graphics in the same window, as shown in Figure 8-14. You need about 25 lines of HTML code, including the four crucial tags <object>, <param>, <embed>, and </object>. See the "Publishing DWFs" document for details.

Any Internet server on which you put DWF files must be configured to recognize the Autodesk DWF file type in order for the *WHIP!* viewer to work correctly with DWF files on that server. The procedure for doing so isn't too difficult, but you'll need to ask the webmaster for your company's or ISP's Web server to do it. Ask the webmaster to add the MIME (Multipurpose

```
<A HREF=http://server/myfile.dwf>myfile.dwf</A>
```

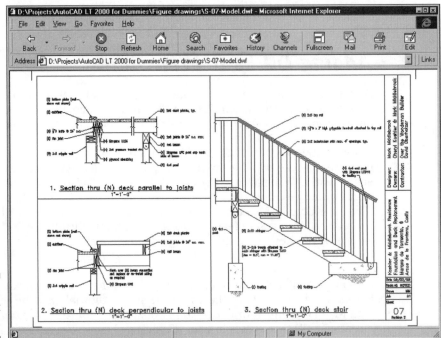

Figure 8-13: Simple, but kinda dorky.

Internet Mail Extension) type "drawing/x-dwf" (with the .dwf extension) to the Web server so that the DWF file type is "registered" with the server software. If the webmaster has any questions or concerns about performing this procedure, direct him or her to Autodesk's "Publishing DWFs" document at the address listed earlier in this section.

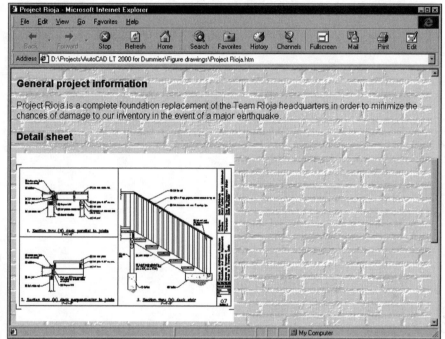

Figure 8-14:
Cool, but requires geek skills.

Part III

Creating Your Own Drawings

The 5th Wave — By Rich Tennant

THE CRAFT-MATIC Office-of-the-Future

In this part . . .

Creating drawings from scratch in AutoCAD LT requires a host of CAD-specific skills, many of which are neither intuitive nor well-documented. The first chapter in this part of the book gets you started on the right track with proper drawing setup, on which everything else depends. The next two chapters serve up the meat and potatoes of creating geometry: drawing and editing. The following three chapters show you how to add those pieces that make a CAD drawing useful and readable: text, dimensions, and hatching. And the final chapter in this part demonstrates how you can reuse information efficiently in order to improve productivity and consistency.

Chapter 9

Setup for Success

*T*he previous chapters of this book show you how to work with existing drawings — other people's or your own — on the theory that many people buy AutoCAD LT so they can stick a toe into the stream of AutoCAD drawing activities that's already flowing through their companies. Enough testing of the water, already — in this chapter, you dive head-first into creating your own drawings from scratch.

Surprisingly, drawing setup is one of the trickier aspects of using AutoCAD LT 2000. It's an easy thing to do incompletely or wrong, and the so-called Setup Wizard is no help at all. And yet, drawing setup is one of the more important things to get right. Setup steps that you omit or don't do right will come back to bite you — or at least gnaw on your leg — later.

Sloppy setup really becomes apparent when you try to plot. Things that seemed more-or-less okay as you zoomed around on the screen suddenly are completely the wrong size on paper. You don't really want to try to convince your boss that the dog ate your plotting homework, do you?

This chapter describes the decisions you need to make before you set up a new drawing, shows the steps for doing a complete and correct setup, and demonstrates how to save setup settings for re-use.

Whatever you do, *don't* assume that you can just create a new blank DWG file and start drawing things. In other words, *do* read this chapter before you get too deeply into the other chapters in this part of the book. Many AutoCAD LT drawing commands and concepts depend on proper drawing setup, so you'll have a much easier time of drawing and editing things if you've done your setup homework. On the positive side, a few minutes invested in setting up a drawing well can save hours of thrashing around later on.

Your Setup Strategy

You need to set up AutoCAD LT correctly, partly because LT is so flexible and partly because, well, you're doing *CAD* — computer-aided drafting (or design). In this context, the following three key reasons help explain why AutoCAD LT drawing setup is important:

- ✔ **Smart paper:** The one thing that can do the most to make using AutoCAD LT fun is working on a correctly set up drawing so that your screen acts like paper, only smarter. When drawing on real paper, you constantly have to translate between units on the paper and the real-life units of the object you're drawing. But when drawing in AutoCAD LT, you can draw directly in real-life units — feet and inches, millimeters, or whatever you use. AutoCAD LT can then calculate distances and dimensions for you and add them to the drawing. You can make the mouse pointer snap directly to "hot spots" on-screen, and a visible, resizable grid gives you a better sense for the scale of your drawing. However, this smart paper function works well only if you tell AutoCAD LT how you set up your specific drawing. LT can't really do its job until you tell it how to work.

- ✔ **Dumb paper:** Creating a great drawing on-screen that doesn't fit well on paper is all too easy. After you finish creating your drawing on the smart paper AutoCAD LT provides on-screen, you must plot it on the dumb paper used for thousands of years. Then you must deal with the fact that people like to use certain standard paper sizes and drawing scales. (Most people also like everything to fit neatly on one sheet of paper.) If you set up AutoCAD LT correctly, good plotting results automatically; if not, plotting time can become one colossal hassle.

- ✔ **It ain't easy:** AutoCAD LT provides templates (as shown in Figure 9-1) and setup wizards for you, but the templates don't work well unless you understand them, and the wizards don't work well even if you do understand them. This particular deficiency, though improved in AutoCAD LT 2000, is still one of the major weaknesses in AutoCAD LT. You must figure out on your own how to make the program work right. If you just plunge in without carefully setting it up, your drawing and printing efforts are likely to wind up a real mess. You may, in fact, end up with a virtually unprintable drawing (and probably mutter a few unprintable words in the process, too).

Fortunately, although the steps for performing your setup correctly are overly complex, you can master them with a little attention and practice. Even more fortunately, you have the information in this chapter to get you started on the right foot! For motivation, keep in mind how impressed your colleagues will be when they see that you can plot correctly the first time.

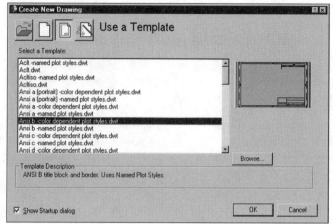

Figure 9-1:
Starting
with a tem-
plate.

While you're working in AutoCAD LT, always keep in mind what your final output looks like on real paper. Even your first printed drawings should look just like hand-drawn ones — only better.

Before you start the actual drawing setup process, you need to make some decisions about your new drawing:

✔ What drawing units will you use?

✔ At what scale — or scales — will you plot it?

✔ On what size paper does it need to fit?

✔ What kind of border or title block does your drawing require?

✔ What system variable settings are most appropriate?

The first three questions are absolutely critical. If you don't answer them, or you answer them wrong, you'll probably need to do lots of reworking of the drawing later. In some cases, you can defer answering the remaining two questions, but it's usually better to deal with them up front as well.

If you're really in a hurry, you sometimes can find an existing drawing that was set up for the drawing scale and paper size that you want to use, make a copy of that DWG file, erase the objects, and start drawing. Use this approach with care, though. When you start from another drawing, you're inheriting any setup mistakes in that drawing. Also, if you start from a pre-AutoCAD 2000 drawing, you probably won't be taking advantage of the new layout and plotting features. In short, if you can find a suitable drawing that was set up in AutoCAD 2000 or LT 2000 by an experienced person who is conscientious about doing setup right, then consider using it. Otherwise, you're better off setting up a new drawing from scratch.

AutoCAD LT and paper

In other Windows programs, you can squeeze content onto paper using any scaling factor you want. You've probably printed an Excel spreadsheet or Web page at some odd scaling factor such as 82 percent of full size because that's what it took to squeeze it onto a single sheet of paper while keeping the text as large as possible.

In drafting, however, your printout needs to be to a specific scaling factor, such as ¼" = 1'–0", in order to be useful and understandable to

others. But the AutoCAD LT screen does not automatically enforce any one scaling factor or paper size. If you just start drawing stuff on the AutoCAD LT screen to fit your immediate needs, it's unlikely that the final result will fit neatly on a piece of paper at a desirable scale.

This chapter tells you how to start your drawing in such a way that you will like how it ends up. With practice, this kind of approach will become second nature.

Choose your units

AutoCAD LT is extremely flexible about drawing units — it lets you have them *your* way. Usually, you choose the type of units that you normally use to talk about whatever you're drawing: feet and inches for a building in the U.S., millimeters for a metric screw, and so on.

During drawing setup, you choose a *type* of unit — Scientific, Decimal, Engineering, Architectural, and Fractional — and a *precision* of measurement in the Drawing Units dialog box, as shown in Figure 9-2. (We show you how in the next section.) Engineering and Architectural units are in feet and inches; Engineering units represent partial inches using decimals, and Architectural units represent them using fractions. AutoCAD LT's other unit types — Decimal, Fractional, and Scientific — are called *unitless* because LT doesn't know or care what the base unit is. If you configure a drawing to use Decimal units, for example, each drawing unit could represent a micron, millimeter, inch, foot, meter, kilometer, mile, parsec, the length of the king's forearm, or any other unit of measurement that you deem convenient. It's up to you to decide.

After you specify a type of unit, you draw things on-screen full size in those units just as though you were laying them out on the construction site or in the machine shop. You draw an eight-foot-high line, for example, to indicate the height of a wall and an eight-inch-high line to indicate the cutout for a doggie door (for a Dachshund, naturally). The on-screen line may actually be only two inches long at a particular zoom resolution, but AutoCAD stores the length as eight feet. This way of working is easy and natural for most people for whom CAD is their first drafting experience, but it seems weird to people who've done a lot of manual drafting. If you're in the latter category, don't worry — you'll soon get the hang of it.

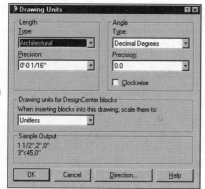

Figure 9-2:
The
Drawing
Units
dialog box.

Weigh your scales

The next decision you should make before setting up a new drawing is choosing the scale at which you'll eventually plot the drawing. This decision gives you the *drawing scale* and *drawing scale factor* — two ways of expressing the same relationship between the objects in the real world and the objects plotted on paper. The "Scaling: To fit or not to fit?" section in Chapter 4 explains drawing scale and drawing scale factor in detail — or in plan, for that matter.

Drawing scale is the traditional way of describing a scale with an equal sign or colon — for example: ¼" = 1'–0"; 1=20; or 2:1. The *drawing scale factor* represents the same relationship with a single number such as 48, 20, or 0.5. The drawing scale factor is the multiplier that converts the first number in the drawing scale into the second number.

You shouldn't just invent some arbitrary scale based on your age, shoe size, or winning lottery number, however. Most industries work with a fairly small set of approved drawing scales that are related to one another by factors of 2 or 10. If you use other scales, you'll at best be branded a clueless newbie and at worst have to redo all your drawings at an approved scale.

Table 9-1 lists some common architectural drawing scales, using both English and metric units. The table also lists the drawing scale factor corresponding to each drawing scale and the common uses for each scale. If you work in other industries than those listed here, ask drafters or other coworkers what the common drawing scales are and for what kinds of drawings they're used.

Table 9-1	Common Architectural Drawing Scales	
Drawing Scale	*Drawing Scale Factor*	*Common Uses*
¹⁄₁₆" = 1'–0"	192	Large building plans
¹⁄₈" = 1'–0"	96	Building plans
¹⁄₄" = 1'–0"	48	House plans
¹⁄₂" = 1'–0"	24	Plan details
1" = 1'–0"	12	Details
1 = 200 mm	200	Large building plans
1 = 100 mm	100	Building plans
1 = 50 mm	50	House plans
1 = 20 mm	20	Plan details
1 = 10 mm	10	Details

After you choose a drawing scale, engrave the corresponding drawing scale factor on your desk, write it on your hand, and put it on a sticky note on your monitor. You need to know the drawing scale factor for many drawing tasks, as well as for plotting. You should be able to recite the drawing scale factor of any drawing you're working on without even thinking about it.

Even if you plan to plot the drawing to fit, you need to choose an "artificial" scale to make text, dimensions, and other annotations appear at a reasonable size. Choose a scale that's in the neighborhood of the Scaled to Fit plotting factor. For example, if you determine that you need to squeeze your drawing down about 90 times in order to fit on the desired sheet size, choose a drawing scale of ⅛ inch = 1 foot – 0 inches (drawing scale factor = 96) if you're using architectural units or 1=100 (drawing scale factor = 100) for other kinds of units.

The worst sin of the AutoCAD LT 2000 drawing setup wizards is that they don't let you specify a drawing scale, and don't make any attempt to set scale-dependent system variables. For this and many other reasons, the LT 2000 drawing setup wizards are worse than useless for starting real drawings.

Think about paper

With a knowledge of your industry's common drawing scales, you can choose a provisional scale based on what you're depicting. But you won't know for sure whether that scale works until you compare it with the size of the paper that you want to use for plotting your drawing. Here again, most industries use a small range of standard sheet sizes. Three common sets of sizes exist, as shown in Figure 9-3 and Table 9-2: ANSI (American National Standards Institute), Architectural, and ISO (International Standard Organization).

Figure 9-3:
Relation-
ships
among
standard
paper sizes.

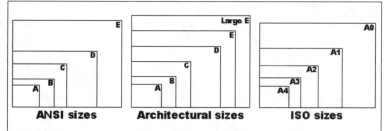

Table 9-2	**Common Plot Sheet Sizes**	
Sheet Size	*Dimensions*	*Comment*
ANSI *E*	34 x 44"	
ANSI *D*	22 x 34"	*E* sheet folded in half
ANSI *C*	17 x 22"	*D* sheet folded in half
ANSI *B*	11 x 17"	*C* sheet folded in half
ANSI *A*	8½ x 11"	*B* sheet folded in half
Architectural Large *E*	36 x 48"	
Architectural *E*	30 x 42"	
Architectural *D*	24 x 36"	
Architectural *C*	18 x 24"	
Architectural *B*	12 x 18"	
Architectural *A*	9 x 12"	
ISO *A0*	841 x 1189 mm	
ISO *A1*	594 x 841 mm	*A0* sheet folded in half
ISO *A2*	420 x 594 mm	*A1* sheet folded in half
ISO *A3*	297 x 420 mm	*A2* sheet folded in half
ISO *A4*	210 x 297 mm	*A3* sheet folded in half

You select a particular set of sheet size based on the common practices in your industry. You then narrow down your choice based on the area required by what you're going to draw. For example, most architectural plans are plotted on Architectural D or E size sheets.

If you know the desired sheet size and drawing scale factor, you can calculate the available drawing area easily. Simply multiply each of the sheet's dimensions (X and Y) by the drawing scale factor. For example, if you choose an 11-x-17-inch sheet and a drawing scale factor of 96 (corresponding to a plot scale of ⅛" = 1'–0"), you multiply 17 times 96 and 11 times 96 to get an available drawing area of 1,632 inches x 1,056 inches (or 136 feet x 88 feet). If your sheet size is in inches but your drawing scale is in millimeters, you need to multiply by an additional 25.4 to convert from inches to millimeters. For example, with an 11-x-17-inch sheet and a scale of 1 = 200 mm (drawing scale factor = 200), you multiply 17 times 200 times 25.4 and 11 times 200 times 25.4 to get 86,360 x 55,880 mm or 86.36 x 55.88 m — not quite big enough for a football field.

Conversely, if you know the sheet size that you're going to use and real-world size of what you're going to draw, and you want to find out the largest plot scale you can use, you have to divide rather than multiply. Divide the needed real-world drawing area dimensions (X and Y) by the sheet's dimensions (X and Y). Take the larger number — X or Y will control — and round up to the nearest "real" drawing scale factor (that is, one that's commonly used in your industry). For example, suppose you want to draw a 60-x-40-foot or 720-x-480-inch) floor plan and print it on 11-x-17-inch paper. You divide 720 by 17 and 480 by 11 to get 42.35 and 43.64, respectively. The larger number, 43.64, corresponds in this example to the short dimension of the house and the paper. The nearest larger common architectural drawing scale factor is 48 (corresponding to ¼" = 1'–0"), which leaves a little bit of room for the plotting margin and title block.

The Cheat Sheet at the front of this book includes two tables that list the available drawing areas for a range of sheet sizes and drawing scales. You can use those tables to help you decide on an appropriate paper size and drawing scale, and revert to the calculation method for situations that the tables don't cover.

When you're selecting a sheet size and drawing scale, always leave some extra room — for the following two reasons:

✔ Most plotters and printers can't print all the way to the edge of the sheet — they require a small margin. For example, a Hewlett-Packard LaserJet III has a printable area of about 7.9 x 10.5 inches on an 8.5-x-11-inch ANSI A size (letter size) sheet. If you know the printable area of your output device, you can use it instead of the physical sheet area in the calculations.

✔ Most drawings require some annotations — text, grid bubbles, and so on — outside the objects you're drawing, plus a title block surrounding the objects and annotations. If you don't leave some room for the annotations and title block, you'll end up having either to cram things together too much or to change to a different sheet size. Either way, you'll be slowed down, and probably late in the project when you can least afford it. Figure 9-4 shows an extreme example of selecting a sheet size that's too small — or, conversely, a drawing scale that's too large. In this example, the building is too long for the sheet and overlaps the title block on both the right and left sides.

Some industries deal with the "sheet-is-too-small / drawing-scale-is-too-large" problem by breaking the drawing up onto multiple plotted sheets.

Don't be afraid to *start* with paper. Experienced drafters often make a quick, throwaway pencil and paper sketch called a *cartoon*. A drawing cartoon usually includes a rectangle indicating the sheet of paper you intend to plot on, a sketch of the title block, and a very rough, schematic sketch of the thing you're going to draw. It helps to scribble down the dimensions of the sheet, the main title block areas, and the major objects to be drawn. By sketching out a cartoon, you'll often catch scale or paper size problems before you set up a drawing, rather than after you've created it.

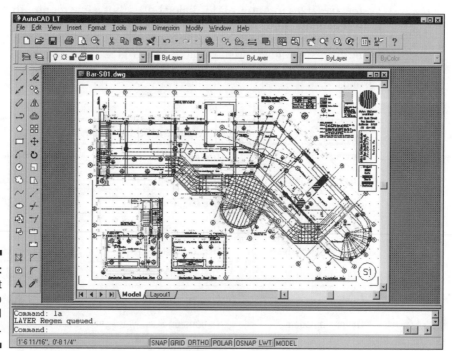

Figure 9-4:
"This sheet size is too small," said Goldilocks.

Defend your border

The next decision to make is what kind of border your drawing deserves. The options include a full-blown title block, a simple rectangle, or nothing at all around your drawing. If you need a title block, do you have one, can you get one, or will you draw one from scratch? Although you can draw title block geometry in an individual drawing, you'll save time by re-using the same title block for multiple drawings. Your company may already have a standard title block drawing ready to use, or someone else who's working on your project may have created one for the project.

Title blocks are usually drawn in a separate DWG file using plotted units, and then either inserted or xrefed into each sheet drawing. See Chapter 15 for more information about the options.

All system variables go

As Chapter 2 describes, AutoCAD LT includes a slew of *system variables* that control the way your drawing, LT itself, or both work. Much of the drawing setup process involves setting system variables based on the drawing scale, sheet size, and other desired properties of the drawing. You can set some system variables in AutoCAD LT dialog boxes, but a few require that you type at the command line. Table 9-3 shows the settings that you most commonly need to change or at least check during drawing setup, along with the names of the corresponding system variables. Later in the chapter, in the section "First Stop, Model Space," we show you the procedure for changing all these settings.

Table 9-3	System Variables for Drawing Setup	
Setting	*Dialog Box*	*System Variables*
Linear units and precision	Drawing Units	LUNITS, LUPREC
Angular units and precision	Drawing Units	AUNITS, AUPREC
Grid spacing and visibility	Drafting Settings	GRIDUNIT, GRIDMODE
Snap spacing and on/off	Drafting Settings	SNAPUNIT, SNAPMODE
Drawing limits	None (use command line)	LIMMIN, LIMMAX
Linetype scale	Linetype Manager	LTSCALE, PSLTSCALE
Dimension scale	Dimension Style Manager	DIMSCALE

Start Me Up?

The Startup dialog box (shown in Figure 9-5) comes up every time you start LT by choosing AutoCAD LT 2000 from the Windows Start menu or double-clicking an AutoCAD LT 2000 program icon. Figure 9-5 shows the dialog box with the Start from Scratch option selected. A very similar dialog box called Create New Drawing (only the Open a Drawing button is missing) comes up whenever you choose File⇨New in AutoCAD LT.

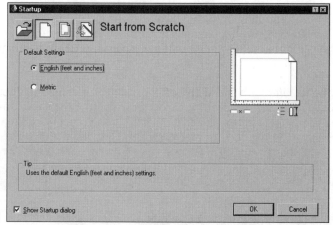

Figure 9-5:
Starting to
be creative.

The Startup dialog box looks kind of funny — more like a little application than a dialog box. The banner across the top of the dialog box changes depending on which button you click. But it is indeed a dialog box — one that you see quite often as you use AutoCAD LT.

(Starting from) scratch where it itches

Eleanor Roosevelt was famous for advising people to "scratch where it itches." That's kind of what you're doing when you use the Start from Scratch option — that is, you do whatever you want, without any help from anyone. AutoCAD LT just comes up with a blank document.

This blank document is set up with the drawing area representing an area 12 units wide by 9 high and a drawing scale factor of 1. The dimensions 12 x 9 inches correspond to an A-size architectural sheet, which almost no one uses — not even most architects. In addition, this size is inconveniently just a bit larger than normal, ANSI A size — 8½ x 11 inches — turned on its side.

Thus, if you choose the Start from Scratch option, immediately use the setup options we describe in the subsequent sections to set units, limits, grid, snap, and the dimension and linetype scale factors. Then you'll be in great shape.

Using a template of doom

The other common way of creating a new drawing is use a template drawing. A *template* is simply a drawing whose name ends in the letters DWT, which you use as the starting point for another drawing. When you create a new drawing from a template, AutoCAD LT makes a copy of the template and opens the copy in a new drawing editor window. The first time you save the file, you're prompted for a new filename to save to; the original template file stays unchanged.

You may be familiar with the Microsoft Word or Excel template documents, and AutoCAD LT template drawings work pretty much the same way — because Autodesk stole the idea from them! When you choose the Use a Template option in the Startup or Create New Drawing dialog boxes, you can select a template drawing to start from, as shown in Figure 9-6. The Select a Template list in the Create New Drawing dialog box displays both a preview and a short description for each template.

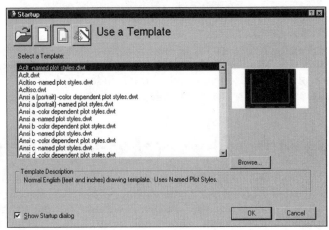

Figure 9-6:
Use a template, please do.

We bet you didn't notice this fact, but even if you choose Start from Scratch or — horror of horrors — Use a Wizard in the Startup or Create New Drawing dialog boxes, LT starts your new drawing from a template — in this case, the LT default templates Aclt.dwt or Acltiso.dwt.

So templates serve as body parts, and you're Dr. Frankenstein — you make a copy of the original and then modify it to suit your evil purposes. Sounds like fun, huh?

Well, templates *are* fun. Using the correct template can save you time and much needless worry because all the options are already set correctly for you. You know the drawing will print correctly; you just have to worry about getting the geometry and text right.

The only problems with templates are creating good ones and then later finding the right one to use when you need it. Later in this chapter, in the section Creating "Terrific Templates," we show you how to create templates from your own setup drawings. Here we show you how to use an already-created template, such as one of the templates that come with AutoCAD LT 2000.

Here are the steps for creating a new drawing from a template drawing:

1. **Close AutoCAD LT and restart it by double-clicking the AutoCAD LT icon or by choosing AutoCAD LT 2000 from the Start menu.**

   The Startup dialog box appears.

   You can accomplish the same thing by choosing File⇨New from within AutoCAD LT. If so, the dialog box that appears is the same except that it's called Create New Drawing and doesn't have a button labeled Open a Drawing.

2. **Click the Use a Template button.**

   The dialog box changes to show the following information:

   - *Select a Template* presents a list of templates that come with AutoCAD LT. (Many of the templates have two versions — one for color-dependent plot styles and another for named plot styles. See Chapter 4 for information about plot styles.) Use color-dependent plot styles if you need to be compatible with the way previous versions of AutoCAD and LT handled plotting (and with the way that most users are likely to do things for some time to come, even in AutoCAD and LT 2000).

   - *Preview* shows a small thumbnail sketch of what the currently highlighted template looks like.

   - *Template Description* gives a brief description of what the template contains.

3. **Highlight the template name you want to look at in the scrolling list.**

   The Preview and Template Description change to reflect the highlighted template.

4. **Click OK or double-click the template name to open the template you choose.**

   A new drawing window, with a temporary name such as Drawing2.dwg, appears. (The template you opened remains unchanged.)

5. **Save the file under a new name.**

   Take the time to save the drawing to the appropriate name and location now so that you can focus on getting your drawing right.

6. **Make needed changes.**

   For most of the templates that come with AutoCAD LT, you need to consider changing the units, limits, grid and snap settings, linetype scale, and dimension scale. See the next section, "First Stop, Model Space," for instructions.

7. **Consider saving the file as a template.**

   If you'll need other drawings in the future similar to the current one, consider saving your modified template as a template in its own right. See the section "Creating Terrific Templates," later in this chapter.

Find or create templates for the main types of drawings that you do, then perfect them over time. You'll save yourself hours of setup hassles and the quality of your work will go up. Encourage others to do the same, and share templates. Instructions on how to set up templates appear in the section "Creating Terrific Templates" later in this chapter.

First Stop, Model Space

Most drawings require a two-part setup: You first set up the model space tab where you'll create most of your drawing, and then create one or more paper space layout tabs for plotting. After you've chosen the drawing scale and sheet size, you can perform model space setup as described in this section.

Setting your units

First, you should set the linear and angular units that you want to use in your new drawing. The following procedure shows how:

1. **Choose Format➪Units from the menu bar.**

   The Drawing Units dialog box appears, as shown in Figure 9-7.

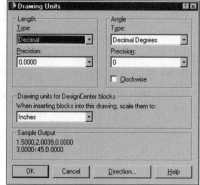

2. Choose a linear unit type from the Length Type drop-down list.

Choose the type of unit representation that's appropriate for your work. Engineering and Architectural units are displayed in feet and inches; the other types of units aren't tied to any particular unit of measurement. You decide whether each unit represents a millimeter, centimeter, meter, inch, foot, or something else. Decimal units usually are a good choice for metric drawings.

AutoCAD LT can "think" in inches! If you're using Engineering or Architectural units (feet and inches), AutoCAD LT understands any coordinate you enter as a number of inches. You use the ' (apostrophe) character on your keyboard to indicate a number in feet instead of inches.

3. From the Length Precision drop-down list, choose the degree of precision you want when AutoCAD displays coordinates and linear measurements.

The precision setting controls how precisely AutoCAD displays coordinates, distances, and some dialog box prompts. In particular, the Coordinates box on the status bar displays the current cursor coordinates using the current precision. A *grosser* — that is, less precise — precision setting makes the numbers displayed in the status bar more readable and less "jumpy." So be gross for now; you can always act a little less gross later.

The linear and angular precision settings affect only AutoCAD LT's *display* of coordinates, distances, and angles. For DWG files, AutoCAD LT always uses maximum precision to store the objects that you draw.

4. Choose an angular unit type from the Angle Type drop-down list.

Decimal Degrees and Deg/Min/Sec are the most common choices.

The Clockwise check box and the Direction button provide additional angle measurement options, but you'll rarely need to change the default settings: Measure angles counterclockwise and use east as the 0 degree direction.

5. **From the Angle Precision drop-down list, choose the degree of precision you want when AutoCAD LT displays angular measurements.**

6. **In the Drawing Units for DesignCenter Blocks area, choose the units of measurement for this drawing.**

7. **Click OK to exit the dialog box and save your settings.**

Telling your drawing its limits

The next model space setup task is to set your drawing's *limits*. You wouldn't want it staying out all night and hanging out with just anybody, would you? The limits represent the rectangular working area that you'll draw on, which usually corresponds to the paper size. Setting limits correctly gives you the following advantages:

✔ When you turn on the grid, as described later in this chapter in the section "Making Your Screen Smart with Snap and Grid," the grid displays in the rectangular limits area. With the grid on and the limits set correctly, you always see your working area and don't accidentally "color outside the lines."

✔ The ZOOM command's All option zooms to the greater of the limits or the drawing extents. (As we describe in Chapter 4, the drawing extents are the corners of an imaginary rectangle that just surrounds all the objects in the drawing.) When you set limits properly and "color within the lines," ZOOM All gives you a quick way to zoom to your working area.

✔ If you plot from model space, you can choose to plot the limits area. This option gives you a quick, reliable way to plot your drawing, but only if you've set limits correctly!

Many CAD drafters don't set limits properly in their drawings. After you read this section, you can smugly tell them why they should and how.

You can start the LIMITS command from a menu choice, but all subsequent action takes place on the command line; despite the importance of the topic, AutoCAD LT has no dialog box for setting limits. The following procedure shows you how to set your drawing limits:

1. **Choose Format⇨Drawing Limits from the menu bar to start the LIMITS command; or type LIMITS on the command line and press Enter.**

   The LIMITS command appears on the command line, and the command line displays the following prompt at the bottom of the screen:

```
Command: limits
Reset Model space limits:
Specify lower left corner or [ON/OFF] <0'-0",0'-0">:
```

The value at the end of the last line of the prompt is the default value for the lower-left corner of the drawing limits; it appears according to the units and precision that you selected in the Drawing Units dialog box — for example, 0'-0" if you selected Architectural units with precision to the nearest inch.

2. **Type the lower-left corner of the limits you want to use and press Enter.**

   The usual value to enter at this point is **0,0**. (That is, type a zero, a comma, and then another zero, with no spaces.) Or you can just press Enter to accept the default value.

   AutoCAD now prompts you for the upper-right corner of the limits:

```
Specify upper right corner <1'-0",0'-9">:
```

   The initial units offered by AutoCAD correspond to an architectural A size sheet of paper in landscape orientation.

3. **Type the upper-right corner of the limits you want to use and press Enter.**

   You calculate the usual setting for the limits upper-right corner by multiplying the paper dimensions by the drawing scale factor. For example, if you're setting up a ⅛" = 1'-0" drawing (drawing scale factor = 96) to be plotted on a 24-x-36-inch sheet in landscape orientation, the upper-right corner of the limits should be 36 inches times 96, 24 inches times 96. Okay, pencils down. The correct answer is 3406,2304 (or 288 feet,192 feet).

   Alternatively, you can cheat when specifying limits and read the limits from the tables on the Cheat Sheet.

   If you have the grid turned on, LT redisplays it in the new limits area after you press Enter.

   If you're using Architectural or Engineering units and you want to enter measurements in feet and not inches, you must add the foot designator after the number, such as **6'**; otherwise, AutoCAD assumes that you mean inches.

4. **Choose View⇨Zoom⇨All.**

   AutoCAD LT zooms to the new limits.

Making your screen smart with snap and grid

So just what does it mean for a computer screen to be smart? No, the screen doesn't know how to tie its shoelaces or spell *cat.* An AutoCAD LT smart computer screen helps you do what you want. For example, you can set up a *grid* to show you where you are within the limits and a *snap interval* that creates hot spots in the drawing area that are easier to connect to when drawing.

The *grid* is simply a set of visible, evenly spaced dots that give some orientation as to how you place objects in your drawing in relation to one another on-screen. You can turn the grid on and off any time, but when it's on, it's only on for display purposes; the grid never appears on your plots.

The *snap interval* attracts the mouse cursor to invisible hot spots a certain distance apart on-screen, enabling you to easily align objects a predetermined distance apart. For example, if you're designing a soccer field, having a snap interval of one meter may make good sense.

If you're using both the on-screen grid and the snap interval, you'll usually want to use spacings that relate them to each other. The snap interval should be an even fraction of the grid distance (½, ¼, or ½₂ of the grid distance, for English (feet and inches) units; or one or more *orders of magnitude,* that is, multiples of 10, for metric units). In this way, the grid serves as a visual reminder of the snap interval.

Technically savvy people love to say "order of magnitude," a term that simply means "a factor of ten." A dollar is an order of magnitude more valuable than a dime and is two orders of magnitude less valuable than a hundred-dollar bill. Now you can toss around the phrase *order of magnitude,* too. (Your friends may accuse you of having an odor of magnitude!)

You nearly always want a grid in your drawing because it's so useful in orienting objects to one another. (You can turn it on and off by clicking the GRID button in the status bar.) You may not always want to use a snap interval, however, because some drawings, such as a contour map, don't contain objects that align on specific points.

You can set your grid to work in one of two ways: to help with your drawing or to help you remain aware of how objects will relate to your plot. For a grid that helps with your drawing, set the grid points a logical number of measurement units apart. Grid points, for example, may be 30 feet (10 yards) apart on a drawing of a football field. A grid that helps with your printout is different; you space this kind of grid so that a grid square represents a specific measurement, such as one inch, on your final plot.

In either case, set the snap interval at the same value or any even division of it: One-half, one-fourth, and one-twelfth work well for architecture; one-half and one-tenth work well for mechanical drawings and for other disciplines.

You set the grid and the snap intervals in the Drafting Settings dialog box, as shown in the following example.

1. **Choose Tools⇨Drafting Settings from the menu bar or right-click the Snap or Grid button in the status bar and choose Settings.**

   The Drafting Settings dialog box appears with the Snap and Grid tab selected, as shown in Figure 9-8.

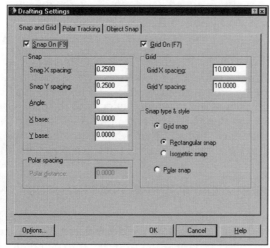

Figure 9-8:
Get your
Drafting
Settings
here!

The Snap and Grid tab has four parts, but we'll concern ourselves only with the Snap and Grid sections for now. Some of the other settings are nerd stuff that you can live a long time without ever needing to think twice about; still others are covered later in this book.

2. **Click the Snap On check box to turn on snap.**

   This action creates default snaps half a unit apart.

3. **Enter the X Spacing for the snap interval in the accompanying text box.**

   Use the information preceding this procedure to decide on a reasonable snap spacing.

   The Y spacing automatically changes to equal the X spacing. Don't change it; having them the same creates a square snap grid, which is just what you want for now.

4. Click the <u>G</u>rid On check box to turn on the grid.

5. Enter the X S<u>p</u>acing for the grid in the accompanying text box.

Use the information preceding this procedure to decide on a reasonable grid spacing.

If you want to have the grid represent one inch on the plot and your drawing units are inches, enter the drawing scale factor. For example, in a ¼" = 1'–0" drawing, you'd enter the drawing scale factor of 48. A 48-inch grid interval in your drawing corresponds to a one-inch interval on the plot when you plot to scale. If your drawing units are metric, but you still want the grid to represent plotted inches, multiply the drawing scale factor by 25.4 to get the grid spacing. Better, yet, round the multiplier off to 25, so that grid squares will represent 25-mm squares when you plot to scale.

The Y spacing automatically changes to equal the X spacing. As with the snap spacing, you usually want to leave it that way.

X measures horizontal distance; Y measures vertical distance. The AutoCAD LT drawing area normally shows an X and Y icon in case you forget. Legend has it that the mathematician René Descartes devised this scheme after watching a fly walk on a patterned ceiling. (This story would be better if he had thought it up while watching horses graze in a field, but to tell that story you'd have to put Descartes before the horse.)

6. Click OK to close the Drafting Settings dialog box.

The array of snap points is sometimes referred to as the *snap grid*. This term makes sense because the snap points do form a grid, but it's easy to get confused between the snap grid and the other grid. What to call that one? The *visible grid* is a good name because its purpose is to be seen (but not heard — or plotted). So if you use the term *snap grid* for your snaps, call the other grid the *visible grid*.

You can also click the SNAP button in the status bar to toggle snap on and off; the same goes for the GRID button and the grid setting.

To use snap effectively, you need to make the snap setting smaller as you zoom in and work on more detailed areas, and larger as you zoom back out. You are likely to find yourself changing the snap setting fairly frequently. The grid setting, on the other hand, can usually remain constant even as you work at different zoom settings.

Setting linetype and dimension scales

Even though you've engraved the drawing scale factor on your desk and written it on your hand, AutoCAD LT doesn't know the drawing scale until you tell
it. Keeping LT in the dark is fine as long as you're just drawing continuous
lines and curves representing real-world geometry, because you draw these
objects at their real-world size, without worrying about plot scale.

As soon as you start adding dimensions (measurements that show the size of
the things you're drawing) and using dash-dot linetypes (line patterns that
contain gaps in them), you need to tell LT how to scale the parts of the
dimensions and the gaps in the linetypes based on the plot scale. If you
forget to do so, the dimension text and arrowheads can come out very tiny or
very large when you plot the drawing, and dash-dot linetype patterns can
look waaaay too big or too small. Figure 9-9 shows what we mean.

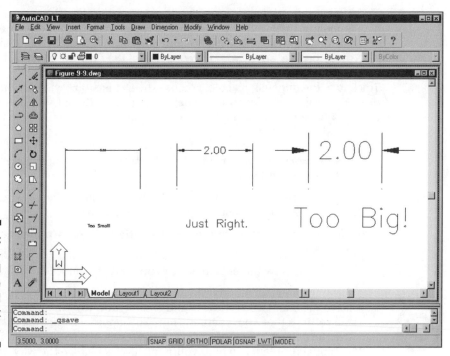

Figure 9-9:
The dimen-
sion and
linetype
scales need
to be Just
Right.

The scale factor that controls dash-dot linetypes is found in a system variable called LTSCALE (as in LineType SCALE). The scaling factor that controls dimensions is found in a system variable called DIMSCALE. You can change either of these settings at any time, but it's best to set them correctly when you're setting up the drawing.

To set the linetype scale from the command line, follow these steps:

1. **Type** LTScale **on the command line and press Enter.**

   AutoCAD LT responds with a prompt, asking you for the scale factor. The value at the end of the prompt is the current linetype scale setting, as in the following example:

   ```
   New scale factor <1.0000>:
   ```

2. **Type the value you want for the linetype scale on the command line and press Enter.**

   The easiest choice is to set the linetype scale to the drawing scale factor. Some people find that the dashes and gaps in dash-dot linetypes get a bit too long when they use the drawing scale factor. If you're one of those people, set LTSCALE to one-half of the drawing scale factor.

To change the dimension scale, you use the Dimension Style Manager dialog box. Dimensions are described in detail in Chapter 13, but you should get in the habit of setting the dimension scale during drawing setup, as shown in the following example:

1. **Choose Format⇨Dimension Style from the menu bar or enter** Dimstyle **at the command line.**

   The Dimension Style Manager dialog box appears. New drawings contain just the default dimension style named Standard.

2. **Click the New button to create a new dimension style that's a copy of Standard.**

   The Create New Dimension Style dialog box appears.

   Although you can modify the default Standard style, we suggest that you leave the Standard style as is and create your own dimension style(s) for the settings that you'll actually use. This approach ensures that you can use the default Standard style as a reference. More important, it avoids a potential problem in which your dimensions change the way they look if the current drawing gets inserted into another drawing.

3. **Enter a New Style Name that makes sense to you and click Continue.**

   The New Dimension Style dialog box appears.

4. **Click the Fit tab.**

   The Fit tab options appear, including an area called Scale for Dimension Features.

5. **In the Scale for Dimension Features area, make sure that the radio button next to the Use Overall $\underline{S}$cale Of setting is selected.**

6. **In the text box next to Use Overall $\underline{S}$cale Of type the drawing scale factor for the current drawing.**

   See — we told you that you'd be using that drawing scale factor a lot!

7. **Click OK to close the New Dimension Style dialog box.**

   The Dimension Style Manager dialog box reappears.

8. **Choose your new dimension style from the $\underline{S}$tyles list and then click the Set C$\underline{u}$rrent button.**

   Your new dimension style, with the appropriate dimension scale factor, becomes the current dimension style that AutoCAD uses for future dimensions.

9. **Click Close.**

   The Dimension Style Manager dialog box closes. Now when you draw dimensions (see Chapter 13), LT will scale the dimension text and arrowheads correctly.

Entering drawing properties

You need to do one last bit of bookkeeping before you're finished with model space drawing setup: You should enter summary information in the Drawing Properties dialog box, as shown in Figure 9-10. Choose $\underline{F}$ile⇨Drawing Proper$\underline{t}$ies to open the Drawing Properties dialog box and then click the Summary tab.

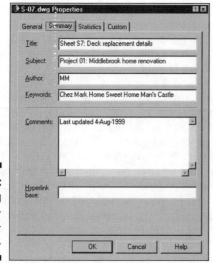

Figure 9-10:
Surveying
your drawing's properties.

Plot Layouts Are In

As we describe in the "About paper space layouts" section of Chapter 4, *paper space* is a separate "space" for composing a printed version of your drawing. You create one or more plottable views, complete with title block, and each one is called a *layout*. Thus, after you complete model space setup, you should create a layout for plotting.

In AutoCAD LT 2000, it's still possible to ignore paper space layouts entirely and do all your drawing *and* plotting in model space. But you owe it to yourself (and to the programmers who slaved over a hot keyboard cooking up all those new layout features) to give layouts a try. We think you'll find that they make plotting more consistent and predictable. They'll certainly give you more plotting flexibility when the time comes that you need it.

You'll sometimes hear the word *tilemode* bandied about in discussions of paper space, including in the AutoCAD LT 2000 online help. In previous releases of LT, you used the TILEMODE command to switch between model space and paper space. (Previous releases had only one paper space layout and didn't display the convenient little tabs at the bottom of the drawing area.) TILEMODE 1 displayed model space and TILEMODE 0 displayed paper space. The insanely obscure name TILEMODE comes from the floating versus tiled viewport distinction, but the programmer who thought of that name still deserves to be sentenced to life behind a DOS prompt. In any case, you almost certainly don't really need to worry about TILEMODE any more. Clicking the Model and Layout tabs takes care of everything for you.

Creating a layout

Creating a simple paper space layout is straightforward, thanks to the new AutoCAD LT 2000 Create Layout wizard, shown in Figure 9-11. The command name is LAYOUTWIZARD, which is not to be confused with the WAYOUT-LIZARD command for drawing geckos and iguanas, but you avoid a lot of typing with <u>T</u>ools⇨Wizards⇨<u>C</u>reate Layout.

Although the Create Layout wizard guides you step by step through the process of creating a paper space layout from scratch, it doesn't eliminate the necessity of your coming up with a sensible set of layout parameters. The sheet size and plot scale that you choose provide a certain amount of space for showing your model (see the information earlier in this chapter), and wizards aren't allowed to bend the laws of arithmetic in order to escape that fact. For example, a map of Texas at a scale of 1 inch = 1 foot won't fit on an 8½-x-11-inch sheet, no way, no how. In other words, garbage in, garbage (lay)out. Fortunately the Create Layout wizard lends itself to experimentation, and you can easily delete layouts that don't work.

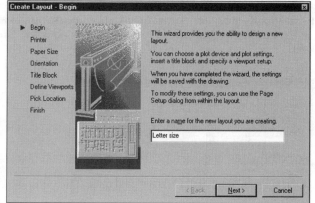

Figure 9-11:
The Create
Layout
wizard.

The following steps show you how to create a layout after you've drawn your model — in this example, an architectural floor plan of a house:

1. **Choose Tools⇨Wizards⇨Create Layout, or type** LAYOUTWIZARD **and press Enter.**

2. **Give the new layout a name (see Figure 9-11) and then click Next.**

   In place of the default name, Layout2, we recommend something more descriptive — for example, Letter size.

3. **Choose a printer or plotter to use when plotting this layout and then click Next.**

   Think of your choice as the *default* plotter for this layout. You can change to a different plotter later or create page setups that plot the same layout on different plotters.

   Many of the names in the configured plotter list should look familiar because they're your Windows printers (*system printers* in AutoCAD LT lingo). Names with a PC3 extension represent nonsystem printer drivers. See Chapter 4 for details.

4. **Choose a paper size and specify whether to use inches or millimeters in order to represent paper units, and then click Next.**

   The available paper sizes depend on the printer or plotter that you selected in Step 3.

5. **Specify the orientation of the drawing on the paper and then click Next.**

   The icon showing the letter A on the piece of paper shows you which orientation is which.

6. **Select either a title block or None (see Figure 9-12). If you choose a title block, specify whether AutoCAD LT should insert it as a Block — which is preferable in this case — or attach it as an Xref. Then click Next.**

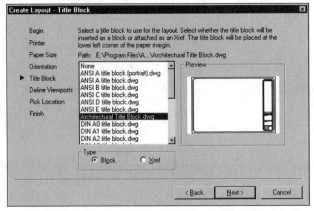

Figure 9-12:
Title block options in the Create Layout wizard.

Attaching a title block as an xref is a good practice if your title block DWG file is in the same folder as the current drawing that you're working on. The Create Layout wizard's title blocks live in the Template folder that's stored with the AutoCAD LT 2000 program files, which isn't — or shouldn't be — where you keep your project files. Thus, in this case Block is a safer choice.

Choose a title block that fits your paper size. If the title block is larger than the paper, the Create Layout wizard simply lets it run off the paper.

If you don't like any of the supplied title blocks, choose None. You can always draw, insert, or xref a title block later. See Chapter 15 for information about inserting or xrefing a title block

The list of available title blocks comes from all the DWG files in the AutoCAD LT Template folder. You can add custom title block drawings to this directory.

7. **Define the arrangement of viewports that AutoCAD LT should create and the paper space to model space scale for all viewports. Then click Next.**

A paper space layout viewport is a "window" into model space. You must create at least one viewport in order to display the model in your new layout. For most 2D drawings, a Single viewport is all you need. 3D models often benefit from multiple viewports, each showing the 3D model from a different perspective.

The default Viewport scale, Scaled to Fit, ensures that all of your model drawing displays in the viewport but results in an arbitrary scale factor Most technical drawings require a specific scale, such as 1=10 or ⅛" = 1'–0".

8. Specify the location of the viewport(s) on the paper by picking its corners. Then click Next.

After you click the Select Location button, the Create Layout wizard displays the preliminary layout with any title block that you've chosen. Pick two points to define a rectangle that falls within the drawing area of your title block (or within the plottable area of the sheet, if you chose no title block in Step 6).

AutoCAD LT represents the plottable area of the sheet with a dashed rectangle near the edge of the sheet. If you don't select a location for the viewport(s), the Create Layout wizard creates a viewport that fills the plottable area of the sheet.

9. Click Finish.

AutoCAD LT creates the new layout, as shown in Figure 9-13.

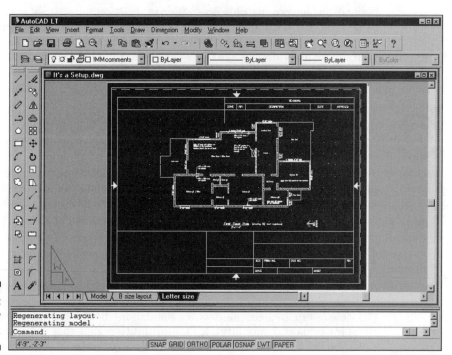

Figure 9-13:
Freshly
laid out.

Working with layouts

After you've created a layout, you can delete, copy, rename, and otherwise manipulate it by right-clicking its tab. Figure 9-14 shows the right-click menu options.

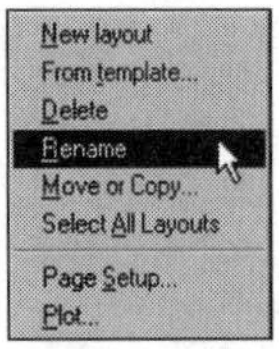

Figure 9-14:
The right-click menu for a layout tab.

New layout
From template...
Delete
Rename
Move or Copy...
Select All Layouts
Page Setup...
Plot...

The From Template option refers to layout templates. You can save a layout to a template file (a DWT file) and then use it to create new layouts in other drawings. For details, see online help: Contents⇨How To⇨Plot Your Drawings⇨To Use an Existing Layout Template.

Many drawings require only one paper space layout. If you always plot the same view of the model, and always plot to the same device and on the same size paper, then a single paper space layout should suffice. If you want to plot your model in different ways (for example, at different scales, with different layers visible, with different areas visible, or with different plotted line characteristics), you may want to create additional paper space layouts.

Some different ways of plotting the same model can be handled in a single paper space layout with different page setups. See the section "It's a (page) setup!" in Chapter 4.

If you want to add another viewport to an existing layout, you need to grapple with the MVIEW command and the ZOOM command's mysterious XP option. See the MVIEW and ZOOM commands in the AutoCAD LT online help.

Lost in paper space

After creating a paper space layout, you suddenly have two views of the same drawing geometry: the view on your original Model tab, and the new layout tab view (perhaps decorated with a handsome title block and other accoutrements of plotting nobility). It's important to realize that both views are of the *same* geometry. If you change the model geometry on one tab, you're changing it on all tabs, because all tabs display the same model space objects. It's like seeing double after downing a few too many drinks — the duplication is in your head, not in the real world (or in this case, in the CAD world).

When you make a paper space layout current by clicking its tab, you can move the cursor between paper space (that is, drawing and zooming on the sheet of paper) and model space (drawing and zooming on the model, inside the viewport) in several ways, including:

✔ Click the Paper / Model button on the status bar.

✔ In the drawing area, double-click over a viewport to move the cursor into model space in that viewport, or double-click outside all viewports (for example, in the gray area outside the sheet) in order to move the cursor into paper space.

✔ Enter **MSpace** or **PSpace** at the command prompt.

When the cursor is in model space, anything you draw or edit changes the model (and thus appears on the Model tab and on all paper space layout tabs, assuming that the given paper space layout displays that part of the underlying model). When the cursor is in paper space, anything you draw appears only on that one paper space layout tab. It's as though you were drawing on an acetate sheet over the top of that sheet of plotter paper — the model beneath remains unaffected.

This distinction can be disorienting at first — even if you haven't had a few too many drinks. To avoid confusion, stick with the following approach (at least until you're more familiar with paper space):

✔ If you want to edit the model, switch to the Model tab first. (Don't try to edit the model in a paper space viewport.)

✔ If you want to edit a particular plot layout, without affecting the model, switch to that layout's tab and make sure the cursor is in paper space.

Creating Terrific Templates

You can create a template from any DWG file by using the Save As dialog box. Follow these steps to save your drawing as a template:

1. **Choose File⇨Save As from the menu bar.**

   The Save Drawing As dialog box appears, as shown in Figure 9-15.

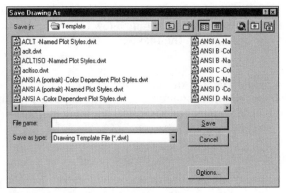

Figure 9-15:
Saving a
drawing as
a template.

2. **From the Save as Type pull-down menu, choose Drawing Template File (*.dwt).**

3. **Navigate to the folder where you want to store the drawing.**

   AutoCAD 2000's default folder for template drawings is \Program Files\ Acad2000\Template. Save your templates there if you want them to appear in the Create New Drawing dialog box's Select a Template list. You can save your templates in other folders, but if you want to use them later, you'll have to click the Browse button in the Create New Drawing dialog box and navigate to a different folder.

4. **Enter a name for the drawing template in the File Name text box.**

   A name such as ESIZ48SC.DWT may seem cryptic at first glance, but a name that includes the paper size (ESIZ, or E size) and scaling factor (48SC) actually may help you find the template you need later.

   Because AutoCAD LT 2000 runs only on Windows 95, Windows 98, and Windows NT, all of which support long filenames, you may be tempted to use a long filename for your AutoCAD LT 2000 files. That's fine, because AutoCAD LT 2000 drawings can be opened only by people who are also running 32-bit versions of Windows, which support long filenames. But if you save the file for use by AutoCAD Release 12 or earlier, be sure to give it a filename using the DOS 8.3 pattern (an eight-character filename followed by a three-character extension, such as BUDSMITH.DWG).

5. **Click the Save button to save your drawing template.**

   The drawing is saved as a template. A dialog box for the template description appears.

6. **Enter the template file description and measurement units (English or Metric).**

   Enter the key info now; you can't do it later unless you save the template to a different name.

7. **Click OK to save the file.**

8. **To save your drawing as a regular drawing, choose File⇨Save As from the menu bar.**

   The Save Drawing As dialog box appears again.

9. **From the Save as Type pull-down menu, choose AutoCAD 2000 Drawing (*.dwg).**

10. **Navigate to the folder where you want to store the drawing.**

    Use a different folder from the one with your template drawings.

11. **Enter the name of the drawing in the File Name text box.**

12. **Click the Save button to save your drawing.**

    The file is saved. Now, when you save it in the future, the regular file, not the template file, gets updated.

So now if someone asks you whether it's faster to set up a new drawing from scratch or start from a well-conceived template drawing, you can answer, "Surely, Template!" (especially if you're a fan of 1940s curly-haired child movie stars).

Chapter 10

Where to Draw the Line?

In This Chapter

▶ Controlling and using object properties

▶ Ensuring precision when you draw

▶ Drawing lines and polygons

▶ Drawing curves and more

As you probably remember from your crayon and coloring book days, drawing stuff is *fun*. CAD imposes a little more discipline on your inner (creative) child, but drawing AutoCAD LT objects is still fun. This chapter shows you how to draw lots of them, and how to draw well while you're at it. We tell you how to take advantage of object properties and ensure precision, and then spend most of the chapter introducing you to the most useful drawing commands in the AutoCAD LT toolbox.

Chapter 5 introduces drawing concepts such as layers, lines, and precision techniques in the context of marking up existing drawings. In this chapter, we occasionally point you to Chapter 5 descriptions in order to avoid repeating ourselves. (We wouldn't want to repeat ourselves.) If you're starting here without having read Chapter 5 first, fear not. We summarize the important concepts and point you to the exact places in Chapter 5 that tell you more.

Objects Own Properties

All the objects that you draw in AutoCAD LT are like good Monopoly players: They own *properties*. In LT, though, these properties aren't little plastic hotels and houses — they're characteristics like layer, color, linetype, and lineweight. You can view — and change — all of an object's properties in the Properties window. In Figure 10-1, the Properties window shows properties for a line object.

Figure 10-1:
A line rich in
properties.

To toggle the Properties window on and off, click the Properties button on
the Standard toolbar. Before you select an object, the Properties window displays the *current properties* — properties that AutoCAD LT applies to new
objects when you draw them. After you select an object, LT displays the
properties for that object. If you select more than one object, LT displays the
properties that they have in common.

Put it on a layer

Every object has *layer* as one of its properties. You might be familiar with
layers from using drawing programs. We describe AutoCAD LT layers in the
section titled "The Layered Look" in Chapter 5, so review that section if
you're unfamiliar with the concept in general or LT's implementation of it in
particular. The "Stacking up your layers" sidebar, in this chapter, summarizes
what you need to know.

Before you draw *any* object in AutoCAD LT, you should set an appropriate
layer current — creating it first, if necessary, using the procedure in the
"Mayor of your own layer" section of Chapter 5. If the layer already exists in
your drawing, you can make it the current layer by choosing it from the Layer
drop-down list on the Object Properties toolbar, as shown in Figure 10-2.

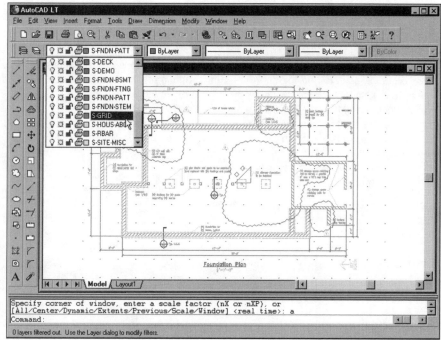

Figure 10-2:
Set a
current
layer before
you draw.

Make sure that no objects are selected before you use the Layer drop-down list to change the current layer. (Press the Esc key twice to be sure.) If objects are selected, the Layer drop-down list displays — and lets you change — those objects' layer. When no objects are selected, the Layer drop-down list displays — and lets you change — the current layer.

If you forget to set an appropriate layer before you draw an object, you can select the object and then change its layer using either the Properties window or the Layer drop-down list.

Accumulating properties

Besides layers, the remaining object properties that you're likely to want to use often are color, linetype, lineweight, and possibly plot style. Table 10-1 summarizes these four properties.

Stacking up your layers

In AutoCAD LT, layers serve several purposes. They organize objects into logical groups of things that belong together — for example, walls, furniture, and text notes usually belong on three separate layers. They give you a way to turn groups of objects on and off — both on the screen and on the plot. In addition, they provide the best way of controlling object color, linetype, and lineweight.

Most offices develop a set of layer guidelines, and some projects impose specific layer requirements. (But be careful; if someone says "you have to have a brick layer for this project," that could mean a couple of different things.)

Ask experienced CAD drafters in your office or industry how they use layers. If you can't find any definitive answer, create a chart of layers for yourself. Each row in the chart should list the layer name, default color, default linetype, default lineweight, and what kinds of objects belong on that layer.

After you've created layers and drawn objects on them, you use the Layer Properties Manager dialog box (see Figure 10-3 later in this chapter) to change layer properties. For example, you can turn a layer off or on in order to hide or show the objects on that layer.

Table 10-1	Useful Object Properties
Property	*Controls*
Color	Displayed color and plotted color or lineweight
Linetype	Displayed and plotted dash-dot line pattern
Lineweight	Displayed and plotted line width
Plot style	Plotted characteristics (see "Plotting with style" in Chapter 4)

In older versions of AutoCAD LT and AutoCAD, color also controlled the plotted lineweight of each object — a strange approach in some ways, but now very common in the AutoCAD world. You may find yourself working this way even in AutoCAD LT 2000, for compatibility with drawings that use the old way — as described in the "About colors and lineweights" section of Chapter 4.

AutoCAD LT gives you two different ways of controlling these properties: by layer and by object. Each layer has a default color, linetype, lineweight, and plot style property. Unless you tell AutoCAD LT otherwise, objects inherit the properties of the layers on which they're created. LT calls this approach controlling properties *by layer*. But LT also enables you to override an object's layer's property setting and give the object a specific color, linetype, lineweight, or plot style that differs from the layer's. LT calls this approach controlling properties *by object*.

If you've worked with other graphics programs, you might be used to assigning properties such as color to objects. If so, you'll be tempted to use the by object approach to assigning properties in LT. Resist the temptation. In almost all cases, it's better to create layers, assign them properties, and let the objects inherit their layers' properties. The *by layer* approach, among other benefits, makes it easy to change the properties of a group of related objects that you put on one layer. You simply change the property of one layer, rather than of a bunch of separate objects. In addition, experienced drafters use the by layer approach, so if you work with drawings from other people, you'll be much more compatible with them if you do it the same way. You'll also avoid getting yelled at by irate CAD managers, one of whose jobs it is to harangue any hapless newbies who assign properties by object.

If you take our advice and assign properties by layer, then all you have to do is set layer properties in the Layer Properties Manager dialog box, as shown in Figure 10-3. Before you draw any objects, make sure the Color Control, Linetype Control, Lineweight Control, and Plot Style Control drop-down lists on the Object Properties toolbar are set to ByLayer, as shown in Figure 10-4.

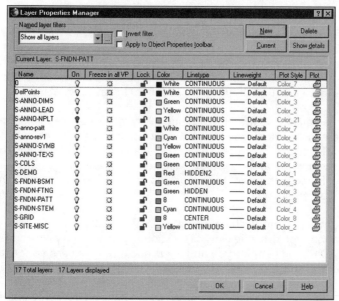

Figure 10-3: Use layer properties to control object properties.

If the drawing is set to use color-based plot styles instead of named plot styles (see "Plotting with style" in Chapter 4), the Plot Style Control drop-down list will be inactive and will display `ByColor`.

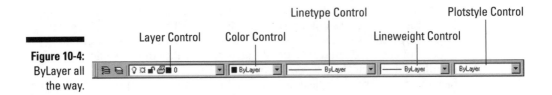

Linetype Control

Plotstyle Control

Layer Control   Color Control   Lineweight Control

Figure 10-4:
ByLayer all
the way.

If you like doing things the wrong way and enjoy getting yelled at by CAD managers, you can assign properties to objects in one of two ways. First, you can choose a specific color, linetype, lineweight, or plot style from the appropriate drop-down list on the Object Properties toolbar, and then draw the objects. Alternatively, you can draw the objects, select them, and then choose a property from the same drop-down lists. Or, if you prefer to do things the right way, assign these properties by layer, as we describe in this section.

My Point Is . . .

One of the more important things to figure out early in your career as a "CADdie" is that you must pay close attention to precision. If you think CAD managers get testy when you assign properties by object instead of by layer, wait until you see them berate someone who doesn't use precision techniques when creating drawings in AutoCAD LT or AutoCAD.

And these managers aren't just being picky; drawings may guide manufacturing and construction projects, and drawing data may drive machinery that automatically manufactures things. Huge amounts of money and, in some cases, even lives can be at stake based on the precision of a drawing, or lack thereof. In recognition of this, a passion for precision permeates the profession. Permanently.

Precision is one of the characteristics that separates CAD from ordinary illustration-type drawing work. The sooner you get fussy about precision in AutoCAD LT, the happier you and everyone else who uses your drawings will be.

In the context of drawing objects, *precision* means specifying points and distances precisely. The "Neatness Counts" section in Chapter 5 introduces the whys and wherefores of precision drawing techniques, so if you're not sure what all the fuss is about, read that section. Table 10-2 lists the more important AutoCAD LT precision techniques, along with the status bar buttons that you use to toggle some of the features off and on.

Table 10-2	Precision Techniques	
Technique	**Status Bar Button**	**Description**
Coordinate entry	—	Type exact X,Y coordinates.
Single-point object snaps	—	Pick points on existing objects (lasts for one point pick).
Running object snaps	OSNAP	Pick points on existing objects (lasts for multiple point picks).
Snap	SNAP	Pick points on an imaginary grid of equally spaced "hot spots."
Ortho	ORTHO	Constrain the cursor to move at an angle of 0, 90, 180, or 270 degrees from the previous point.
Direct distance entry	—	Point the cursor in a direction and type a distance (see "And one further point . . ." in Chapter 5).
Polar tracking	POLAR	Causes the cursor to "prefer" certain angles.

Before you draw objects, always check the SNAP, ORTHO, POLAR, and OSNAP buttons on the status bar and set them according to your precision needs. A button that appears to be pushed in indicates that the feature is turned on. A button that appears to be popped up indicates that the feature is turned off.

Keyboard capers: Coordinate entry

One of the simpler ways to enter points precisely is to type numbers at the command line. AutoCAD LT understands these keyboard coordinate entry formats:

- Absolute rectangular coordinates in the form *X,Y* (for example: 7,4)

- Relative rectangular coordinates in the form @*X,Y* (for example: @3,2)

- Relative polar coordinates in the form @*distance<angle* (for example: @6<45)

AutoCAD LT locates *absolute rectangular coordinates* with respect to the 0,0 point of the drawing — usually its lower-left corner. LT locates *relative rectangular coordinates* and *relative polar coordinates* with respect to the previous point that you picked or typed. Figure 10-5 demonstrates how to use all three coordinate formats to draw a pair of line segments that start at absolute coordinates 2,1, go 3 units to the right and 2 units up, and then go 4 units at an angle of 60 degrees.

You can view absolute coordinate locations by moving the cursor around in the drawing area and reading the Coordinates area at the left of the status bar. The X,Y coordinates should change as you move the cursor. If not, click the Coordinates area until the command line says <Coords on>.

Absolute rectangular coordinates

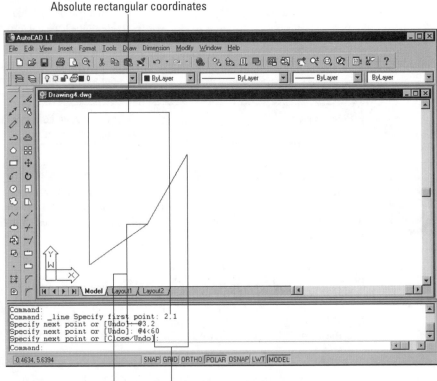

Figure 10-5:
Coordinating
from the
keyboard.

Relative rectangular coordinates

Relative polar coordinates

When you type coordinates at the command line, do *not* add any spaces, because AutoCAD LT interprets them as though you've pressed Enter. This "Spacebar = Enter" weirdness is a productivity feature that's been in AutoCAD since forever — it's easier to find the spacebar than the Enter key when you're entering lots of commands and coordinates in a hurry. This special use of the spacebar will drive you crazy for a while if you're in the habit of typing spaces in your coordinates.

If you're working in architectural or engineering units, the default unit of entry is *inches,* not feet. (If you're not careful, you can end up designing a very finely detailed, one-twelfth scale model of that office tower you've been commissioned to build!) To specify feet, you must enter the symbol for feet after the number, for instance: **6'** for 6 feet. You can enter a dash to separate feet from inches, as architects often do: **6'– 6"** is 6 feet, 6 inches. Both the dash and the inch mark are optional when you're entering coordinates and distances: AutoCAD understands **6'6"** and **6'6** as the same as **6'– 6"**. If you're typing a coordinate or distance that contains fractional inches, you *must* enter a dash — not a space — between the whole number of inches and the fraction: **6'6 –1/2** (or **6'– 6 –1/2**) represents 6 feet, 6½ inches. If all this dashing about confuses you, enter partial inches using decimals instead: **6'6.5** is the same as **6'6 –1/2** to AutoCAD LT, whether you're working in architectural or engineering units.

Snapping to attention: Object snaps

After you've drawn a few objects precisely in a new drawing, the most efficient way to draw more objects with equal precision is to grab points, such as endpoints, midpoints, or quadrants, on the existing objects. AutoCAD LT calls this technique *object snapping.* AutoCAD LT provides two kinds of object snapping modes: *single point* (or *override*) object snaps and *running* object snaps.

In Chapter 5, the section "Pick a point, and make it snappy" shows how to use single object snaps, which last for just a single point pick. Frequently, you want to use the same object snap mode (such as endpoint) repeatedly. Running object snaps addresses this need. To set a running object snap, right-click the OSNAP button on the status bar and choose the Settings option to display the Object Snap tab on the Drafting Settings dialog box, as shown in Figure 10-6. Select one or more object snap modes by checking the appropriate boxes, and then click OK to close the dialog box.

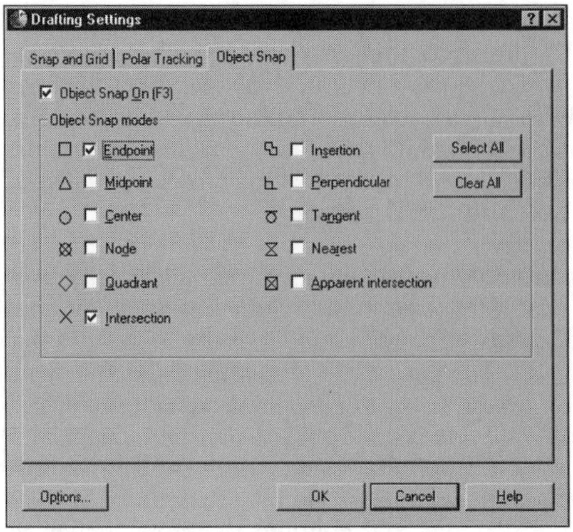

Figure 10-6:
Grabbing
object
features is a
snap.

You click the OSNAP button on the status bar to toggle running object snap mode off and on. If you turn on running object snap, AutoCAD LT "hunts" for points that correspond to the object snap modes you checked in the Drafting Settings dialog box. As with single-point object snaps, LT indicates that it has found an object snap point by displaying a special symbol — such as a square for an endpoint object snap. If you keep the cursor still for a moment, LT also displays a ToolTip that lists the kind of object snap point.

Other precision practices

The other LT precision techniques listed in Table 10-2 and not covered in Chapter 5 are

- ✔ **Snap:** If you turn on snap mode, LT constrains the cursor to an imaginary grid of points at the spacing that you specified. Right-click the SNAP button on the status bar and choose the Settings option to display the Snap and Grid tab on the Drafting Settings dialog box. Enter a snap spacing in the Snap X Spacing field and then click OK. Click the SNAP button on the status bar to toggle snap mode off and on. To use snap effectively, you need to change the snap spacing frequently — changing to a smaller spacing as you zoom in and work on smaller areas. You also need to toggle snap off and on frequently, because selecting objects and some editing tasks are easier with snap off.

- ✔ **Ortho:** Ortho mode constrains the cursor to move at right angles (orthogonally) to the starting point. Click the ORTHO button on the status bar to toggle ortho mode off and on.

✔ **Polar tracking:** When you turn on polar tracking, the cursor jumps to increments of the angle you selected. When the cursor jumps, a ToolTip label starting with `Polar:` appears. Right-click the POLAR button on the status bar and choose the Settings option to display the Polar Tracking tab on the Drafting Settings dialog box. Select an angle from the Increment Angle drop-down list and then click OK. Click the POLAR button on the status bar to toggle polar tracking mode off and on.

Drawing Commands

The following sections in this chapter provide a guided tour of the AutoCAD LT drawing toolbox. We show you commands for drawing straight lines and shapes composed of straight-line segments and then we cover the curvy commands.

Each time you draw an object, make sure you've set the right current properties — layer, color, and so on. (We recommend that you set color, linetype, lineweight, and plot style to ByLayer.) Also make sure that you use snap, object snaps, typed coordinates, or direct distance entry to ensure that you specify each object point precisely. The procedures in the following sections remind you to do both.

You can start the AutoCAD LT object drawing commands in a variety of ways, but the commands always prompt you at the command line. Read the command line prompts during every step of the command, especially when you're trying a drawing command for the first time.

The straight and narrow: Lines and polygons

As we've harped on a bunch of times elsewhere in this book, CAD programs are for precision drawing, so you'll spend a lot of your LT time drawing objects composed of straight-line segments. This section reviews the LINE and POLYLINE commands, which we introduce in Chapter 5, and then covers the commands for drawing rectangles and other kinds of polygons.

The lowly line and the peerless polyline

The "Line It Up" section of Chapter 5 demonstrates how to draw *lines* (one or more distinct straight-line segments) and *polylines* (a series of connected segments, straight or curved, that are joined together into a single object). The LINE and PLINE commands — both readily available on the Draw toolbar — are your basic line-drawing tools. The following procedure shows how to use these commands with the precision techniques described earlier in this chapter:

1. **Set an appropriate current layer, as described in the "Put it on a layer" section earlier in this chapter.**

2. **Check the SNAP, ORTHO, POLAR, and OSNAP buttons on the status bar and set them according to your needs, as described in the "My Point Is . . ." section earlier in this chapter.**

3. **Click the Line or Polyline button on the Draw toolbar.**

   Choose the LINE command if you need to draw only a single segment or you want to draw multiple segments that don't need to be joined together into a single object. Otherwise, choose the PLINE command.

   The command line prompts you to specify the first endpoint:

   ```
   Specify first point:
   ```

4. **Specify the starting point by typing absolute X,Y coordinates or using an object snap mode.**

   The command line prompts you to specify the other endpoint of the first line segment:

   ```
   Specify next point or [Undo]:
   ```

   The preceding prompt is for the LINE command. The PLINE command includes additional options, as shown in Figure 10-7.

5. **Specify additional points by typing relative or absolute X,Y coordinates, using object snap modes, or using direct distance entry.**

   Refer to the "And one further point . . ." section in Chapter 5 for instructions on using direct distance entry.

6. **Right-click anywhere in the drawing area and choose Enter from the cursor menu.**

   AutoCAD LT draws the final segment and returns to the Command prompt, indicating that the LINE or POLYLINE command is finished.

Figure 10-7 demonstrates a polyline drawn using a combination of absolute coordinates, relative coordinates, direct distance entry, and object snap.

You can use the Double Line button on the Draw toolbar to draw pairs of parallel lines, such as the walls of a building or edges of a roadway. The Double Line button runs the DLINE command, which works pretty much like the PLINE command but with a doubled line.

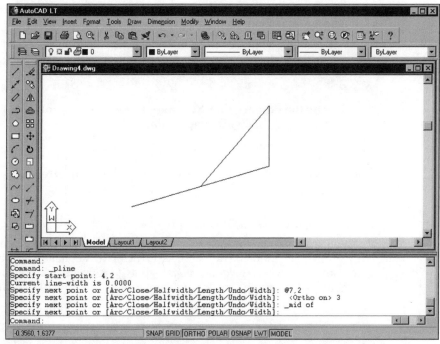

Figure 10-7:
(Poly)line
it up.

Rectangle (oh, what a tangled wreck . . .)

You can use the POLYLINE or LINE command to draw a rectangle segment-by-segment — see the procedure in the "And one further point . . ." section of Chapter 5 for instructions. In most cases, though, you'll find it easier to use the special-purpose RECTANG command. The following procedure demonstrates how:

1. **Set an appropriate layer current and check the status bar buttons, as described in the previous procedure.**

2. **Click the Rectangle button on the Draw toolbar.**

   The command line prompts you to specify a point for one corner of the rectangle:

   ```
   Specify first corner point or
           [Chamfer/Elevation/Fillet/Thickness/Width]:
   ```

Note that you can add fancy effects with the additional command options. The default options work best for most purposes. Look up "RECTANG command" in the AutoCAD LT Help system if you want to know more about the options.

3. **Specify the first corner by typing absolute X,Y coordinates or using an object snap mode.**

   The command line prompts you to specify the other corner of the rectangle — the one that's diagonally opposite from the first corner:

   ```
   Specify other corner point:
   ```

4. **Specify the other corner by typing a relative or absolute X,Y coordinate or using an object snap mode.**

   AutoCAD LT draws the rectangle.

Figure 10-8 demonstrates how to draw a rectangle that's six units long by three units high, with its lower-left corner at the point 2,1.

Polygon (guess she didn't like the cracker)

Rectangles and other closed polylines are types of *polygons,* or closed figures with three or more sides. The AutoCAD LT POLYGON command provides a quick way of drawing *regular polygons* — polygons in which all sides and angles are equal. The following procedure demonstrates the POLYGON command:

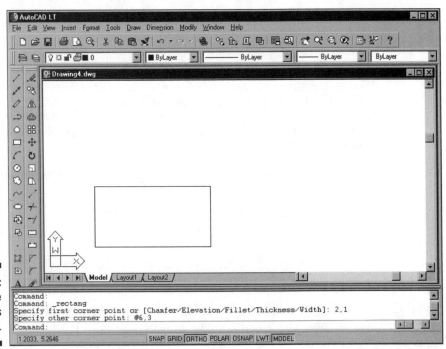

Figure 10-8:
A rectangle that's right on.

1. **Set an appropriate layer current and check the status bar buttons, as described in the first two steps of the procedure in the "The lowly line and the peerless polyline" section earlier in this chapter.**

2. **Click the Polygon button on the Draw toolbar.**

   The command line prompts you to enter the number of sides for the polygon:

   ```
   Enter number of sides <4>:
   ```

3. **Type the number of sides in the polygon that you want to draw and press Enter.**

   The command line prompts you to specify the center point of the polygon:

   ```
   Specify center of polygon or [Edge]:
   ```

   You can use the Edge option to draw a polygon by specifying one side, instead of the center and radius of an imaginary inscribed or circumscribed circle. The imaginary circle method is much more common.

4. **Specify the center point by typing absolute X,Y coordinates or using an object snap mode.**

   The command line prompts you to specify whether the polygon will be inscribed in or circumscribed about an imaginary circle whose radius you will specify in the following step:

   ```
   Enter an option [Inscribed in circle/Circumscribed about
           circle] <I>:
   ```

5. **Type I or C and press Enter.**

   The command line prompts you to specify the radius of the imaginary circle:

   ```
   Specify radius of circle:
   ```

6. **Specify the radius by typing a distance or by using an object snap mode or direct distance entry to indicate the length of the radius.**

   AutoCAD LT draws the polygon.

Figure 10-9 demonstrates how to draw a hexagon centered on the endpoint of an existing line (endpoint object snap) and inscribed in an imaginary circle whose radius is 3 units.

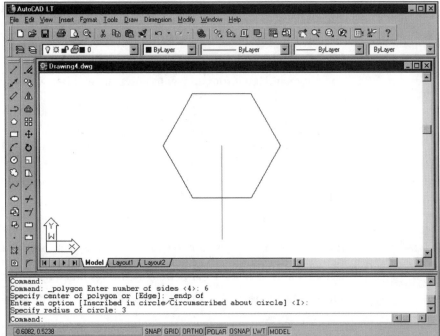

Figure 10-9:
Placing a
hexagon on
a line.

Rectangles and polygons in AutoCAD LT are really just polylines that you specify in a way that's appropriate to the shape you're creating. You'll notice this when you grip edit a rectangle or polygon and move one of the vertexes: Only the selected vertex moves. AutoCAD LT doesn't make the entire rectangle or polygon larger or smaller.

(Throwing) curves

Although straight line segments predominate in many CAD drawings, even the most humdrum, rectilinear design is likely to have a few curves. And if you're drawing car bodies or Gaudí buildings, your drawings will be almost nothing but curves! This section shows you how to use the most common LT curve-drawing commands.

Full circle

If you followed the polygon-drawing procedure in the previous section, then drawing circles is a piece of cake — or maybe a whole pie. The following procedure shows you how to draw a circle by specifying its center point and radius:

1. **Set an appropriate layer current and check the status bar buttons.**

2. **Click the Circle button on the Draw toolbar, as described in the first two steps of the procedure in the "The lowly line and the peerless polyline" section earlier in this chapter.**

   The command line prompts you to specify the center point of the circle:

   ```
   Specify center point for circle or [3P/2P/Ttr (tan tan
   radius)]:
   ```

   As the prompt shows, you can use methods other than center point and radius to draw circles in LT. The additional options are 3-point, 2-point, and tangent-tangent-radius. (No, "tan tan radius" is not a mathematician's dance.) Look up "CIRCLE command" in the online help if you think you might have a use for these less common circle-drawing methods.

3. **Specify the center point by typing absolute X,Y coordinates or using an object snap mode.**

   The command line prompts you to specify the circle's radius:

   ```
   Specify radius of circle or [Diameter]:
   ```

   Type D and press Enter if you prefer to enter the diameter instead of the radius and you have trouble dividing by two — or, more seriously, if the diameter is easier to specify or enter exactly than the radius is.

4. **Specify the radius by typing a distance or by using an object snap mode or direct distance entry to indicate the length of the radius.**

   AutoCAD LT draws the circle.

If you prefer your circles — or your arcs — squashed, use the ELLIPSE command, which is available on the Draw toolbar. You can draw a full ellipse using a variety of methods, including specifying points on its axes. You also can draw elliptical arcs — and then make elliptical comments about why you needed to.

Arc-y-ology

The AutoCAD LT ARC command draws *circular arcs* — arcs whose curvature corresponds to sections of circles. (In case you wondered, other, more mathematically complex kinds of arcs exist, such as the elliptical arcs mentioned in the previous tip. Which kind of arc Noah used remains a mystery.)

The ARC command provides ten different ways to draw a measly little arc! Choose Draw⇨Arc to see the full list. For many purposes, the default 3-point method works fine, and that's the method that we cover here. If 3-point arcs don't serve your needs — for example, if you need to draw arcs with precise center points, experiment with the other options in the Draw⇨Arc submenu or look up "arcs" in the online help.

The following example shows how you draw an arc:

1. **Set an appropriate layer current and check the status bar buttons, as described in the first two steps of the procedure in the "The lowly line and the peerless polyline" section earlier in this chapter.**

2. **Click the Arc button on the Draw toolbar.**

   The command line prompts you to specify the first endpoint of the arc:

   ```
   Specify start point of arc or [CEnter]:
   ```

3. **Specify the start point by typing absolute X,Y coordinates or using an object snap mode.**

   The command line prompts you to specify a second point on the arc:

   ```
   Specify second point of arc or [CEnter/ENd]:
   ```

4. **Specify a second point by picking a point on the screen.**

   The second point lies somewhere along the curve of the arc. LT will determine the exact curvature of the arc after you choose the final endpoint in the following step. If you want the second point to align with an existing object, use an object snap mode.

   The command line prompts you to specify the other endpoint of the arc, and as you move the cursor around, AutoCAD LT displays an image of what the arc will look like:

   ```
   Specify end point of arc:
   ```

5. **Specify the other endpoint of the arc by typing absolute X,Y coordinates or using an object snap mode.**

   AutoCAD LT draws the arc.

Figure 10-10 demonstrates how to draw an arc with its endpoints at the ends of two existing lines.

Spinning splines

Most people use CAD programs for precision drawing tasks: straight lines, carefully defined curves, precisely specified points, and so on. AutoCAD LT is not the program to reach for when you want to free your inner artist — unless perhaps your inner artist is Mondrian. Nonetheless, even in meticulously created CAD drawings, you sometimes need — or just want! — to add freeform curves. The AutoCAD LT SPLINE command is just the thing for the job.

Drawing splines is fairly straightforward, as long as you ignore the advanced options. The following procedure demonstrates how to draw a freeform curve with the SPLINE command:

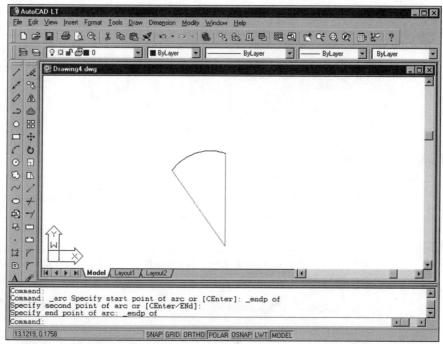

Figure 10-10:
Arcs are
easy as pie.

1. **Set an appropriate layer current and check the status bar buttons, as described in the first two steps of the procedure in the "The lowly line and the peerless polyline" section earlier in this chapter.**

2. **Click the Spline button on the Draw toolbar.**

   The command line prompts you to specify the first endpoint of the spline:

   ```
   Specify first point or [Object]:
   ```

3. **Specify the start point by picking a point — use an object snap mode if you want the start point to coincide with a point on an existing object.**

   The command line prompts you to specify additional points:

   ```
   Specify next point:
   ```

4. **Specify additional points by picking them on the screen.**

   After you pick the second point, the command-line prompt changes to show additional options:

   ```
   Specify next point or [Close/Fit tolerance] <start
             tangent>:
   ```

Because you're drawing a freeform curve, you usually don't need to use object snaps or other precision techniques when picking spline points.

5. Press Enter after you've chosen the final endpoint of your spline.

LT prompts you to specify tangent lines for each end of the spline:

```
Specify start tangent:
Specify end tangent:
```

The Specify start tangent and Specify end tangent prompts enable you to control the curvature of the start and end points of the spline. In most cases, simply pressing Enter at both prompts to accept the default tangents works fine.

6. Press Enter twice to accept the default tangent directions.

AutoCAD LT draws the spline.

Figure 10-11 shows some examples of splines and demonstrates how to draw one of them by picking a series of points.

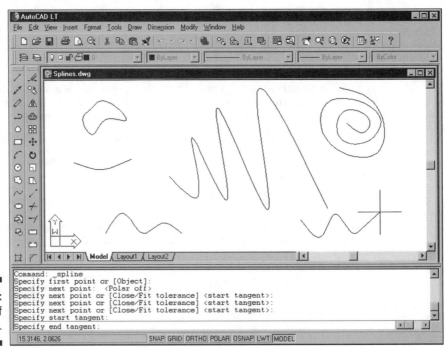

Figure 10-11:
A slew of splines.

After you've drawn a spline, you can grip edit it in order to adjust its shape. See Chapter 6 for information about grip editing. If you need finer control over spline editing, look up "SPLINEDIT command" in the AutoCAD LT online help.

You can use AutoCAD LT splines in two ways. One way is the freeform, sketchy, not-too-precise approach that we describe here. You just eyeball the location and shape of the curve and don't worry too much about getting it "just so." But beneath their easygoing, informal exterior, AutoCAD LT splines are really highly precise, mathematically defined entities called NURBS curves (Non-Uniform Rational B-Spline curves). Mathematicians and some mechanical and industrial designers care a lot about the precise characteristics of the curves they work with. For those people, the AutoCAD LT SPLINE and SPLINEDIT commands include a number of advanced options. Look up "spline curves (NURBS curves)" in the AutoCAD LT online help for more information.

More drawing commands

This chapter covers the AutoCAD LT commands for drawing straight lines and arcs, but you'll need to draw other kinds of objects as well, such as text, dimensions, and hatching. We cover the most useful additional tools in Chapters 12 through 15 of this book. Table 10-3 describes the additional drawing objects and where to find information about them.

Table 10-3	Additional Drawing Objects
Drawing Objects	*See for More Information*
Leaders	Chapter 5 ("Pointy-Headed Leaders")
Revision clouds	Chapter 5 ("Cloud Cover")
Text	Chapter 12
Dimensions	Chapter 13
Hatching	Chapter 14
Blocks and xrefs	Chapter 15
Donut	"DONUT command" in online help
Point	"POINT command" in online help
Construction lines	"xlines" in online help

Construction lines, also known as *xlines,* are used less in AutoCAD LT 2000 than previously because the need for them is often handled by the polar tracking and direct distance entry precision tools that are built into the program. See the " My Point Is . . ." section, earlier in this chapter, for more information.

Chapter 11

Edit for Credit

· ·

In This Chapter

▶ Using command-first editing

▶ Selecting objects with maximum flexibility

▶ Ensuring precision when you edit

▶ Moving, copying, and stretching objects

▶ Manipulating whole objects with ROTATE, SCALE, ARRAY, and OFFSET

▶ Changing pieces of objects with TRIM, EXTEND, BREAK, FILLET, and CHAMFER

▶ Editing object properties

· ·

*E*diting objects is the flip side of creating them, and in AutoCAD LT, you spend a lot of time editing — far more than drawing objects from scratch, in fact. That's partly because the design and drafting process is by its nature iterative, and also because CAD programs make it so easy to edit objects cleanly.

Chapter 6 introduces AutoCAD LT editing concepts and the basic editing techniques you use for making simple changes to existing drawings. That chapter describes two important AutoCAD LT editing concepts — editing styles and object selection techniques — and shows you how to edit objects by manipulating their grips. This chapter goes beyond the introductory information in Chapter 6 and shows you the additional editing techniques and commands that you need for making substantial modifications to new or existing drawings. In this chapter, we occasionally point to conceptual information from Chapter 6 so we don't have to repeat that information and you don't have to see it again if you've already read Chapter 6.

Editing Styles, Revisited

As we describe in detail in the "Which Came First: The Command or the Selection?" section of Chapter 6, AutoCAD LT offers two main styles of editing: *command-first editing* and *selection-first editing*. In command-first editing, you start the command first and then select the objects that you want to edit.

In selection-first editing, you do the reverse: Select objects and then start the command. Chapter 6 covers the *direct manipulation* form of selection-first editing, which AutoCAD LT calls *grip editing*.

The editing techniques described in Chapter 6 are useful even after you graduate to full-blown editing. But as you do more editing, you'll discover that AutoCAD LT 2000 is fundamentally a command-first program. AutoCAD started out offering *only* command-first editing and only later added selection-first methods; AutoCAD LT 2000 inherits this ancestral trait. Some of the more useful editing commands remain command-first only. In addition, command-first editing gives you a much wider range of object selection options, which can be useful when you work on more complicated, busy drawings.

So, sooner or later, you'll need to come to grips — pun intended — with command-first editing. It may be a bit more difficult to understand than what you're used to from other programs, but you'll eventually find that command-first editing gives you greater flexibility and consistency inside LT. To encourage you to get used to the command-first methods, this chapter uses them exclusively.

Perfecting Selecting

When you edit in command-first mode, you have all the selection options we describe in the "Grab It" section of Chapter 6 — single object, bounding box (Window), and crossing box (Crossing) — plus a slew of others. If you type **?** and press Enter at any Select objects prompt, AutoCAD LT lists all the selection options:

```
Window/Last/Crossing/BOX/ALL/Fence/WPolygon/CPolygon/Group/Ad
        d/Remove/Multiple/Previous/Undo/AUto/SIngle
```

Table 11-1 summarizes the most useful command-first selection options.

Table 11-1	Some Useful Command-First Selection Options
Option	*Description*
Window	All objects within a rectangle that you specify by picking two points
Last	The last object you drew that's still visible in the drawing area
Crossing	All objects within or crossing a rectangle that you specify by picking two points

Option	Description
ALL	All objects on layers that aren't frozen
Fence	All objects touching an imaginary polyline whose vertices you specify by picking points
WPolygon	All objects within a polygonal area whose corners you specify by picking points
CPolygon	All objects within or crossing a polygonal area whose corners you specify by picking points
Previous	The previous selection set that you specified

To use any of the command-first selection options at the Select objects prompt, you type the uppercase letters corresponding to the option and press Enter. When you're finished selecting objects, you must press Enter once more to tell AutoCAD LT that you've finished selecting objects and want to start the editing operation.

As with selection-first editing, you can specify a bounding box (Window) or crossing box (Crossing) using *implied windowing:* Simply pick two points, either left-to-right for Window or right-to-left for Crossing. You don't have to type **W** or **C** first. Review the "How much is that object in the window?" section in Chapter 6 for detailed instructions.

The following example demonstrates how to use the ERASE command in command-first mode with several different selection options. The selection techniques used in this example apply to most AutoCAD LT editing commands:

1. **Press Esc twice to make sure that no objects are selected.**

2. **Click the Erase button on the Edit toolbar.**

   The command line displays the Select objects prompt.

3. **Select two or three individual objects by clicking each one.**

   LT adds each object to the selection set — all the objects you select remain ghosted. The command line displays the Select objects prompt.

4. **Specify a bounding selection box (Window) that completely encloses several objects.**

   Move the cursor to a point below and to the left of the objects, click, release the mouse button, move the cursor above and to the right of the objects, and click again.

   All objects that are completely within the box are selected.

5. **Specify a crossing selection box (Crossing) that encloses a few objects and cuts through several others.**

   Move the cursor to a point below and to the right of some of the objects, click, release the mouse button, move the cursor above and to the left of some of the objects, and click and release again.

   All objects that are completely within or cross through the box are selected.

6. **Type WP and press Enter to activate the WPolygon selection option.**

   The command line prompts you to pick points that define the selection polygon.

7. **Pick a series of points and press Enter.**

   Figure 11-1 shows an example. All objects that are completely within the polygon are selected.

8. **Press Enter to end object selection.**

   AutoCAD LT erases all the selected objects.

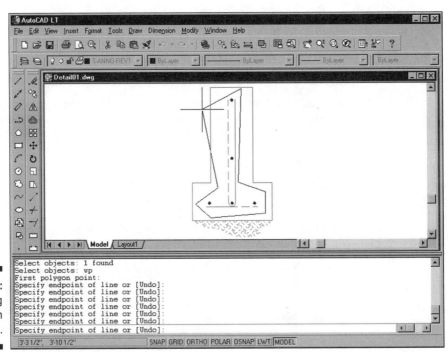

Figure 11-1:
Lassoing objects with a WPolygon.

Notice how you were able to build up a selection set using a combination of object selection methods, and then press Enter to execute the command on them. Most AutoCAD LT editing commands work this way in command-first mode.

Paying Attention to Precision

As we describe in the "Precision Editing" section of Chapter 6 and the "My Point Is. . ." section of Chapter 10, maintaining precision when you draw and edit is absolutely crucial to good CAD work. If you've used a drawing program and are accustomed to moving, stretching, and otherwise editing objects by eye, you'll need to suppress that habit when you edit in AutoCAD LT. Nothing ruins a drawing faster than "approximate" editing, in which you shove objects around until they look okay, without worrying about precise distances and points.

The AutoCAD LT precision techniques for editing are the same ones that you use for drawing objects. (See the "My Point Is. . ." section of Chapter 10 and Table 10-2 in particular if you need a review of precision techniques.) The procedures that we describe throughout the rest of this chapter suggest which precision techniques you're likely to find most useful with each editing command.

Ready, Get Set, Edit!

The remainder of this chapter covers the most important AutoCAD LT editing commands, using command-first editing mode.

Whether you start an AutoCAD LT editing command by clicking a toolbar button, choosing a pull-down menu command, or typing a command name, in almost all cases, the command will prompt you for points, distances, and options at the command line. Read the command-line prompts during every step of the command, especially when you're figuring out how to use a new editing command.

The big three: Move, Copy, and Stretch

Moving, copying, and stretching are three of the more common AutoCAD LT editing operations. Chapter 6 shows you how to perform these operations using grip editing. There's nothing wrong with the grip editing approach — in fact, it's often the most efficient approach for editing one or two objects, so get a grip! But the full-blown AutoCAD LT MOVE, COPY, and STRETCH commands are useful to know when you need to edit larger groups of objects.

Base points and displacements

The MOVE, COPY, and STRETCH commands require that you specify how far and in what direction you want the objects moved, copied, or stretched. After you've selected the objects to be edited and started the command, AutoCAD LT prompts you for two pieces of information:

```
Specify base point or displacement:
Specify second point of displacement or <use first point as
        displacement>:
```

In a not-so-clear way, these prompts say that two possible ways exist for you to specify how far and in what direction you want the objects copied, moved, or stretched. The most common way — the base point way — is to pick or type the coordinates of two points that define a *displacement vector*. AutoCAD calls these points the *base point* and the *second point*. Imagine an arrow pointing from the base point to the second point — that arrow defines how far and in what direction the objects get copied, moved, or stretched.

The other way — the displacement way — to specify how far and in what direction is to type an X,Y pair of numbers that represents a distance rather than a point. This distance is the absolute displacement that you want to copy, move, or stretch the objects.

So how does AutoCAD LT know whether your response to the first prompt is a base point or a displacement? It depends on how you respond to the second prompt. (Is that confusing, or what?!) If you pick or type the coordinates of a point at the second prompt, LT says to itself, "Aha — displacement vector!" and moves the objects according to the imaginary arrow pointing from the base point to the second point. If you instead press Enter at the second prompt (without having typed anything), LT says, "Aha — displacement distance," and uses the X,Y pair of numbers that you typed at the first prompt as an absolute displacement distance.

What makes this displacement business even more confusing is that AutoCAD LT lets you pick a point at the first prompt and press Enter at the second prompt. LT still says, "Aha — displacement distance," but now it treats the coordinates of the point you picked as an absolute distance. For example, during the MOVE command, if you pick the point whose coordinates are 14.5,24.2, and press Enter at the second prompt, AutoCAD LT moves the objects 14.5 units in the X direction and 24.2 units in the Y direction. If the point you picked has relatively large coordinates, the objects can get moved way outside the normal drawing area as defined by the limits. The objects fly off into space, which you probably won't notice at first because you're zoomed into part of your normal drawing area — it just looks to you like the objects have vanished! In short, be careful when you press Enter during the COPY, MOVE, and STRETCH commands. Press Enter in response to the second prompt only if you want LT to use your response to the first prompt as an absolute displacement. If you make a mistake, use the UNDO command — described in Chapter 6 — to back up and try again. Also, you can use ZOOM Extents to look for objects that have flown off into space.

Move

The following procedure demonstrates selection-first editing with the MOVE command using the base point method of indicating how far and in what direction. This procedure also gives detailed recommendations on how to use precision techniques when you edit:

1. **Press Esc twice to make sure that no objects are selected.**

2. **Check the SNAP, ORTHO, POLAR, and OSNAP buttons on the status bar and set them according to your needs, as described in the "My Point Is. . ." section of Chapter 10.**

3. **Click the Move button on the Edit toolbar.**

   The command line displays the `Select objects` prompt.

4. **Select one or more objects.**

   You can use any of the object selection techniques described in the "Perfecting Selecting" section, earlier in this chapter.

5. **Press Enter when you're finished selecting objects.**

   AutoCAD LT displays the following prompt:

   ```
   Specify base point or displacement:
   ```

6. **Specify a base point by object snapping to a point on an existing object or by typing absolute X,Y coordinates.**

   This point serves as the tail end of your imaginary arrow indicating how far and in what direction you want the objects moved. After you pick a base point, it's fairly easy to see what's going on because AutoCAD LT displays a temporary image of the object that moves around as you move the cursor. Figure 11-2 shows what the screen looks like at this stage of the proceedings.

   You may want to specify a base point somewhere on or near the object(s) that you're moving. You can use an object snap mode to choose a point exactly on one of the objects.

   LT displays the following prompt:

   ```
   Specify second point of displacement or <use first point
                as displacement>:
   ```

Displacement vector

Original location   Drag image to new location

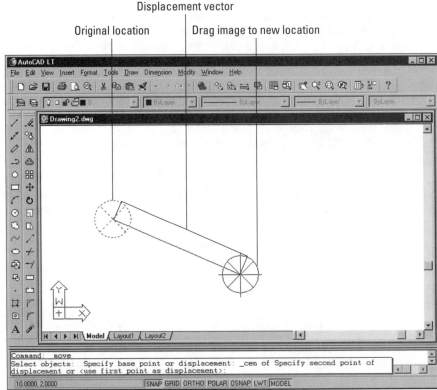

Figure 11-2:
Figure 11-2:
Dragging
objects in
the middle
of the MOVE
command.

7. **Specify the second point by using direct distance entry, object snapping to a point on an existing object, or typing relative X,Y
coordinates.**

   The second point serves as the arrow end of your imaginary displacement arrow. After you specify the second point, AutoCAD LT moves the
objects.

   Don't press Enter alone at this prompt! If you do, AutoCAD LT will treat
the X,Y coordinates of the first point you picked as an absolute displacement, and the objects will fly off in an unpredictable fashion. See the
warning in the "Base points and displacements" section earlier in this
chapter for more information.

   You may want to use an object snap mode to pick a second point exactly
on another object in the drawing. Alternatively, you can type a relative
or polar coordinate, as described in Chapter 10. For example, if you
type **@6,2**, AutoCAD moves the objects 6 units to the right and 2 units
up. If you type **@3<45**, AutoCAD moves the objects 3 units at an angle of
45 degrees. Finally, you can use direct distance entry to move objects in
an orthogonal direction. See the "Precision Editing" section of Chapter 6
for instructions.

Copy

The COPY command works almost identically to the MOVE command, except of course that AutoCAD LT leaves the selected objects in place and "moves" new copies of them to the new location. In addition, the COPY command includes a Multiple option for making multiple copies of the same set of objects.

Copy between drawings

One useful variation on the COPY command is copying objects from one drawing to another using the COPYCLIP command. The following procedure shows how:

1. **Open two drawings that contain geometry you want to copy from one to the other. Arrange the two drawings so that you can see both of them, as shown in Figure 11-3.**

   If you don't have enough screen real estate to arrange the two drawings side by side, you can leave them overlapped and change between the two drawing windows by using the Window menu, the Ctrl+Tab keyboard shortcut, or the Ctrl+F6 keyboard shortcut.

2. **In the first drawing, right-click in the drawing area and choose Copy from the cursor menu.**

   Choose Cut if you want to move rather than copy the objects to the other drawing. Choose Copy with Base Point if you want to choose a specific base point rather than let AutoCAD LT choose a base point.

   The base point that AutoCAD LT chooses is the lower-left corner of an imaginary rectangle that just barely encloses all the objects you've selected.

3. **If you chose Copy with Base Point in Step 2, pick a base point to use for the copy operation.**

   The base point is like a base point for a block definition, as described in Chapter 15. Choose a useful point such as the endpoint of a line, the lower-left corner of a rectangle, or the center of a circle.

4. **Select the objects that you want to copy and then press Enter to end object selection.**

5. **Click in the second drawing's window to make it current.**

6. **Right-click in the second drawing's window and choose Paste from the cursor menu.**

   Choose Paste to Original Coordinates if you want to copy the objects so they land at the same point (with respect to 0,0) in the second drawing as they were located in the first drawing.

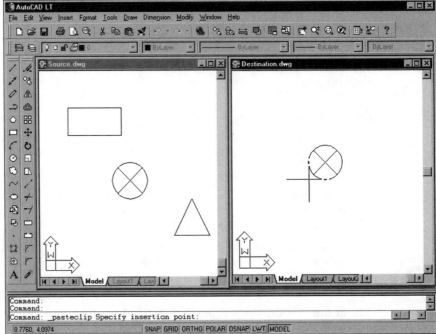

7. **Specify an insertion point for the copied objects by object snapping to a point on an existing object or typing absolute X,Y coordinates.**

   AutoCAD LT copies the objects.

Stretch

The STRETCH command is superficially similar to COPY and MOVE; it has the same inscrutable base point and displacement prompts, and it shifts objects — or parts of objects — to other locations in the drawing. But it also has important differences that often confound new AutoCAD LT users to the point where they give up trying to learn to use STRETCH. That's a mistake, because STRETCH is one of the more valuable commands in the LT editing toolbox. Here are the things you need to know in order to make STRETCH your friend:

✔ To use STRETCH effectively, you must select objects using a crossing window (or crossing polygon), as described in the section "Perfecting Selecting" earlier in this chapter.

✔ STRETCH operates on the defining points of objects — endpoints of a line, vertices of a polyline, center of a circle, and so on — according to the following rule: If a defining point is within the crossing window that you specify, AutoCAD LT moves the defining point and updates the object accordingly. For example, if your crossing window surrounds one endpoint of a line but not the other endpoint, STRETCH moves the first endpoint and redraws the line in the new position dictated by the first endpoint's new location. It's as though you have a rubber-band tacked to the wall with two pins, and you move one of the pins.

✔ STRETCH can make lines longer or shorter, depending on your crossing window and displacement vector. In other words, the STRETCH command really combines stretching and compressing.

✔ You usually want to turn ORTHO on before stretching. Otherwise, you'll end up stretching objects in strange directions.

In AutoCAD LT 2000, STRETCH is one of those commands that works only in command-first editing mode. If you select objects and then start the STRETCH command, it not only ignores your selection but also issues an error message! You have to restart the command and then select objects using a crossing window.

The following set of steps shows you how to STRETCH lines:

1. **Draw some lines in an arrangement similar to the dashed lines shown in Figure 11-4.**

   You don't need to draw the small dotted rectangle in Figure 11-4 — it represents the crossing window that you'll specify in Step 4.

   Start your stretching with simple objects. You can work up to more complicated objects — polylines, circles, arcs, and so on — after you've limbered up with lines.

2. **Press Esc twice to make sure that no objects are selected.**

3. **Click the Stretch button on the Edit toolbar.**

   The command line displays the `Select objects` prompt, with a warning to use the Crossing or CPolygon object selection mode:

   ```
   Select objects to stretch by crossing-window or crossing-
           polygon...
           Select objects:
   ```

4. **Specify a crossing window that encloses some, but not all, endpoints of the lines.**

   Figure 11-4 shows a sample crossing window that completely encloses the single, short horizontal line and the two very short vertical lines. This crossing window cuts through the four longer horizontal lines, enclosing only one endpoint of each.

   You specify a crossing window by picking a point and then dragging your mouse to the *left*.

Drag image to new location

Displacement vector

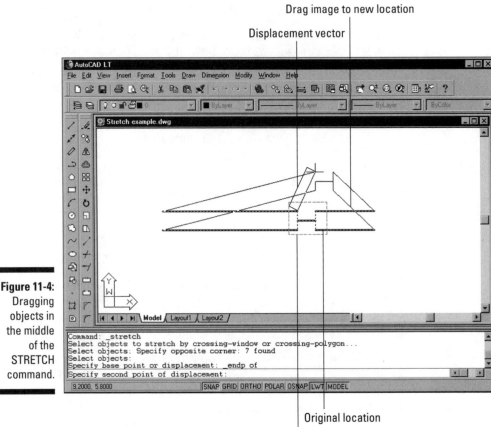

Figure 11-4:
Dragging
objects in
the middle
of the
STRETCH
command.

Original location

Crossing window

5. Press Enter to end object selection.

LT displays the following prompt:

```
Specify base point or displacement:
```

6. Specify a base point by object snapping to a point on an existing object, or typing absolute X,Y coordinates.

This step is just like Step 6 in the Move procedure earlier in this chapter. After you pick a base point, AutoCAD LT displays a temporary image of the objects that updates as you move the cursor.

LT displays the following prompt:

```
Specify second point of displacement or <use first point
                        as displacement>:
```

7. **Toggle ortho mode on and then off by clicking the ORTHO button on the status bar; try moving the cursor around first with ortho mode on and then with it off in order to see the difference.**

   Figure 11-4 shows what the screen looks like as you move the cursor around with ortho off.

8. **Toggle ortho mode on and then specify the second point by using direct distance entry, object snapping to a point on an existing object, or typing relative X,Y coordinates.**

   This step is just like Step 7 in the Move procedure earlier in this chapter. After you pick the second point, AutoCAD LT stretches the objects. Notice that the STRETCH command moved the three short lines — because the crossing window contained both endpoints of all three lines. STRETCH lengthened or shortened the four longer horizontal lines — because the crossing window enclosed only one endpoint of each.

The STRETCH command takes some practice, but it's worth the effort. Draw some additional kinds of objects and practice stretching with different crossing window locations as well as different base points and second points. Also try stretching using an absolute displacement distance, as described in the "Base points and displacements" section, earlier in this chapter: Type an **X,Y** displacement at the first prompt and then press Enter at the second prompt.

More manipulations

The commands that we cover in this section — ROTATE, SCALE, ARRAY, and OFFSET — manipulate or create new versions of whole objects. The procedures for each command assume that you're familiar with the object selection and editing precision techniques presented in the MOVE, COPY, and STRETCH procedures (see the previous sections in this chapter).

Rotate

Even if you don't get around to rotating your tires regularly, you'll probably find lots of occasions to use the ROTATE command on AutoCAD LT objects. Fortunately, rotating in LT doesn't require a trip to the tire shop, as the following example demonstrates:

1. **Press Esc twice to make sure that no objects are selected and set the status bar buttons according to your needs, as described in the "My Point Is. . ." section of Chapter 10.**

2. **Click the Rotate button on the Edit toolbar.**

3. **Select one or more objects and then press Enter to end object selection.**

LT prompts you for the base point for rotating the selected objects:

```
Specify base point:
```

4. **Specify a base point by object snapping to a point on an existing object or by typing absolute X,Y coordinates.**

   The base point becomes the point about which LT rotates the objects. You also have to specify a rotation angle:

```
Specify rotation angle or [Reference]:
```

5. **Specify a rotation angle by typing an angle measurement.**

   Alternatively, you can indicate an angle on the screen by moving the cursor until the Coordinates section of the status bar indicates the desired angle and then clicking. Ortho mode or polar tracking make it easier to pick orthogonal angles.

   As you move the cursor to points that are at different angles from the base point that you specified in Step 4, AutoCAD LT displays a temporary image that shows you how the objects would look at the various angles. After you specify the rotation angle by picking or typing, LT rotates the objects into their new position.

Scale

If you read all of our harping about drawing scales and drawing scale factors in the previous chapters of this book, you may think that the SCALE command performs some magical scale transformation on your entire drawing. No such luck — it merely scales one or more objects up or down by a factor that you specify. Here's how it works:

1. **Press Esc twice to make sure that no objects are selected and set the status bar buttons according to your needs, as described in the "My Point Is. . ." section of Chapter 10.**

2. **Click the Scale button on the Edit toolbar.**

3. **Select one or more objects and then press Enter to end object selection.**

   LT prompts you for the base point about which it will scale all of the selected objects:

```
Specify base point:
```

AutoCAD LT does not scale each object individually around its own base point because most LT drawing objects don't have individual base points. Instead, LT uses the base point that you specify to determine how to scale *all* objects in the selection set. In other words, if you select a circle to scale, pick a point outside the circle as the base point and then specify a scale factor of 2, LT doesn't only make the circle twice as big. It also moves the circle twice as far away from the base point that you specified.

4. **Specify a base point by object snapping to a point on an existing object, or typing absolute X,Y coordinates.**

   The base point becomes the point about which the objects are scaled. LT prompts you for the scale factor:

   ```
   Specify scale factor or [Reference]:
   ```

5. **Type a scale factor and press Enter.**

   Numbers greater than 1 increase the objects' size. Numbers smaller than 1 decrease the objects' size. LT then scales the objects by the factor that you type, using the base point that you specified.

If you need to convert a drawing from inches to millimeters, use the SCALE command to scale all objects in the drawing by a factor of 25.4.

Changing the drawing scale factor of a drawing after you've drawn it is a fairly tedious and complicated process in AutoCAD LT. In brief, you need to change the scale-dependent system variables described in Chapter 9, and then scale some, but not all, drawing objects. You don't scale the real-world geometry that you've drawn, because its measurements in the real world remain the same. You do scale objects such as text and hatching that have a fixed height or spacing regardless of drawing scale factor. Because of these complications, you should try to make sure that you choose a proper scale and set up the drawing properly for that scale before you begin drawing. See Chapter 9 for details.

Array

The ARRAY command is like a supercharged COPY: You use it to create a rectangular "grid" of objects at regular X and Y spacings or a polar "wheel" of objects at a regular angular spacing. For example, you can use a rectangular array to populate an auditorium with chairs or a polar array to draw bicycle spokes.

The following procedure demonstrates how to create a rectangular array, which you'll probably do more often than creating a polar array:

1. **Press Esc twice to make sure that no objects are selected.**

   Alternatively, you can select objects before starting the ARRAY command and thereby skip Step 3.

2. **Click the Array button on the Edit toolbar.**

   The Array dialog box appears, as shown in Figure 11-5.

3. **Choose the Select Objects button and then select one or more objects. Press Enter to end object selection and return to the Array dialog box.**

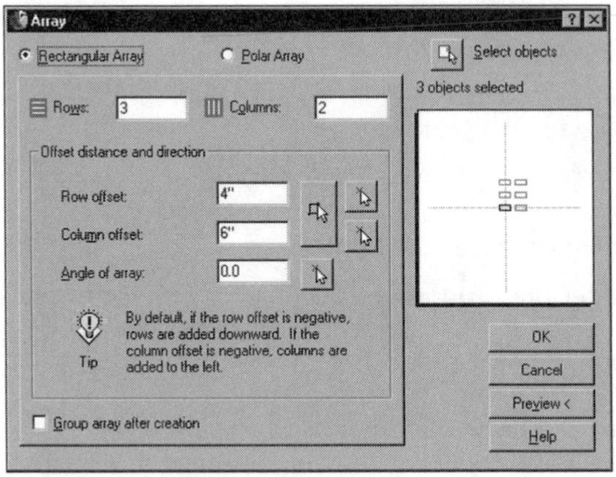

Figure 11-5:
Hooray for
Array.

4. **Make sure that the Rectangular Array radio button is selected.**

   Or, if rectangular arrays leave you cold, choose the Polar Array radio button instead and experiment with the other array option.

5. **Fill in the five edit boxes: Rows, Columns, Row Offset, Column Offset, and Angle of Array.**

   Note that the Rows and Columns numbers include the row and column of the original objects themselves. In other words, entries of 1 don't create any new objects in that direction. The Row Offset and Column Offset measurements are the distances between adjacent rows and columns.

6. **Click Preview.**

   AutoCAD LT shows what the array will look like using your current settings and displays a dialog box with Accept, Modify, and Cancel buttons.

7. **Click the Accept button if you're satisfied with the array, or the Modify button if you want to change the array parameters.**

Offset

Although offset may remind you of where film starlets and producers engage in lewd activities, the AutoCAD LT OFFSET command is far more innocent — and helpful. You use OFFSET to create parallel copies of lines, polylines, circles, arcs, or splines:

1. **Click the Offset button on the Edit toolbar.**

   LT prompts you for the *offset distance* — the distance from the original object to the copy you're creating:

   ```
   Specify offset distance or [Through] <Through>:
   ```

2. **Type an offset distance and press Enter.**

   Alternatively, you can indicate an offset distance picking two points on the screen. If you choose this method, you normally should use object snaps in order to specify a precise distance from one existing object to another.

   LT prompts you to select the object from which you want to create an offset copy:

   ```
   Select object to offset or <exit>:
   ```

3. **Select a single object, such as a line, polyline, or arc.**

   Note that you can select only one object at a time with the OFFSET command. LT asks where you want the offset object:

   ```
   Specify point on side to offset:
   ```

4. **Point to one side or the other of the object and then click.**

   It doesn't matter how far away from the object the cursor is when you click. You're simply indicating a direction.

   AutoCAD LT repeats the `Select object` prompt, in case you want to offset other objects by the same distance:

   ```
   Select object to offset or <exit>:
   ```

5. **Go back to Step 3 if you want to offset another object, or press Enter if you're finished offsetting objects for now.**

Figure 11-6 shows the OFFSET command in progress.

Slicing and dicing

But wait, there's more! If you liked those fancy knives from late-night TV, you'll *love* the following commands. The commands that we cover in this section — TRIM, EXTEND, BREAK, FILLET, and CHAMFER — are useful for shortening and lengthening objects and for breaking them in two.

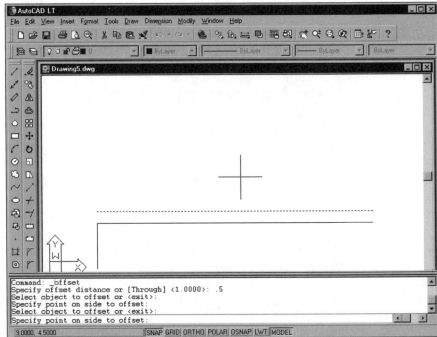

Figure 11-6:
Offsetting a
line.

Trim and Extend

TRIM and EXTEND are the twin commands for making lines, polylines, and arcs shorter and longer. They're the yin and yang, the Laurel and Hardy, the Jack Sprat and his wife of the AutoCAD LT editing world. The two commands and their prompts are almost identical, so the following procedure covers both. We show the prompts for the TRIM command; the EXTEND prompts are similar:

1. Click the Trim or Extend button on the Edit toolbar.

   LT prompts you to select cutting edges that will do the trimming. If you chose the EXTEND command, you are prompted to select boundary edges for extending to:

   ```
   Select cutting edges ...
   Select objects:
   ```

2. Select one or more objects that will act as the "knife" for trimming objects or the "wall" to which objects will be extended. Press Enter to end object selection.

   Figure 11-7 shows a cutting edge (for TRIM) and a boundary edge (for EXTEND).

Cutting edge (for TRIM)   Boundary edge (for EXTEND)

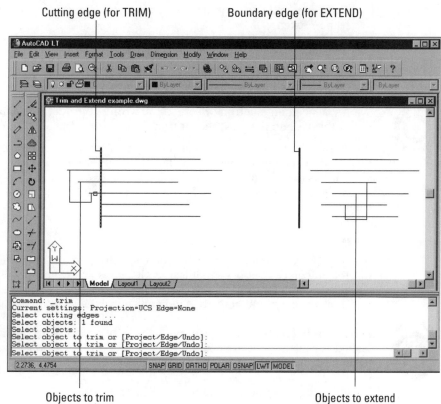

Figure 11-7:
Anatomy of
the TRIM
and
EXTEND
operations.

Objects to trim   Objects to extend

LT prompts you to select objects that you want to trim or extend:

```
Select object to trim or [Project/Edge/Undo]:
```

3. **Select a single object to trim or extend. Choose the portion of the object that you want AutoCAD LT to trim away.**

   AutoCAD LT trims or extends the object to one of the objects that you selected in Step 2. If AutoCAD LT can't trim or extend the object — for example, if the trimming object and the object to be trimmed are parallel, the command line displays an error message such as `Object does not intersect an edge`.

   TRIM and EXTEND normally allow you to select only one object at a time for trimming or extending. The one exception is that you can type **F** and press Enter to use the Fence object selection mode (see Table 11-1). Fence is useful for trimming or extending a large group of objects in one fell swoop.

The command line continues to prompt you to select other objects to trim or extend:

```
Select object to trim or [Project/Edge/Undo]:
```

4. **Choose additional objects or press Enter when you're finished trimming or extending.**

If you accidentally trim or extend the wrong object, type **U** and press Enter to undo the most recent trim.

The example in Figure 11-7 shows trimming to a single cutting edge, in which the end of the trimmed lines get lopped off. Another common use of the TRIM command is for trimming out a piece of a line between two cutting edges. In the two-cutting-edges scenario, TRIM cuts a piece out of the middle of the trimmed line.

Break

No, the BREAK command isn't what you use before heading out for coffee. It's for breaking pieces out of — that is, creating gaps in — lines, polylines, circles, arcs, or splines. BREAK also comes in handy if you need to separate one object into two without actually removing any visible material.

If you want to create regularly spaced gaps in an object — so that it displays dashed, for instance, don't use BREAK. Use an AutoCAD LT dash-dot linetype instead. See Chapter 10 for more information.

The following example shows how you BREAK an object:

1. **Click the Break 2 Points button on the Edit toolbar.**

   LT prompts you to select a single object that you want to break:

   ```
   Select object:
   ```

2. **Select a single object, such as a line, polyline, or arc.**

The point you pick when selecting the object serves double-duty: It selects the object, of course, but it also becomes the default first *break point* (that is, it defines one side of the gap that you'll create). Thus, you should either use one of the AutoCAD LT precision techniques (such as an object snap) to pick the object at a precise point, or use the First Point option (described in the next step) to re-pick the first break point.

LT prompts you to specify the second break point, or to type **F** if you want to re-specify the first break point:

```
Specify second break point or [First point]:
```

3. **If the point that you picked in the preceding step doesn't also correspond to a break point (see the previous tip), type F and press Enter to re-specify the first break point, and then pick the point using an object snap or other precision technique.**

If you do type **F** and press Enter and then re-specify the first break point, LT prompts you now to select the second break point:

```
Specify second break point:
```

4. **Specify the second break point by using direct distance entry, object snapping to a point on an existing object, or typing relative X,Y coordinates.**

   AutoCAD LT cuts a section out of the object, using the first and second break points to define the length of the gap.

If you want to cut an object into two pieces without removing anything, click the Break 1 Point button on the Edit toolbar. The point that you pick serves to select the object and define the point at which AutoCAD LT breaks it into two. You can then move, copy, or otherwise manipulate each section of the original object as a separate object.

Fillet and Chamfer

Whereas TRIM, EXTEND, and BREAK alter one object at a time, the FILLET and CHAMFER commands require a pair of objects. As Figure 11-8 shows, FILLET creates a curved corner between two lines, while CHAMFER creates an angled, straight corner. In case you wondered, it's pronounced *fill-let*, not *fill-lay*. Saying that you know how to *fill-lay* may get you a job in a butcher shop, but it will get you only strange looks in a design office.

The following procedure demonstrates how to use the FILLET command:

1. **Click the Fillet button on the Edit toolbar.**

   LT displays the current FILLET settings and prompts you to select the first object for filleting or to specify one of three options:

```
Current settings: Mode = TRIM, Radius = 0.5000
Select first object or [Polyline/Radius/Trim]:
```

2. **Type R and press Enter to set the fillet radius.**

   LT prompts you to specify the fillet radius that it uses for future fillet operations:

```
Specify fillet radius <0.5000>:
```

3. **Type a fillet radius and press Enter.**

   The number you type will be the radius of the arc that joins the two lines.

   The command line displays the Command prompt:

```
Command:
```

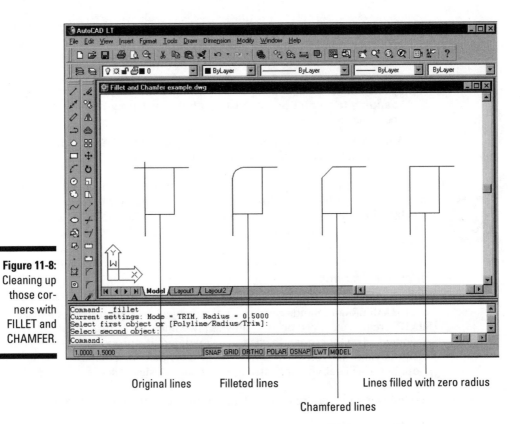

Original lines   Filleted lines   Lines filled with zero radius

Chamfered lines

The FILLET command is stupid enough to think that you may want to
change the fillet radius without actually filleting any objects, so you
have to restart the command in order to do anything useful.

4. Click the Fillet button on the Edit toolbar again.

LT repeats the prompt that you saw in Step 1:

```
Select first object or [Polyline/Radius/Trim]:
```

5. Select the first line of the pair that you want to fillet.

LT prompts you to select the second object for filleting:

```
Select second object:
```

6. Select the second line of the pair that you want to fillet.

AutoCAD LT fillets the two objects, drawing an arc of the radius that you
specified in Step 3.

You can fillet two lines using a radius of 0 in order to make them meet at a point.

The CHAMFER command works similarly except that, instead of specifying a fillet distance, you specify either two chamfer distances or a chamfer length and angle:

```
(TRIM mode) Current chamfer Dist1 = 0.5000, Dist2 = 0.5000
Select first line or [Polyline/Distance/Angle/Trim/Method]:
```

As you probably noticed when you read the command prompts throughout this chapter, the procedures that we present don't cover every option of these editing commands. We cover the most useful procedures and options so that you don't have to worry about a half-dozen permutations of every command. When you're ready to explore a particular editing command further, look up the command name in the index of the AutoCAD LT online help system.

Polishing those properties

When you think of editing objects, you probably think first about editing their geometry: moving, stretching, making new copies, and so on. That's the kind of editing we cover in this chapter.

Another kind of editing is changing objects' properties. As we describe in the "Objects Own Properties" section of Chapter 10, every object in an AutoCAD LT drawing has a set of nongeometrical properties, including layer, color, linetype, and lineweight. Sometimes, you need to edit those properties — when you accidentally draw something on the wrong layer, for example.

The most flexible way to edit properties is with the Properties window. Select any object or (objects), right-click in the drawing area, and

choose Properties from the cursor menu. The Properties window displays a tabular grid that lists the names and values of all properties. Click in the value cell to change a particular property.

Another way to change properties is to select objects and then choose from the drop-down lists (layer, color, and so on) on the Object Properties toolbar. See Chapter 10 for more information.

Finally, you can use the Match Properties button on the Standard toolbar — the button with the paintbrush on it — to "paint" properties from one object to another. Match Properties works similarly to the Format Painter button in Microsoft applications.

Chapter 12

The Character of Text

· ·

In This Chapter

▶ Using text styles to control text appearance

▶ Creating line text

▶ Creating paragraph text

▶ Editing text contents and properties

▶ Checking spelling

· ·

*A*lthough it's often true that "A picture is worth a thousand words," it's also true that adding a few words to your drawing can save you from having to draw a thousand lines and arcs. It's a lot easier to write "Simpson A35 framing clip" next to a simple, schematic representation of one than to draw one in photorealistic detail and hope that the contractor can figure out what it is!

Most CAD drawings include some text in the form of explanatory notes, objects labels, and titles. The "Please Note . . ." section in Chapter 5 shows you how to add paragraph notes to drawings and describes how to select an appropriate text height. This chapter covers other ways to add text to drawings and shows you how to take advantage of AutoCAD LT text styles and the spelling checker.

Getting Ready to Write

In AutoCAD LT 2000, adding text to a drawing is only slightly more complicated than adding it to a word processing document. Here are the steps:

1. **Create a new AutoCAD LT text style, or select an existing style, that includes the font and other text characteristics you want to use.**

2. **Make an appropriate text layer current.**

3. **Run the MTEXT or TEXT command in order to draw paragraph or line text, respectively.**

4. **Specify the text alignment points, justification, and height.**

5. **Type the text.**

You're probably familiar with most of these steps already — especially if you've ever used a word processor or read Chapter 5. In the remainder of this section, we review the particularities of AutoCAD LT text styles, the two kinds of LT text, and ways of controlling height and justification.

Simply stylish text

AutoCAD LT assigns text properties to individual lines or paragraphs of text based on *text styles*. These text styles are similar to the paragraph styles in Microsoft Word: They contain font and other settings that determine the look and feel of text.

Before you add text to a drawing, you should use the Text Style dialog box to select an existing style or create a new one with settings that are appropriate to your purpose. Your AutoCAD LT notes may generate strange responses (or no response at all) if they appear in Old Persian Cuneiform (a real font!) or the Cyrillic alphabet.

Just as you should put every object on an appropriate layer, you should make sure that every text object uses an appropriate text style. In the Chapter 5 section titled "Making multiline text," we treat text styles the way the Wizard of Oz wanted Dorothy to treat him — we pay no attention to that text style behind the MTEXT curtain. The Multiline Text Editor lets you override text style characteristics such as font, and that's what we do in Chapter 5. That approach is fine for adding a couple of mark-up notes to someone else's drawing. If you're doing more than simple drawing markup, though, you definitely *should* pay attention to text styles.

The following procedure shows you how to select an existing text style or create a new one before you enter text into a drawing:

1. **Choose Format⇨Text Style.**

   The Text Style dialog box appears, as shown in Figure 12-1.

2. **In the Style Name drop-down list, select each of the styles in turn in order to see what text styles have been created in this drawing.**

   Note what appears in the Font Name box and view the Preview panel to get a feel for what the different fonts look like.

3. **If you find a suitable text style, select it in the Style Name drop-down list and then skip to Step 9.**

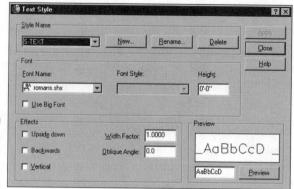

Figure 12-1:
Text with
style.

The selected text style name becomes the current style.

Look for a text style that uses the AutoCAD LT font ROMANS.SHX (Roman Simplex) or SIMPLEX.SHX (an older version of Roman Simplex). These are good, general-purpose fonts for drafting in AutoCAD LT. Avoid complicated, thick fonts. They can slow down AutoCAD LT a lot, and they're usually more difficult to read than the simpler fonts.

Stay away from Windows TrueType fonts. TrueType font names appear with a TT symbol to the left of name. AutoCAD LT doesn't handle TrueType fonts very efficiently, and if you add much TrueType text to a drawing, performance will suffer. Stick with AutoCAD native fonts, with names ending in SHX. AutoCAD font names appear with a drafting compass to the left of the name.

Also avoid *custom fonts,* which are font files that don't come with AutoCAD and LT. (Both programs come with the same fonts.) If you use a custom font, exchanging your drawings with other people will be more complicated. If you are compelled to use a custom font, make a note of it and remember either to send it whenever you send the DWG file (assuming that the font isn't copyrighted, which many custom fonts are), or to warn the recipients that the text will appear different on their systems. Obviously, it's far less hassle to eschew custom fonts altogether. See the "Package and go" section in Chapter 8 for more information.

4. **If you don't find a suitable text style, or if you prefer to create your own text style anyway, click New.**

   The New Text Style dialog box appears, with an edit box for you to type a name.

5. **Type a name for your new text style and then click OK.**

   Your new text style is added to the Style Name list and becomes the current style.

6. **From the <u>F</u>ont Name list, choose romans.shx.**

   Roman Simplex becomes the font that's assigned to your new text style.

7. **Set the remaining text style settings as shown in Figure 12-1: Heigh<u>t</u> = 0.0, <u>W</u>idth factor = 1.0, <u>O</u>blique angle = 0.0, and all four of the check boxes unchecked.**

   A text style height of zero makes the style *variable height,* which means that you can specify the height separately for each line text object. Although it's possible to assign a *fixed* (that is, nonzero) height to a text style, it's usually better to maintain the flexibility of variable height styles.

8. **Click <u>A</u>pply.**

9. **Click <u>C</u>lose.**

   The Text Style dialog box closes, and the text style that you selected or created is now the current style for new text objects.

As with layers, your office might have its own text style standards. If so, you'll make everyone very happy by following those standards.

As you saw in Step 3 of the previous procedure, AutoCAD LT can use two different kinds of fonts: native AutoCAD SHX (compiled SHape) fonts and Windows TTF (TrueType) fonts. SHX fonts usually provide better performance, because they're optimized for AutoCAD's and LT's use. TTF fonts give you more and fancier font options, but they slow down AutoCAD LT when you zoom, pan, and select and snap to objects. It's okay to use a TrueType font sparingly for something like a title block logo, but in general you should stick with standard AutoCAD SHX fonts whenever possible.

Most drawings require very few text styles. You might want to create one style for all notes, object labels, and annotations, and another one for special titles. A title block may require one or two additional fonts, especially if you want to mimic the font used in a company logo or project logo.

One line or two?

For historical reasons (namely, because the AutoCAD and AutoCAD LT text capabilities used to be even more primitive than they are now!), LT offers two different kinds of text objects and two corresponding text-drawing commands. Table 12-1 explains the two options.

Table 12-1	The Two Kinds of AutoCAD LT Text	
Text Object	*Command*	*Comments*
Line text	TEXT	Limited to single lines. Text appears directly in the drawing as you enter it.
Paragraph text	MTEXT	Supports multiple lines, with word wrapping. You enter text in a dialog box.

Although you might be inclined to ignore the older line text option, it's worth knowing how to use both kinds of text. The TEXT command is a bit simpler than the MTEXT command, so it's still useful for entering short, single-line pieces of text such as object labels and one-line notes. Obviously, it's the command of choice for CAD comedians who want to document their one-liners — and aren't fortunate enough to have a *For Dummies* book in which to inflict their humor on readers!

The small additional complexity of the MTEXT command is worth it whenever you enter multiple-line text that benefits from automatic word-wrapping. In addition, the MTEXT command provides more text formatting options.

Your text will be justified

Both the TEXT and MTEXT commands offer a bewildering array of text *justification* options — in other words, which way the text flows from the justification point or points that you pick in the drawing. For most purposes, the default left justification for line text or top left justification for paragraph text works fine. Occasionally, you might want to use a different justification, such as centered, for labels or titles. Both commands provide command-line options for changing text justification. We point out these options when we demonstrate the commands later in this chapter.

Taking your text to new heights

As we explain in the "Scaling the heights" section in Chapter 5, text height works differently in AutoCAD LT than it does in word processors and most other programs. You must multiply the desired plotted text height by the drawing's scale factor in order to get the required height of text that you enter in the drawing. Remember, in AutoCAD LT you're working in real-world units, not printout measurements. This approach is great for geometry — the most important part of your drawing — but confusing for frosting-like text that isn't part of the real-world object. (Unless you're drafting a neon sign!)

If you're the least bit uncertain about text scaling, do not pass the TEXT or MTEXT command, do not create 200 text strings, but instead go read "Scaling the heights" in Chapter 5. That information is critical not only for scaling text, but also for scaling dimensions and hatching, which we cover in Chapters 13 and 14, respectively.

Using the Same Old Line

Despite its limitations, the TEXT command is useful for labels and other short notes for which MTEXT would be overkill. The following procedure shows you how to enter text by using the AutoCAD LT TEXT command.

You *can* use TEXT for multiple lines of text: Just keep pressing Enter after you type each line of text, and TEXT puts the new line below the previous one. The problem is that TEXT creates each line of text as a separate object. If you later want to add or remove words in the multiple lines, AutoCAD LT can't do any word-wrapping for you; you have to edit each line separately, cutting words from one line and adding them to the adjacent line.

The AutoCAD LT 2000 TEXT command was called DTEXT (Dynamic TEXT) in previous versions of AutoCAD LT and AutoCAD. Thus, you might hear AutoCAD old-timers refer to the DTEXT command instead of TEXT. And you thought they called it DTEXT because it wasn't good enough to be A, B, or C text. . . .

The TEXT command does all of its prompting on the command line, so be sure to read the command-line prompts at each step along the way.

Here's how you enter text using the TEXT command:

1. **Set an appropriate layer current, as described in the "Put it on a layer" section in Chapter 10.**

2. **Set an appropriate text style current, as described in the section "Simply stylish text," earlier in this chapter.**

3. **Use the OSNAP button on the status bar to turn off running object snap mode.**

   You usually don't want to snap text to existing objects. See Chapter 10 for more information.

4. **Choose Draw⇨Text⇨Single Line Text from the menu bar to start the TEXT command.**

   The text icon on the Draw toolbar starts the multiline text command, MTEXT, which is covered in the next section.

   LT prompts you to either select a starting point for the text or to choose an option for changing the text justification or current text style first:

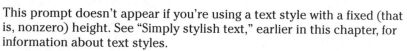
```
Specify start point of text or [Justify/Style]:
```

5. **If you want to change justification from the default (lower left), then type J, press Enter, and choose one of the other justification options.**

   Look up "justifying, single-line text" in the online help system if you need help with the justification options.

6. **Specify the insertion point for the first text character.**

   You can enter the point's coordinates from the command line, use the mouse to click a point on-screen, or press Enter to locate new text immediately below a previous line text object.

7. **Specify the height for the text.**

   This prompt doesn't appear if you're using a text style with a fixed (that is, nonzero) height. See "Simply stylish text," earlier in this chapter, for information about text styles.

8. **Specify the text rotation angle by entering the rotation angle from the command line and pressing Enter or by rotating the line on-screen by using the mouse.**

9. **Type the first line of text and press Enter.**

10. **Type additional lines of text, pressing Enter at the end of each line.**

    Figure 12-2 shows text appearing on-screen as you type it, following the TEXT command.

11. **To complete the command, press Enter at the start of a blank line.**

    AutoCAD LT adds the new line text object — or objects, if you typed more than one line — to the drawing.

To align lines of text correctly, make sure that you type in all the lines just as you want them to appear, pressing Enter after each line to make the next line appear just after it. Otherwise, aligning different lines of text precisely is harder to do (unless you set your snap just right, or use a complicated combination of object snaps and point filters, or are extraordinarily dexterous).

To edit line text after you've created it, select the text, right-click, and choose Text Edit. The Edit Text dialog box appears, enabling you to edit the text. If you want to edit other text properties, such as text height, select the text, right-click, and choose Properties to display the Properties window.

If you want to add text to your drawing that tracks the time and date — so that you can tell when a particular plot was created — choose Tools⇨Time and Date Stamp. This command adds a special block with text attributes to your drawing. The attributes show not only the date and time as of when the block was created, but also your name, your company's name, and the drawing name. You must remember to choose Tools⇨Time and Date Stamp again before plotting the drawing in order to update the date and time information.

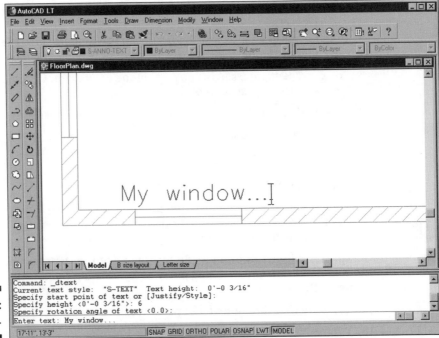

Figure 12-2:
Line text.

Saying More in Paragraphs

When you just can't shoehorn your creative genius into one-line pieces of text, the AutoCAD LT paragraph object gives you room to go on . . . and on . . . and on. The following procedure shows you how to create text paragraphs with the MTEXT command. Refer to the "Making multiline text" section in Chapter 5 for more information about each step.

The first part of the MTEXT command prompts you for various points and options on the command line. The order is a bit confusing, so read these steps and the command-line prompts carefully.

Here's how you use the MTEXT command:

1. **Set an appropriate layer and text style current and turn off running object snaps, as in Steps 1 through 3 of the procedure we describe in the previous section of this chapter.**

2. **Click the Multiline Text button on the Draw toolbar.**

   The command line displays the current text style and height settings and prompts you to select the first corner of an imaginary rectangle that will determine the word-wrapping width for the text object:

```
Current text style: "S-NOTES"  Text height:  0.125
Specify first corner:
```

3. Pick a point in the drawing.

The command line prompts you for the opposite corner of the text rectangle that will determine the word-wrapping width:

```
Specify opposite corner or [Height/Justify/Line
        spacing/Rotation/Style/Width]:
```

4. Type H and press Enter to change the default text height.

The command line prompts you for a new default text height:

```
Specify height <0.2000>:
```

5. Type an appropriate text height.

See the "Calculating text height" section in Chapter 5 for instructions. Remember to use the scaled AutoCAD LT text height, not the plotted text height.

The command-line prompt for the opposite corner of the MTEXT box reappears:

```
Specify opposite corner or [Height/Justify/Line
        spacing/Rotation/Style/Width]:
```

6. If you want to change justification from the default (top left), then type J, press Enter, and choose one of the other justification options.

Look up "justifying, multiline text" in the index of the online help system for more information about the justification options.

7. Pick another point in the drawing.

The Multiline Text Editor dialog box appears, as shown in Figure 12-3.

Figure 12-3:
Adding
paragraph
text.

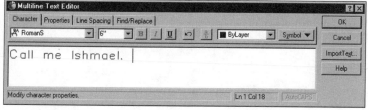

8. Verify the text font and height.

They should be set correctly if you correctly performed Steps 1, 4, and 5. If not, you can change these settings in the Font drop-down list and the Font Height edit box.

9. Type text into the text area of the dialog box.

AutoCAD LT word wraps multiline text automatically. If you want to force a line break at a particular location, press Enter.

10. **Click OK.**

The Multiline Text Editor dialog box closes and LT adds your text to the drawing.

As you can tell by looking at the Multiline Text Editor dialog box, the MTEXT command gives you plenty of other options, including a Stack/Unstack button for fractions, a special Symbol menu, a Find/Replace tab, and an Import Text button for importing text from a TXT (ASCII text) file or RTF (Rich Text Format) file. Use the dialog box help to learn more about these options: Click the question mark at the upper right of the dialog box title bar and then point to the part of the dialog box that you want to know about.

After you've created a paragraph text object, you edit it as you do a line text object: Select the paragraph text object, right-click, and choose Text Edit or Properties. The Text Edit option opens the Multiline Text Editor dialog box so that you can change the text contents and formatting. The Properties option opens the Properties window, where you can change overall properties for the text object.

The AutoCAD LT text commands are designed for the kinds of text that most people add to drawings: short, single-line notes or longer blocks of a paragraph or two. The LT commands don't work very well for long stretches of text or sophisticated formatting. If you're contemplating adding pages of text or fancy text formatting to a drawing, you should consider putting the text in a separate word processing document instead. If you absolutely must place the text from a long document on a drawing (on a general notes sheet, for example), you'll have to break it up into several columns, each of which is a separate MTEXT object. In other words, to avoid disappointment, treat LT like a little kid who hasn't graduated beyond Big Chief tablets and enormous pencils.

If you're tempted to circumvent our warning by pasting a word processing document directly into an AutoCAD LT drawing, please read the "Why not just shout, 'OLE!'?" sidebar in Chapter 7 first.

Checking It Out

AutoCAD LT 2000, like almost every other computer program on this planet — and possibly on several other planets and moons in our solar system alone — includes a spelling checker. (Rumor has it that you now need to take a graduate-level college course to learn how to write a computer program *without* a spelling checker. Some programmers experience severe anxiety at the beginning of the course due to their inability to imagine such a thing.)

Unlike Microsoft Word, LT's spelling checker doesn't make those little red squiggles under your errors, but it does let you search for spelling errors in the various line and paragraph text objects in your drawing. The following procedure demonstrates how to use the spelling checker:

1. **Press the Esc key twice to deselect any selected objects.**

2. **Choose Tools⇨Spelling to start the SPELL command.**

   This is text spell-checking, not casting a spell. (That's the EYEOFNEWT command.) The command line prompts you to select objects.

3. **Select the objects you want to check.**

   You can use any of the standard AutoCAD LT object selection methods to select text to check. (See Chapter 11 if you're unfamiliar with object selection.) Type **ALL** and press Enter if you want to check the spelling of all text in the drawing. Don't worry if you accidentally select objects other than text — the spelling checker ignores any objects that aren't text. When you're finished selecting objects, press Enter to initiate the spelling check.

   If the spelling checker finds a misspelling, the Check Spelling dialog box appears with the first misspelled or unrecognized word. See Figure 12-4 for an example.

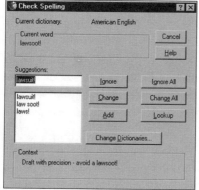

Figure 12-4:
It's good to sue your spelling checker.

4. **Use the dialog box buttons and the following options to tell AutoCAD LT how to handle a misspelling:**

   - **Suggestions:** AutoCAD puts its #1 suggestion here. Click another suggestion in the list to use that suggestion instead, or type the correct spelling yourself.

   - **Ignore/Ignore All:** Ignores the current word and continues checking, or ignores the current word and any future instances of it as well.

- **Change/Change All:** Changes the current word to the highlighted word and continues checking, or changes the current word and all other instances of it as well.

- **Add:** Adds the misspelled word to the custom dictionary.

- **Lookup:** Checks the spelling of the new word entered in the text-entry area under Suggestions.

- **Change Dictionaries:** Changes to a different dictionary (for example, a dictionary for a different language).

- **Context:** Displays the words among which AutoCAD found the mis-spelled word.

AutoCAD continues with spell checking until it has checked all the selected text objects. When it finds no further misspellings, the dialog box disappears and the `Spelling check complete` alert appears.

Every industry has its own set of abbreviations and specialized vocabulary that appear on drawings. AutoCAD LT, being a computer program, is pretty stupid and doesn't understand your industry's lingo. Thus, at first, it will complain about perfectly good words (from a drafter's point of view) such as *thru* and *S.A.D.* (which stands for See Architectural Drawing). If you're patient with it, AutoCAD LT, like an errant puppy, will become more obedient. Be prepared to click the Add button frequently during the first few weeks in order to tell AutoCAD LT which words and abbreviations are acceptable in your industry and office. Then you'll be thru feeling S.A.D.

Chapter 13

Dimension This!

● ●

In This Chapter

▶ Understanding dimension parts and types

▶ Using dimension styles from other drawings

▶ Creating and modifying your own dimension styles

▶ Drawing dimensions

▶ Editing dimensions

● ●

*I*n drafting — either CAD or manual drafting — *dimensions* are special text labels with attached lines that indicate unambiguously the size of something. Although it's theoretically possible to draw all the pieces of each dimension using AutoCAD LT commands such as MTEXT and LINE, dimensioning is so common a drafting task that LT provides special commands for doing the job more efficiently. These dimensioning commands group the parts of each dimension into a convenient, easy-to-edit package. Even better, as you stretch an object and the dimension that's attached to it, AutoCAD LT automatically updates the measurement displayed in the dimension text label to indicate the object's new size, as shown in Figure 13-1.

AutoCAD LT controls the look of dimensions by means of dimension styles, just as it controls the look of text with text styles. But dimension styles are much more complicated than text styles, because dimensions have so many more pieces that you need to control. After you find or create an appropriate dimension style, you use one of several dimensioning commands to draw dimensions that "point" to the important points on an object (the two endpoints of a line, for example).

Dimension text label updates as you stretch

Original dimension text label

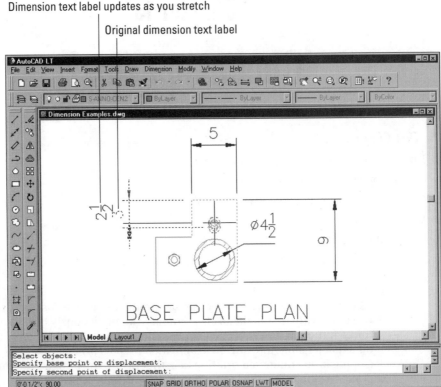

Figure 13-1:
Stretching
objects with
dimensions
automatically
updates
dimension
text.

AutoCAD LT dimensioning is a big, complicated subject. (It's so complicated, in fact, that Autodesk has an especially wise person in charge of dimensioning in AutoCAD and AutoCAD LT — he's called the "DimWit.") Every industry has its own dimensioning conventions, habits, and quirks. As usual, LT tries to support them all, and in so doing, makes things a bit convoluted for everyone. This chapter covers the essential concepts and commands that you need to know in order to start drawing dimensions. Be prepared to spend some additional time studying how to create any specialized types of dimensions that your industry uses.

You may be able to avoid getting too deeply into the details of dimensioning just by copying dimension styles from existing drawings in your office. This may be a good time to get some advice and coaching from the AutoCAD geek in the cubicle across from yours.

Why dimensions in CAD?

You might think that CAD would have rendered text dimensions obsolete. After all, you comply with all of our suggestions about using AutoCAD LT precision techniques when you draw and edit, and you're careful to draw each object at its true size, right? The contractor or machinist can just use AutoCAD or LT to query distances and angles in the CAD DWG file, right? Sorry, but no (to the last question, anyway).

First of all, some people need to or want to use paper drawings when they build something. We're still some time away from the day when contractors haul computers around in their tool belts (never mind trying to whip them out and zoom around a drawing while hanging off of scaffolding).

Second, in many industries, paper drawings still rule legally. Your company may supply both plotted drawings and DWG files to clients, but your contracts probably specify that the plotted drawings govern in the case of any discrepancy. The contracts probably also warn against relying on any distances that the recipient of the drawings measures — using measuring commands in the CAD DWG file or a scale on the plotted drawing. The text dimensions are supposed to supply all the dimensional information that's needed to construct the object.

Third, dimensions sometimes carry additional information besides the basic length or angle. For example, they can indicate the allowable construction tolerances, or show that a particular distance is typical of similar situations elsewhere on the drawing.

Fourth, even conscientious CAD drafters rarely draw *every* object its true size. They sometimes exaggerate distances for graphical clarity or settle for approximate distances because time pressures (especially late in a project) make it difficult to be completely accurate and precise.

For all these reasons, the traditional dimensioning that CAD drafting has inherited from manual drafting is likely to be around for awhile. So remember the old rule of drafting prowess: "It's not the size of the drawn object that matters, but the dimensions that are on it."

Discovering New Dimensions

Before we dig into the techniques that you use to create dimension styles and dimensions, we need to review some LT dimensioning terminology. If you're already familiar with CAD dimensioning lingo, just skim this section and look at the figures in it. Otherwise, read on.

Anatomy of a dimension

AutoCAD LT uses the names shown in Figure 13-2 and that are described in the following list to refer to the parts of each dimension:

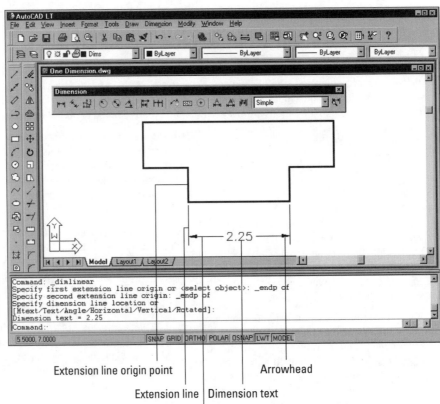

Figure 13-2:
The parts of
a dimension.

Extension line origin point

Arrowhead

Extension line | Dimension text

Dimension line

- **Dimension text:** Dimension text usually is the number that indicates the actual distance or angle. Dimension text can, however, include other text information in addition to or instead of the number. For example, you can add a suffix such as mm to indicate units or insert a description such as See Detail 3/A2.

- **Dimension lines:** The dimension lines go from the dimension text outward (parallel to the direction of the object being measured), to indicate the extent of the dimensioned length. AutoCAD LT's default dimension style settings center the dimension text vertically and horizontally on the dimension lines (as shown in Figure 13-1), but you can change those settings in order to cause the text to appear in a different location — riding above an unbroken dimension line, for example. See the section "Adjusting style settings" later in this chapter for instructions.

- **Dimension arrowheads:** The dimension arrowheads appear at the ends of the dimension lines and clarify the extent of the dimensioned length. AutoCAD LT's default arrowhead style is the closed, filled type shown in

Figure 13-1, but you can choose other symbols, such as tick marks, to indicate the ends of the dimension lines. (AutoCAD LT calls the line ending an *arrowhead* even when, as in the case of a tick mark, it doesn't look like an arrow.)

✔ **Extension lines:** The extension lines extend outward from the extension line origin points that you select (usually by snapping to points on an object) to the dimension lines. By drafting convention, a small gap usually exists between the extension line origin points and the beginning of the extension lines. Also, the extension lines usually extend just beyond where they meet the dimension lines.

A field guide to dimensions

AutoCAD LT provides quite a few different types of dimensions and commands for drawing them. Figure 13-3 shows the most common types, and the following list describes them:

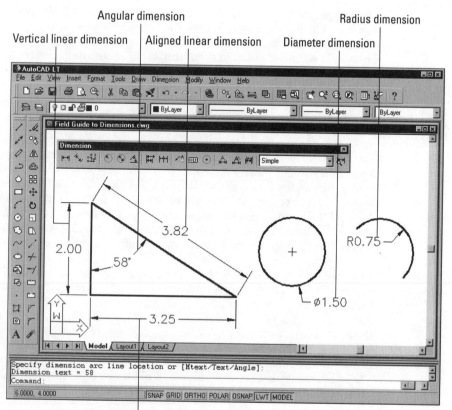

Figure 13-3: Common types of dimensions.

✔ **Linear dimensions:** A *linear* dimension measures the linear extent of an object or the linear distance between objects. Most linear dimensions are either *horizontal* or *vertical,* but you can draw dimensions that are *rotated* to other angles, too. An *aligned* dimension is a special kind of linear dimension in which the dimension line tilts to the same angle as a line drawn through the endpoints of its extension lines.

✔ **Radial dimensions:** A *radius* dimension calls out the radius of a circle or arc. The arrowhead points to an arbitrary point on the curve. A *diameter* dimension calls out the diameter of a circle or arc. A diameter dimension appears in one of two ways, depending on whether there's enough room inside the circle or arc for dimensions text and two arrowheads. If there is enough room, AutoCAD LT draws a line with arrowheads pointing to two diametrically opposite points on the curve. If there's not enough room, as in Figure 13-3, LT draws a little cross at the center of the circle or arc and draws an arrow pointing to an arbitrary point on the curve.

✔ **Angular dimensions:** An *angular* dimension calls out the angular measurement between two lines or other linear objects; the dimension line appears as an arc that indicates the sweep of the measured angle.

Other types of AutoCAD LT dimensions include ordinate, tolerance, center mark, and leader dimensions. (See the "Pointy-Headed Leaders" section of Chapter 5 for instructions on how to draw leaders. Look up "dimensions, creating" on the Index tab in the AutoCAD LT online help system for more information about other kinds of dimensions.)

Pulling out your dimension tools

The AutoCAD LT Dimension menu provides access to dimensioning commands. If you find yourself adding dimensions in batches, the Dimension toolbar is more efficient, because it makes the dimensioning commands more easily accessible. You toggle the Dimension toolbar off and on by right-clicking any AutoCAD LT toolbar icon and choosing Dimension from the cursor menu. As with other toolbars, you can move the Dimension toolbar to a different location on the screen or dock it on any margin of the drawing area.

All dimensioning commands have long command names (such as DIMLINEAR and DIMRADIUS) and corresponding shortened abbreviations (DLI and DRA) that you can type at the command prompt. If you do lots of dimensioning and don't want to toggle the Dimension toolbar on and off repeatedly, memorize the abbreviated forms of the dimension commands that you use frequently. You'll find a list of the long command names on the Contents tab in the AutoCAD LT online help system. Choose Commands and then D Commands. The short names are the first, fourth, and fifth letters of the long names. (In other words, take the first five letters of the long name and remove "IM".)

Doing Dimensions with Style (s)

Creating a usable dimension style that gives you the dimension look you want is the biggest challenge in using AutoCAD LT's dimensioning features. Each drawing contains its own dimension styles, so changes you make to a dimension style in one drawing affect only that drawing.

A dimension style is a collection of drawing settings called *dimension variables,* which are a special class of the *system variables* that we introduce in Chapter 2.

If you want to see a list of the dimension variable names and what each variable controls, look up "dimensioning system variables, default settings" on the Index tab in the AutoCAD LT online help system and then click the proceeding `Example: The Default Dimension Style` link.

AutoCAD users, like all computer nerds, like to shorten names. You might hear them refer to *dimstyles* and *dimvars* instead of dimension styles and dimension variables. You can tell them that doing so makes you think of them as "dimwits" — like the Autodesk expert on the topic to whom we referred earlier in this chapter.

Borrowing existing dimension styles

If you're lucky enough to work in an office where someone has set up dimension styles that are appropriate for your industry and project, you can skip the pain and strain of creating your own dimension styles. If that ready-made dimension style lives in another drawing, you can copy it into your drawing using AutoCAD DesignCenter, as we describe in the following procedure:

1. **Open the drawing that contains the dimension style you want to copy (the *source* drawing).**

2. **Open the drawing to which you want to copy the dimension style (the *destination* drawing).**

3. **Click the AutoCAD DesignCenter button on the Standard toolbar to display the DesignCenter window.**

   The DesignCenter window appears.

4. **In the left pane of the DesignCenter window, click the plus sign next to the name of the drawing that you opened in Step 1.**

   A list of copy-able objects, including dimstyles, appears.

5. **Click and drag the desired dimension style from the left pane of the DesignCenter window into the window containing the drawing that you opened in Step 2, as shown in Figure 13-4.**

If the name of the dimension style that you copy duplicates the name of an existing dimension style in the destination drawing, AutoCAD LT refuses to overwrite the existing dimension style. In that case, rename the existing dimension style using the information in the section "Creating and managing dimension styles" later in this chapter.

6. **Change the Use Overall Scale Of factor on the Fit tab of the Modify Dimension Style dialog box so that it matches the drawing scale factor of the current drawing.**

   See the "Setting linetype and dimension scales" section of Chapter 9 for detailed instructions.

If you want a dimension style to be available in new drawings, copy the style to a template drawing and use that template to create your new drawings. See Chapter 9 for more information about template drawings.

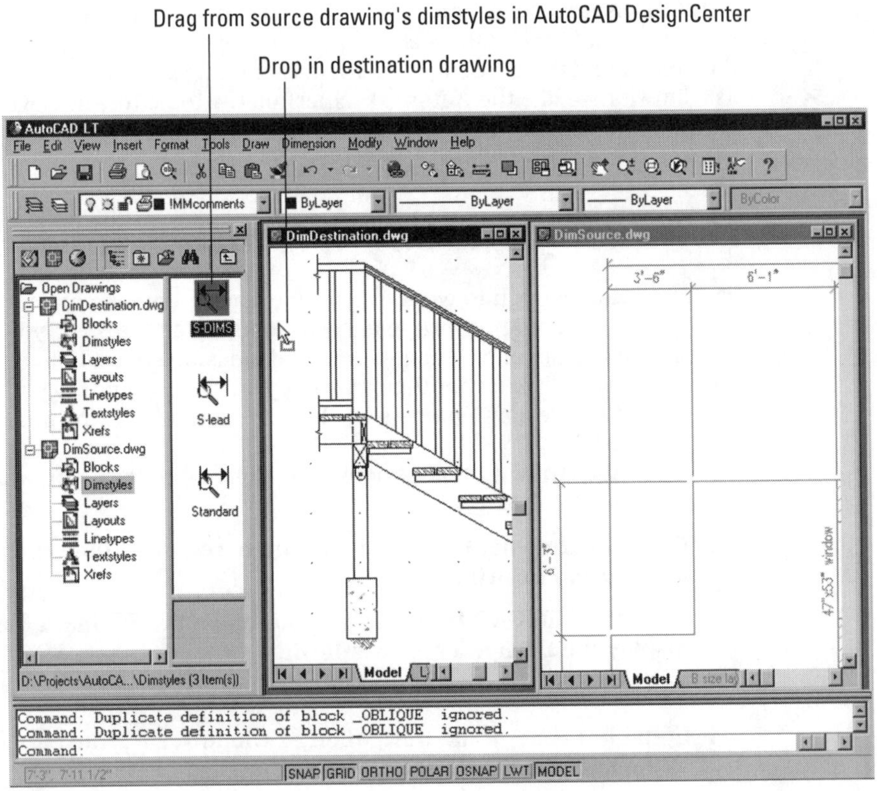

Drag from source drawing's dimstyles in AutoCAD DesignCenter

Drop in destination drawing

Figure 13-4:
Copying a
dimension
style from
one drawing
to another.

Creating and managing dimension styles

If you *do* need to create your own dimension styles, or you want to tweak ones that you copied from another drawing, you use the Dimension Style Manager dialog box, shown in Figure 13-5.

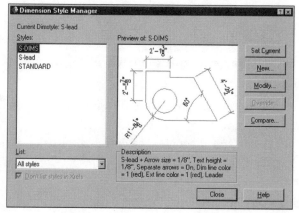

Figure 13-5:
Yet another manager, this one for dimension styles.

Every drawing comes with a default dimension style named Standard. Although you can use and modify the Standard style, we suggest that you leave the Standard style as is and create your own dimension style(s) for the settings that are appropriate to your work. This approach ensures that you can use the default Standard style as a reference. More important, it avoids a potential naming conflict that can change the way your dimensions look if the current drawing gets inserted into another drawing.

The following procedure shows you how to create your own dimension style(s):

1. **Choose Format⇨Dimension Style from the menu bar, or click the Dimension Style button on the Dimension toolbar.**

   The Dimension Style Manager dialog box appears.

2. **In the Styles list, select the existing dimension style whose settings you want to use as the starting point for the settings of your new style.**

   For example, select the default dimension style named Standard.

3. **Click the New button to create a new dimension style that's a copy of the existing style.**

   The Create New Dimension Style dialog box appears.

4. **Enter a <u>N</u>ew Style Name and click Continue.**

   The New Dimension Style dialog box appears, which is the same as the Modify Dimension Style dialog box shown in Figure 13-6 later in this chapter.

5. **Modify dimension settings on any of the six tabs in the New Dimension Style dialog box.**

   See the descriptions of these settings in the next section of this chapter. In particular, be sure to set the Use Overall Scale Of factor on the Fit tab to set the drawing scale factor.

6. **Click OK to close the New Dimension Style dialog box.**

   The Dimension Style Manager dialog box reappears.

7. **Select your new dimension style from the <u>S</u>tyles list and then click Set C<u>u</u>rrent.**

   Your new dimension style becomes the current dimension style that AutoCAD LT uses for future dimensions in this drawing.

8. **Click Close.**

   The Dimension Style Manager dialog box closes.

9. **Draw some dimensions to test your new dimension style.**

Avoid changing existing dimension styles that you didn't create, unless you know for sure what they're used for. When you change a dimension style setting, all dimensions that use that style change to reflect the revised setting. Thus, one small dimension variable setting change can affect a large number of existing dimensions! When in doubt, instead of modifying an existing dimension style, create a new style by copying the existing one, and then modify the new one.

A further variation on the already baroque dimension style picture is that you can create dimension *secondary styles* (also called *substyles* or *style families*) — variations of a main style that affect only a particular type of dimension, such as radial or angular. You probably want to avoid this additional complication if you can, but if you open the Dimension Style Manager dialog box and see names of dimension types indented beneath the main dimension style names, be aware that you're dealing with secondary styles. Look up "dimension styles, secondary styles" on the Index tab in the AutoCAD LT online help system for more information.

Adjusting style settings

After you click New or Modify in the Dimension Style Manager, AutoCAD LT displays a tabbed New/Modify Dimension Style subdialog box with a mind-boggling — and potentially drawing-boggling, if you're not careful — array of settings. Figure 13-6 shows the settings on the first tab.

Fortunately, the dimension preview that appears on all tabs — as well as on the main Dimension Style Manager dialog box — immediately shows the results of most setting changes. This new feature in AutoCAD LT 2000 makes creating dimension styles easier. With this new feature and some trial-and-error changing of settings, you usually can home in on an acceptable group of settings. For more information, use the dialog box help: Click the question mark on the title bar and then click the setting that you want to know more about.

The most important thing to know before you start messing with dimension style settings is what you want your dimensions to look like when they're plotted. If you're not sure how it's done in your industry, ask others in your office or profession, or look at a plotted drawing that someone in the know represents as being a good example. (If you're not sure how it's done in your industry, maybe you should be working in a different industry — or maybe you're a creative genius whose mind can't be bound by trivia, as a typical business plan in Silicon Valley might put it. Who are we to say?)

The following sections introduce you to the more important New/Modify Dimension Style tabs and highlight useful settings. Note that whenever you specify a distance or length setting, you should enter the desired *plotted* size. AutoCAD LT scales all these numbers by the overall scale factor that you enter on the Fit tab.

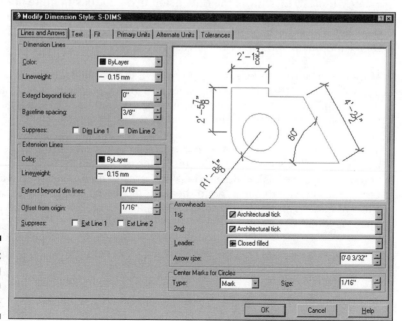

Figure 13-6:
Modifying dimension settings.

Following Lines and Arrows

The settings on the Lines and Arrows tab control the basic "look and feel" of all parts of your dimensions except for text. Use this tab to change the type and size of arrowheads or the display characteristics of the dimension and extension lines.

Tabbing to Text

Use the Text tab to control how your dimension text looks — the text style and height to use (see Chapter 12) and where to place the text with respect to the dimension and extension lines. You'll probably want to change the Text Style setting to something that uses a more pleasing font than the dorky default Txt.shx font, such as the Romans.shx font. The default Text Height is too large for most situations — set it to ⅛ (= 0.125) or another height that makes sense.

Enter the desired plotted text height — don't multiply it by the drawing scale factor, as you do for ordinary text.

Industry or company standards usually dictate the size of dimension text (for example, ⅛ inch is common in the architectural industry). In any case, make sure you pick a height that's not too small to read on your smallest size check plot.

Getting Fit

The Fit tab contains a bunch of confusing options that control when and where AutoCAD LT shoves the dimension text if it doesn't quite fit between the dimension lines. Stick with the defaults until you get the hang of what LT does in these situations, and if you aren't happy with the default behavior, then experiment with other settings.

More importantly, the Fit tab includes the Use Overall Scale Of setting, as shown in Figure 13-7. This setting acts as a global scaling factor for all the other length-related dimension settings. Always set Use Overall Scale Of to the drawing scale factor of the current drawing.

The Use Overall Scale Of setting corresponds to the DIMSCALE system variable, and you'll hear AutoCAD drafters refer to it as such. AutoCAD LT accepts zero and negative DIMSCALE settings and uses them for special dimensioning techniques in paper space. Avoid these nonpositive settings like the plague. They're hard to understand and usually reflect a dumb way of using paper space layouts.

Drawing scale factor goes here!

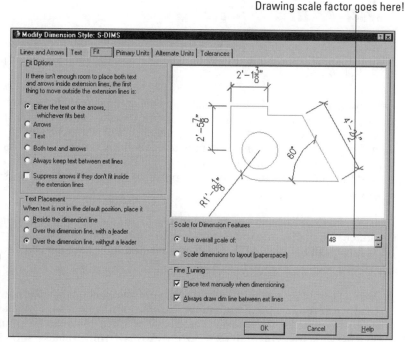

Figure 13-7:
Keep Fit and
don't forget
the scale.

Using Primary Units

The Primary Units tab gives you incredibly (or overly) detailed control over how AutoCAD LT formats the characters in the dimension text string. You usually want to set the Unit format and Precision and maybe specify a suffix for unitless numbers (such as mm for millimeters). You may also change to set the Zero Suppression settings, depending on whether you want dimension text to read 0.5000, .5000, or 0.5. (You can sound like a real human rights advocate if you say "We use zero suppression in our shop.")

Other style settings

If your work requires that you show dimensions in two different units (such as inches and millimeters), use the Alternate Units tab to turn on and control alternate units. If your work requires listing construction tolerances (for example, 3.5mm +/-0.01), use the Tolerances tab to configure the tolerance format that you want.

The New/Modify Dimension Style dialog box Tolerance tab *settings* affect the text of ordinary dimensions. AutoCAD LT includes a separate TOLERANCES *command* that draws special symbols called geometric tolerances. If you need these symbols, you probably know it; if you've never heard of them, just ignore them. Look up "tolerance symbols" on the Index tab in the AutoCAD LT online help system for more information.

Drawing Dimensions

After you've copied or created a suitable dimension style, you're ready to dimension. Fortunately, adding dimensions to a drawing usually is pretty straightforward.

AutoCAD LT does not require that you specify *objects* to dimension; it draws a dimension between any *points* you specify. Usually, however, you should choose points on objects using object snaps (see the "My Point Is. . ." section in Chapter 10). The points you pick are called the *origins* of the dimension's extension lines. When you move the origin points — by stretching the object and the dimension, for example — AutoCAD LT updates the dimension text to show the new length.

If you don't use object snaps or another LT precision technique to choose dimension points, the dimension text probably won't reflect the precise measurement of the object. This lack of precision can cause serious problems, so when in doubt, snap to it!

When you set up a new drawing, make sure that you change the Use Overall Scale Of setting on the Fit tab in the New/Modify Dimension Style dialog box so that it matches the drawing scale factor. Before you draw any dimensions in a drawing that you didn't set up, check this setting to make sure it's correct.

The AutoCAD LT dimension drawing commands prompt you with useful information at the command line. Read the command-line prompts during every step of the command, especially when you're trying a dimensioning command for the first time.

Lining up some linear dimensions

Linear dimensions are by far the most common type of dimensions, and horizontal and vertical are the most common of those. The following steps show you how to create horizontal, vertical, and aligned linear dimensions:

1. **Use the LINE command to draw a non-orthogonal line — that is, a line segment that's not horizontal or vertical. An angle of about 30 degrees works well for this example.**

   If you want to apply dimensioning to an object other than a line, use these steps as a general guideline, filling in the appropriate commands and data as applicable to your drawing.

2. **Set a layer that's appropriate for dimensions current, as we describe in the "Put it on a layer" section in Chapter 10.**

3. **Set a dimension style that's appropriate for your needs current, as described in Step 7 of the "Creating and managing dimension styles" procedure, earlier in this chapter.**

4. **Choose Dimension⇨Linear or click the Linear Dimension button on the Dimension toolbar.**

   AutoCAD LT prompts you:

   ```
   Specify first extension line origin or <select object>:
   ```

5. **To specify the origin of the first extension line, snap to the lower-left endpoint of the line by using endpoint object snap.**

   If you don't have endpoint as one of your current running object snaps, specify a single endpoint object snap by holding down the Shift key, right-clicking, and choosing Endpoint from the cursor menu. (See Chapter 10 for more about object snaps.)

   AutoCAD LT prompts you:

   ```
   Specify second extension line origin:
   ```

6. **To specify the origin of the second extension line, snap to the other endpoint of the line by using endpoint object snap again.**

   AutoCAD LT draws a *horizontal* dimension — the length of the displacement in the left-to-right direction — if you move the cursor above or below the line. It draws a *vertical* dimension — the length of the displacement in the up-and-down direction — if you move the cursor to the left or right of the line. If you move the cursor near the line, LT determines the type of dimension that's displayed by where the cursor was the last time it was outside an imaginary rectangle that just encloses the line.

   AutoCAD LT prompts you:

   ```
   Specify dimension line location or
   [Mtext/Text/Angle/Horizontal/Vertical/Rotated]:
   ```

7. **Move the mouse to generate the type of dimension you want, horizontal or vertical, and then click wherever you want to place the dimension line.**

   AutoCAD LT draws the dimension.

   If you want to be able to align subsequent dimension lines easily, turn on Snap and set a suitable snap spacing — more easily done than said! — before you pick the point that determines the location of the dimension line. See the "My Point Is. . ." section in Chapter 10 for more information about snap.

8. **Repeat Steps 4 through 7 to create another linear dimension of the opposite orientation (vertical or horizontal).**

9. **Choose Dimension⇨Aligned or click the Aligned Dimension button on the Dimension toolbar.**

   Notice that the prompt includes an option to select an object instead of picking two points. You can use this technique with the Linear Dimension command, too:

   ```
   Specify first extension line origin or <select object>:
   ```

10. **Press Enter to choose the Select Object option.**

    AutoCAD LT prompts you:

    ```
    Select object to dimension:
    ```

11. **Select the line or other object that you want to dimension.**

    AutoCAD LT automatically finds the endpoints of the line and uses them as the extension line origin points, as shown in Figure 13-8.

    AutoCAD LT prompts you:

    ```
    Specify dimension line location or
    [Mtext/Text/Angle]:
    ```

12. **Click wherever you want to place the dimension line.**

    AutoCAD LT draws the dimension.

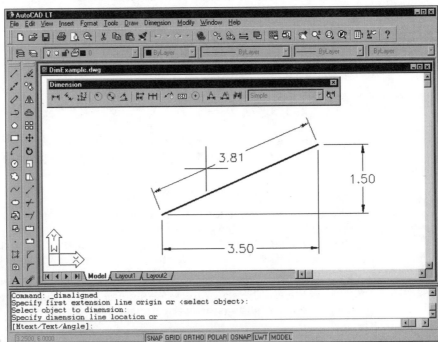

Figure 13-8:
Placing an aligned linear dimension.

Drawing other kinds of dimensions

After you have the hang of ordinary linear dimensions, you should be able to master other common dimension types quickly. Draw some lines, arcs, and circles, and try the other dimension commands on the Dimension toolbar or menu.

AutoCAD LT considers leaders to be a special kind of dimension object. The "Pointy-Headed Leaders" section in Chapter 5 demonstrates how to draw leaders using the QLEADER (Quick Leader) command. Note that this command includes a Settings option, which opens a Leader Settings dialog box in which you can change options such as whether to draw a straight or curved leader line and what kind of leader arrowhead to draw.

Editing Dimensions

After you've drawn dimensions, you can edit the position of the various parts of each dimension and change the contents of the dimension text. AutoCAD LT groups all the parts of a dimension into a single object, so that the entire dimension ghosts when you select it for editing.

Editing dimension geometry

The easiest way to change the location of dimension parts is to use group editing, which we describe in the "Get a Grip" section of Chapter 6. Just click a dimension, click one of its grips, and maneuver away. You'll discover that certain grips control certain directions of movement. A couple of minutes of experimentation will make clear how they work.

If you move or copy an object, the dimension that you drew for that object doesn't automatically go with it. Even when you pick points right on an object, AutoCAD LT creates the dimension as a separate object with no specific connection to the object. In other words, the object and the dimension are living together, but not married. Thus, when you edit dimensioned objects, be sure to select the dimension along with the object if you want the editing operation to affect the dimension as well. Likewise, if you move and want your live-in boyfriend or girlfriend to come along, be sure to tell him or her.

If you want to change the actual look of a dimension part (for example, substitute a different arrowhead or suppress an extension line), use the Properties window. It's described in the "Polishing those properties" sidebar in Chapter 11. All the dimension settings in the New/Modify Dimension Style dialog box (see "Adjusting style settings," earlier in this chapter) are available in the Properties window when you select one or more dimensions.

When you change a setting in the Properties window, you're *overriding* the default style setting for that dimension. If you need to make the same change to a bunch of dimensions, it's better to create a new dimension style and assign that style to them. You can use the Properties window or the right-click menu to change the dimension style that's assigned to one or more dimensions.

If you select one or more dimensions and right-click, the cursor menu displays a number of useful options for overriding dimension settings or assigning a different style.

The AutoCAD LT EXPLODE command on the Modify toolbar will blow a dimension apart, into a bunch of line and MTEXT objects. Don't do it! Exploding a dimension makes it much harder to edit cleanly and eliminates AutoCAD LT's ability to update the dimension text measurement automatically.

Editing dimension text

AutoCAD LT creates dimension text as a paragraph text (MTEXT) object, so you have the same editing options as with ordinary text. Unfortunately, the right-click menu for dimension objects doesn't include a Text Edit option. You can use the Text Override field in the Properties window or choose Modify➪Object➪Text to edit dimension text in the Multiline Text Editor dialog box.

The default text is blank, which causes AutoCAD LT to insert the true dimension length (and to keep it up to date if you change the distance between the dimension's origin points). You can override the true length by typing a specific length or other text string. You can preserve the true length but add a prefix or suffix by typing <> (that is, the left- and right-angled bracket characters, above the comma and period characters on most keyboards) as a placeholder for the true length. In other words, if you enter <> **Max.**, and the actual distance is 12.00, then AutoCAD LT will display **12.00 Max.** for the dimension text. If you later stretch the dimension so that the actual distance changes to 14.50, LT will automatically change the dimension text to read **14.50 Max.**

Avoid the temptation to override the default dimension text. Doing so eliminates AutoCAD LT's ability to keep dimension measurements current, but even worse, you get no visual cue that the default distance has been overridden (unless you edit the dimension text). If you find that you're overriding dimension text a lot, it's probably a sign that the creator of the drawing didn't pay enough attention to using precision techniques when drawing and editing. We're not going to point any fingers, but you probably know whom to talk to.

Chapter 14

Down the Hatch

*I*f you were hoping to hatch a plot (or plot a hatch), see Chapter 4 instead. If you want to hatch an egg, buy our companion book, *Raising Chickens For Dummies*. If, on the other hand, you need to fill in closed areas of your drawings with special patterns of lines, then this is your chapter.

Drafters often use *hatching* to represent the type of material that makes up an object, such as insulation, metal, concrete, and so on. In other cases, hatching helps emphasize or clarify the extent of a particular element in the drawing — for example, showing the location of walls in a building plan, or highlighting a swampy area on a map so you know where to avoid building a road. Figure 14-1 shows an example of hatching in a structural detail.

A hatch is similar to a linetype in that it conveys information about part of the drawing. But unlike a linetype, a hatch isn't a property of a single line. Instead, it's a separate object that fills a space and is associated with the objects that bound that space, such as lines, polylines, or arcs. If you move or stretch the boundaries, AutoCAD LT normally updates the hatching to fill the resized area.

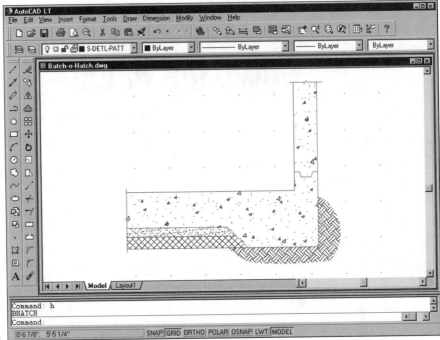

Figure 14-1:
A big batch
o' hatch.

Hatch . . . Hatch . . . Hatchoo

This section outlines the steps you use to add hatching to a drawing with the Boundary Hatch dialog box, shown in Figure 14-2. You can use this information to get started quickly with hatching, and then jump to the relevant sections of "Pushing the Boundary (of) Hatch," later in this chapter, when you need more information about any part of the process.

To demonstrate the workings of boundary hatches, the following steps show you how to hatch an object, such as the wheels of a (very) simple drawing of a car, by using the picking-points method of selecting the hatch area:

1. Open a drawing containing geometry that forms fully closed boundaries or draw some boundaries using the drawing commands we describe in Chapter 10.

The areas you want to hatch must be completely enclosed. The CIRCLE, POLYGON, and RECTANG commands, and the LINE and PLINE commands with the Close option, make great hatch boundaries. (See Chapter 10 for details.)

2. Set an appropriate layer current, as described in Chapter 10.

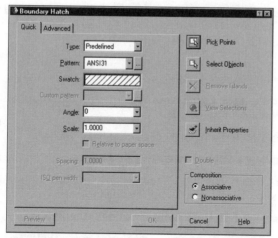

3. **Start the BHATCH command by clicking the Hatch button on the Draw toolbar.**

   The Boundary Hatch dialog box appears.

   For historical reasons, AutoCAD LT 2000 also has a HATCH command, which prompts you at the command line rather than opening a dialog box. Trust us — you want the BHATCH command's dialog box.

4. **Choose Predefined, User Defined, or Custom from the Type drop-down list.**

   Predefined or User Defined works best for most purposes. See the next section for details.

5. **If you chose Predefined or Custom in the previous step, select any predefined or custom hatch pattern from the Pattern drop-down list or the dialog box button next to it. If you chose User Defined, proceed to the next step.**

6. **Specify an Angle and Scale for the hatch pattern. (If you chose User Defined in Step 4, specify Angle and Spacing.)**

   See "Getting it right: Hatch angle and scale," later in this chapter, for more information.

7. **Click the Pick Points button.**

   The Boundary Hatch dialog box (temporarily) disappears and your drawing reappears, with the following prompt at the command line:

   ```
   Select internal point:
   ```

8. **Select a point inside the boundary that you want to hatch by clicking it with the mouse.**

AutoCAD LT analyzes the drawing and decides which boundaries to use. In a complex drawing, this analysis can take several seconds. LT highlights the boundary that it finds.

If LT highlights the wrong boundary, right-click, choose Clear All from the cursor menu, and try again.

9. **Right-click and choose Enter from the cursor menu to indicate that you're finished selecting points.**

    The Boundary Hatch dialog box reappears.

10. **Click the Preview button to preview the hatch.**

    The Boundary Hatch dialog box (temporarily) disappears again, and AutoCAD LT shows you what the hatch will look like.

11. **Right-click to return to the Boundary Hatch dialog box.**

12. **Adjust any settings and preview again until you're satisfied with the hatch.**

13. **Click OK.**

    AutoCAD LT hatches the area inside the boundary. If you modify the boundary, the hatch will automatically resize to fill the resized area.

Occasionally, AutoCAD LT gets confused and doesn't resize a hatch after you resize the boundary. If that happens, you'll need to erase and then re-create the hatch in the resized area.

Pushing the Boundary (of) Hatch

The remainder of this chapter shows you how to refine the techniques presented in the preceding procedure. Precisely.

Cop a hatch: Copying hatch properties

One of the slicker and faster ways to hatch is by using the Inherit Properties button in the Boundary Hatch dialog box to copy hatch properties from an existing hatch object. Think of it as "point and shoot" hatching. If someone — such as you — added some hatching in the past that's just like what you want to use now, click the Inherit Properties button and pick the existing hatching.

Inherit Properties simply updates the hatch pattern settings in the Boundary Hatch dialog box to make them the same as the existing hatch pattern object that you picked. You can use the cloned hatch pattern specifications as is or modify them by making changes in the Boundary Hatch dialog box.

Consistency is a very good thing in drafting, especially in computer-aided drafting, in which some or all of your drawing may be used and reused for a very long time. So consider using the same hatch patterns, scales, and angles for the same purposes in all your drawings. Find out whether your project, office, company, or profession has hatching standards that apply to the drawing you're working on.

Despite its position in the Boundary Hatch dialog box (underneath the buttons used to establish the hatching boundary), the Inherit Properties button affects only the pattern information on the left side of the dialog box. It doesn't affect how LT handles boundaries.

Rolling your own

You can use predefined, user-defined, or custom hatch patterns. Most of the time, you'll choose either predefined or user-defined hatch patterns, unless some generous soul gives you a custom pattern. The next three sections describe the hatch pattern type choices.

Pick a pattern, any pattern: Predefined hatch patterns

To use AutoCAD LT's *predefined* hatch patterns, select Predefined from the drop-down list box at the top of the Quick tab in the Boundary Hatch dialog box. This selection sets the stage for choosing the hatch pattern.

You can scan through the hatch patterns in one of three ways:

- ✔ By selecting the name from the Pattern drop-down list box; this action changes the hatch pattern shown in the Swatch area.

- ✔ By clicking the Pattern button (the tiny button with the ellipses [three dots] to the right of the Pattern prompt and pattern name); this button brings up the Hatch Pattern Palette with pattern previews.

- ✔ By clicking the swatch that's displayed; this action also brings up the Hatch Pattern Palette.

AutoCAD LT has about 70 predefined hatch patterns from which to choose. The list includes ANSI (American National Standards Institute) and ISO (International Standards Organization) standard hatch patterns. Figure 14-3 shows the Other Predefined hatch patterns, which cover everything from Earth to Escher to Stars(ky and Hatch?). However, there's no option for a Dick Van Pattern.

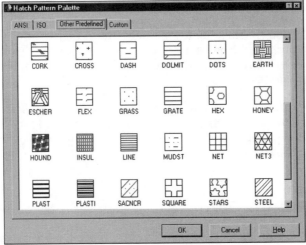

Figure 14-3:
Plenty of
hatch
patterns.

After you've selected a pattern, you need to specify Angle and Scale, as we describe in the section "Getting it right: Hatch angle and scale," later in this chapter.

It's up to you: User-defined hatches

A *user-defined* hatch pattern makes a hatch pattern out of simple parallel lines. This option is useful when you want to create a simple pattern and specify the space between the lines in drawing units, rather than using a nebulous hatch scale factor to set the spacing. For example, you might hatch a wall in a building plan with a user-defined pattern and specify that the hatch lines are to be three inches apart.

Make it solid, man

Although you might not guess it, AutoCAD LT treats *solid fills* (that is, filling an area with a solid color) as a predefined hatch "pattern." Simply choose Solid from the top of the Pattern drop-down list or the Other Predefined tab of the Hatch Pattern Palette.

Like any other object, a solid hatch takes on the current object color — or the current layer's color if you leave color set to ByLayer. Therefore, you should make sure that the current object layer and color are set appropriately before you use the Solid hatching option. (See Chapter 10 for details.)

After you choose User Defined from the Type drop-down list in the Boundary Hatch dialog box, you specify the angle and spacing of the lines. You can turn on Double in order to achieve a *crosshatching* effect (two perpendicular sets of hatching lines).

A custom PAT

A *custom* hatch pattern is one that clever, patient, and excessively nerdy users can define and save in a file with a file extension of PAT. No, football fans, we're sorry. PAT doesn't stand for *point after touchdown;* it stands for *pat*tern. If you enjoy learning arcane, pen-plotter-like codes, you can find out more about creating custom hatch patterns by looking up "hatch patterns, customizing" in the AutoCAD LT online help.

Getting it right: Hatch angle and scale

All predefined and custom hatch patterns require that you enter the angle and scale for AutoCAD LT to use when generating the hatching. You usually won't have any trouble deciding on an appropriate angle, but figuring out a suitable scale can be tricky.

The hatch scale usually should be a multiplier times the drawing scale factor, as described in the "Weigh your scales" section of Chapter 9. For example, the EARTH pattern (in the Other Predefined tab of the Hatch Pattern Palette dialog box) looks pretty good in a full scale (1 = 1) drawing with a hatch scale of 0.75. If you're adding hatching in the EARTH pattern to a 1" = 1'–0" detail (drawing scale factor equals 12), try using a hatch scale of 0.75 x 12, or 9.0. This multiplier and drawing scale factor approach ensures that hatching looks consistent (that is, the spaces between the lines are the same) at all scales when you plot.

So, assuming that you know your drawing's scale factor, the only complication is figuring out what the multiplier should be for a particular hatch pattern. In a more rational world, the multiplier would always be something sensible, like 1.0. Unfortunately, that's not the case for all hatch pattern definitions. Even worse, there's no way to predict before you use a hatch pattern for the first time what an appropriate multiplier might be. You have to use trial and error the first time, and then make a note of the hatch pattern and multiplier for future use.

The first time you use a hatch pattern definition, try 1.0 as the multiplier — in other words, assume that we live in a rational world and that 1.0 will work. Don't forget to multiply by the drawing scale factor. Preview the hatch and then adjust the hatch scale iteratively, previewing after each change. After you settle upon a suitable scale for the current drawing, you can calculate the corresponding multiplier (for future use) by dividing the hatch scale by the current drawing's scale factor.

User-defined patterns require that you enter an angle and spacing, rather than angle and scale. Spacing is expressed in drawing units, so if you set up your drawing for architectural units and you want user-defined hatch lines that are three inches apart, specify a spacing of 3.

Do fence me in: Defining hatch boundaries

After you specify the hatch pattern, angle, and scale you want to use, you define the boundary (or boundaries) into which you want to "pour" that hatch pattern in one of two ways: by picking points within the area(s) you want hatched or by selecting objects that surround those areas. The actual operation involved in using either of these options is confusing to most people, and you'll probably need a little practice before you get used to it. (Not that you're simply "most people" — after all, you *did* buy our book.)

The idea behind either definition option is simple, if applied to simple areas — that is, closed areas with no additional objects inside them. To hatch such a simple area, click the Pick Points button in the Boundary Hatch dialog box and then pick a point inside the boundary. Alternatively, you can click the Select Objects button and select one or more objects that form a fully closed boundary. AutoCAD LT then applies the hatch for you within the boundary — and you're done.

This simple hatching gets a little more complicated if you have one closed object inside another, as shown in Figure 14-4. If you pick points inside the *enclosing* (outermost) object but outside the *enclosed* (inner) object, AutoCAD LT hatches only the area between the boundaries of the two objects. If you pick some points inside each object, AutoCAD hatches the entire area within the outermost surrounding boundary, including the area within the inner boundary.

The results are reversed if you select objects instead of picking points. If you pick the outermost enclosing object(s) as well as the enclosed one(s), AutoCAD LT uses both boundaries and hatches only the area between them. Pick only the outermost object to hatch everything within it. In any event, after you finish picking or selecting, press Enter to return to the Boundary Hatch dialog box.

Fortunately, the AutoCAD LT hatch preview and a bit of experimentation can clarify all these potentially puzzling permutations.

Pick one point between two areas

Pick inside a simple area   Pick points inside both areas

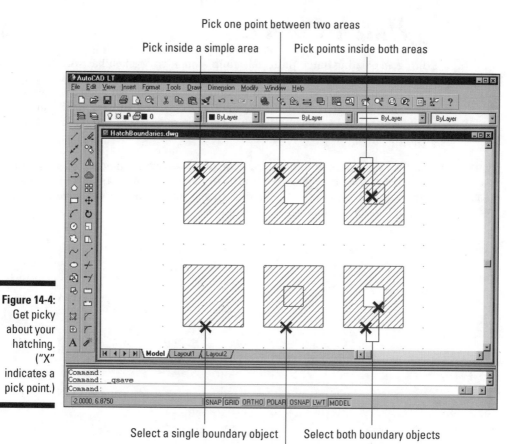

Figure 14-4:
Figure 14-4:
Get picky
about your
hatching.
("X"
indicates a
pick point.)

Select a single boundary object | Select both boundary objects

Select one boundary object with another nested inside

As we warned you earlier in this chapter, boundaries must be *completely* closed before AutoCAD LT will hatch them. That's one of the reasons you should employ the precision techniques that we harp on throughout this book whenever you draw or edit objects. If the lines surrounding your boundary don't meet *exactly,* or cross, AutoCAD LT will scold you with a Valid hatch boundary not found error message.

Editing Hatch Objects

Editing an existing hatch pattern is simple once you're familiar with the Boundary Hatch dialog box. Simply select the hatch object, right-click, and choose Hatch Edit from the cursor menu. AutoCAD LT will open the Hatch Edit dialog box and display the hatch object's current settings. Make any changes, use the Preview button to look them over them, and click OK to keep the changes.

Don't go overboard with hatching. The purpose of hatching is to clarify, not overwhelm, the other geometry in the drawing. If your plots look like a patchwork quilt of hatch patterns, it's time to simplify. Or better yet, save time by keeping hatching simple in the first place.

Chapter 15

The X-ref Files

A thing of beauty is a joy forever, as the old saying goes. And when you do manage to create a drawing in AutoCAD LT that's a thing of beauty, you'll want to be able to reuse it to make it a joy forever. That's where LT blocks and external references come in.

A *block* is a collection of objects grouped together to form a single object. A block can live within a specific drawing, or you can export a block so that multiple drawings can share access to it. At any time, you can *explode* the block — that is, divide it back into the objects that make it up — and edit the objects.

An *external reference* is like an industrial-strength block. An external reference is a pointer to a separate drawing outside the drawing you're working on. The referenced drawing appears on-screen and on plots as part of the original drawing, but it continues to "live" as a separate document on your hard disk. By using an external reference, you can include a whole separate drawing without increasing the size of the drawing you're working on. But you can't explode the external reference; you can only change its appearance by editing the externally referenced drawing. If you do edit the externally referenced drawing, the appearance of the drawing changes in all the other drawings that reference it, too.

Blocks and external references enable you to reuse your work and the work of others, giving you the potential to save tremendous amounts of time — or to cause tremendous problems if you change a file on which other peoples' drawings depend. Use these features when you can to save time, but do so in an organized and careful way so as to avoid problems.

The way in which you use blocks and especially xrefs will depend a lot on the profession and office in which you work. Some disciplines and companies use these drawing organization features heavily and in a highly organized way, while others don't. Ask your colleagues what the local customs are and follow them.

Rocking with Blocks

First, a little more block theory and then you can rock right into those blocks.

To use a block in a drawing, you need two things: a block *definition* and one or more block *inserts*. AutoCAD LT doesn't always make the distinction between these two things very clear, but you need to understand the difference to avoid terminal confusion about blocks. (Maybe we should call this syndrome *blockheadedness?*)

A block definition lives in an invisible area of your drawing file called the *block table*. Think of it as a table of graphical recipes for making different kinds of blocks. Thus, each block definition is like a recipe for making one kind of block. When you insert a block, as we describe later in this chapter, AutoCAD LT creates a special object called a *block insert*. The insert simply points to the recipe and tells LT, "Hey, draw me according to the instructions in this recipe!"

Thus, although a block looks at first like a collection of objects stored together and given a name, it's really a graphical recipe (the block definition), together with one or more pointers to that recipe (one or more block inserts). Each time you insert a particular block, you create another pointer to the same recipe.

The advantages of blocks include:

✔ **Grouping objects together when they belong together logically.** For instance, you can draw a screw using lines, polylines, and arcs, and then make a block definition out of all these objects. When you insert the screw block, AutoCAD LT treats it as a single object for purposes of copying, moving, and so on.

✔ **Efficiency of storage when you reuse the same block repeatedly.** For instance, if you insert the same screw block 15 times in a drawing, AutoCAD LT stores the detailed block definition only once. The 15 block inserts that point to the block definition are very compact, so they take up much less disk space than 15 copies of all the lines, polylines, and arcs would.

✔ **The ability to edit all instances of a symbol in a drawing simply by modifying a single block definition.** For instance, if you decide that your design requires a different kind of screw, you simply redefine the screw's block definition. With this new recipe, AutoCAD LT then replaces all 15 screws automatically. (Don't you wish you could've done that in your last home improvement project?)

Blocks are great for convenience and storage savings within a drawing. Blocks *aren't* as great for drawing elements used in multiple drawings, however, especially in a multiuser environment. That's because blocks, after they get into multiple drawings, stay in each drawing; a later modification to a block definition in one drawing does not automatically modify all the other drawings that use that block. So if you use a block with your company's logo in a number of drawings and then you decide to change the logo, you must make the change within each drawing that uses the block.

External references, however, do enable you to modify multiple drawings from the original referenced drawing. You can find out more about external references in the section "Going External," later in this chapter.

If all you need to do is make some objects into a group so that you can more easily select them for copying, moving, and so on, use the AutoCAD LT *group* feature. Choose Tools➪Group Manager to open the Group Manager dialog box. Then select some objects, click the Create Group button, and type a name for the group. Press Ctrl+H to toggle "group-ness" on or off. If you've toggled "group-ness" on, picking any object in a group selects all objects in the group. If you've toggled it off, picking an object selects only that object, even if it happens to be a member of a group.

Creating block definitions

To create a block definition from objects in the current drawing, use the Block Definition dialog box. Alternatively, you can create a block definition by inserting another AutoCAD DWG file into your current drawing. (See the next section for details.) The following steps show you how to create a block definition using the Block Definition dialog box:

1. **Click the Make Block button on the Draw toolbar.**

   The Block Definition dialog box appears (see Figure 15-1).

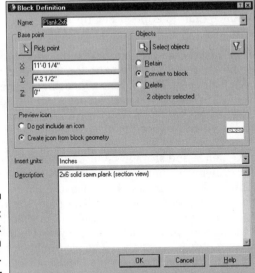

Figure 15-1:
The Block
Definition
dialog box.

Pay attention to which AutoCAD LT layers you use for creating objects that you'll later include in a block definition. In LT, layer 0 functions as a special construction layer for blocks. If you create geometry on layer 0 and include it in a block definition, when you insert the block, the geometry takes on the layer characteristics, such as color and linetype, of the layer on which the block is inserted. If you create a block from geometry drawn on any other layer, it always retains the color and linetype in effect when it was created. Think of block definition geometry created on layer 0 as a chameleon. (If you don't know what a chameleon is, ask a zoology teacher or a politician.)

2. **Type the block definition's name in the text entry box.**

   If you type the name of an existing block definition, AutoCAD LT replaces that block definition with the new group of objects you select. This process is called *block redefinition.* LT first warns you and then updates all instances of the block in the current drawing to match the changed block definition.

   To see a list of the names of all the current blocks in your drawing, drop down the Name list.

3. **Specify the base point, also known as the *insertion point,* of the block, using either of the following methods:**

   • Enter the coordinates of the insertion point at the X, Y, and Z text boxes.

   • Click the Pick Point button and then select a point on the screen.

The *base point* is the point on the block by which you insert it later, as we describe in the next section.

TIP

Try to use a consistent point on the group of objects for the base point, such as the lower-left corner, so that you always know what to expect when you insert the block.

4. Click the Select Objects button and then select the objects that you want as part of the block.

AutoCAD LT will use the selected objects to create a block definition. Figure 15-2 shows the base point and group of selected objects during the process of creating a new block definition.

5. Click a radio button to tell AutoCAD LT what to do with the objects used to define the block: retain them in place, convert them into a block instance, or delete them.

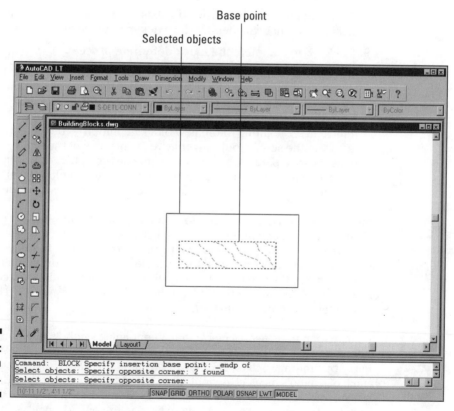

Base point

Selected objects

Figure 15-2:
Building a
block.

The default choice, Convert to Block, is usually the best, because it preserves the pointer to the block definition "recipe." If you choose Retain instead, AutoCAD LT leaves the objects on the screen, but as separate objects with no relationship to the block definition.

6. **Click a radio button to choose either Do Not Include an Icon or Create Icon from Block Geometry.**

   Go ahead and create the icon; it will help you and others find the right block to use later.

7. **Specify the Insert units to which the block will be scaled.**

   If and when the block is dragged from one drawing into another via the AutoCAD DesignCenter, the units you specify here and the units of the drawing you're dragging into will control the default insertion scale factor.

8. **Enter the block Description.**

   Now is the time to think like a database manager and enter a useful description that will identify the block to yourself and others.

9. **Click OK to complete the block definition process.**

   If you don't choose the Convert to Block or the Retain radio button, your objects disappear! AutoCAD LT has stored the block definition in the current drawing's block table, however, and the block is ready to use. If you choose the Convert to Block radio button (the default), LT creates a block insert pointing to the new block definition — the objects look the same on the screen, but now they're an instance of the block rather than existing as separate objects. If you choose the Retain radio button, the objects remain in place but aren't converted into a block insert — they stay individual objects with no connection to the new block definition.

You can include in a block definition a special kind of variable text object called an *attribute definition*. When you insert a block that contains one or more attribute definitions, AutoCAD LT prompts you to fill in values for the text fields. Attributes are useful for variable title block information (sheet number, sheet title, and so on) and symbols that contain different codes or call-outs. Look up "attribute data" on the Index tab in the AutoCAD LT online help system for more information.

You may want to develop a *block library* containing symbols that you use frequently. You can create a separate DWG file for each symbol (using WBLOCK or simply by drawing each one in a new drawing). Alternatively, you can store a bunch of symbols as block definitions in one drawing and use AutoCAD DesignCenter to import block definitions from this drawing when you need them. In either case, it's a good idea to keep your common symbol drawings in one or more specific folders that you set aside just for that purpose.

BLOCK and WBLOCK

The BLOCK command, which opens the Block Definition dialog box, is great for use within a drawing, but what if you want to use the block definition in multiple drawings? The easiest method is to use AutoCAD DesignCenter to copy a block definition from one drawing to another. (See the tip in the next section.)

Another method involves the WBLOCK and INSERT commands. We don't cover this method here, because it's less intuitive than using AutoCAD DesignCenter. But you may hear

AutoCAD drafters talk about *wblocking* part of a drawing. So that you can keep these block-y names straight:

✔ The BLOCK command creates a block definition from objects in the current drawing.

✔ The WBLOCK command creates a new DWG file from objects in the current drawing, or from a block definition in the current drawing.

Inserting blocks

AutoCAD LT provides a number of ways to insert a block, but the most commonly used and most flexible is the Insert dialog box. Here's the procedure for inserting a block:

1. **Click the Insert Block button on the Draw toolbar.**

   The Insert dialog box appears, as shown in Figure 15-3.

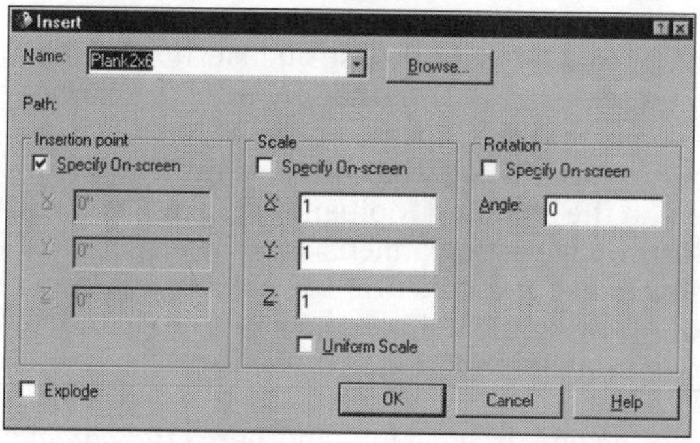

Figure 15-3:
The Insert dialog box.

2. **Enter the block definition name or external filename by using one of the following methods:**

   • Use the Name drop-down list to select from a list of block definitions in the current drawing.

   • Click the Browse button to select an external DWG file and have AutoCAD LT create a block definition from it.

You can use an external drawing to replace a block definition in your current drawing. If you click Browse and choose a file whose name matches the name of a block definition that's already in your drawing, AutoCAD LT warns you and then updates the block definition in your drawing with the current contents of the external file. This process is called *redefining* a block — it automatically updates all the block inserts that point to the block definition.

3. **Enter the insertion point, scale, and rotation angle of the block.**

   You can either click the Specify On-Screen check box in each area, to specify the parameters on-screen at the command prompt, or type the values you want in the Insertion Point, Scale, and Rotation text boxes.

   Check the Uniform Scale check box to constrain the X, Y, and Z scaling parameters to the same value.

4. **(Optional) Click the Explode check box if you want AutoCAD LT to create a copy of the individual objects in the block instead of a block insert that points to the block definition.**

5. **Click OK.**

6. **If you checked Specify On-Screen for the insertion point, scale, or rotation angle, answer the prompts on the command line to specify these parameters.**

After you've inserted a block, all the objects displayed in the block insert behave like a single object. When you select any object in the block insert, AutoCAD LT highlights all the objects in it.

Another way to insert a block is to drag a DWG file's name from Windows Explorer and drop it anywhere in the current drawing window. AutoCAD LT then provides a prompt that lets you choose an insertion point and optionally change the default scale factor and rotation angle. Similarly, you can drag a block definition's name from the Blocks section of AutoCAD DesignCenter and drop it into the current drawing window. Click the AutoCAD DesignCenter button on the Standard toolbar to display the DesignCenter window. See the "Borrowing existing dimension styles" section of Chapter 13 for an example of how to use DesignCenter to copy objects between drawings. Look up "AutoCAD DesignCenter" on the Index tab in the AutoCAD LT online help system for more information.

Be careful when inserting one drawing into another. If the *parent drawing* (the drawing into which you're inserting the other drawing) and the *child drawing* (the drawing being inserted) have different definitions for layers that share the same name, the objects in the child drawing will take on the layer characteristics of the parent drawing. For example, if you insert a drawing with lines on a layer called Walls that's blue and dashed into a drawing with a layer called Walls that's red and continuous, the inserted lines on the wall layer will turn red and continuous after they're inserted. The same rules apply to linetypes, text styles, dimension styles, and block definitions that are nested inside the drawing you're inserting.

Exploding blocks

All objects in each block insert act like a well-honed marching squadron: If you move or otherwise edit one object in the block insert, all objects move or change in the same way. Usually this cohesion is an advantage, but occasionally you need to break up the squadron in order to modify one object without affecting the others.

To *explode* a block insert into individual objects, click Explode (the firecracker button) on the Edit toolbar and then select the block insert. When you explode a block insert, AutoCAD LT replaces it with all the objects — lines, polylines, arcs, and so on — specified in the block definition. You can then edit the objects or perhaps use them to make more block definitions.

Don't make a habit of exploding blocks cavalierly, especially if you're working in someone else's drawing and aren't sure why the objects are organized as blocks. Most people use blocks for a reason, and if you go around exploding them left and right, you're likely to be treated the same way that anyone who blows up a lot of things gets treated.

Going External

In AutoCAD LT, an *xref*, or external reference, is not someone who used to be an official in a sporting contest. An xref is a reference to another, *external* file — one outside the current drawing — that you can make act as though it's part of your drawing. Technically, a reference is simply a pointer from one file to another. The xref is the actual pointer, but the combination of the pointer and the external file often is called the xref.

Drawings that you include as xrefs in other drawings often are referred to as *child* drawings. Drawings that contain pointers to the child drawings are called *parent* drawings.

Xrefs have a big advantage over blocks: If you change a child drawing, AutoCAD LT automatically loads the change into all the parent drawings that reference the child drawing.

AutoCAD LT loads all xrefs into the parent drawing each time the parent drawing is opened. If the child drawing has been changed, LT automatically incorporates those changes into the parent drawing.

Another advantage of xrefs over blocks is that their contents aren't stored in your drawing even once. The disk storage space taken up by the original drawing (that is, the xref) isn't duplicated, no matter how many parent drawings reference it. This characteristic makes xrefs much more efficient than blocks for larger drawings that are reused several times.

But you can always buy more hard disk space, so the storage issue is not crucial. The key benefit of xrefs is that they enable you to leverage your own or someone else's work easily and transparently, thereby increasing both consistency and productivity.

The automatic update feature of xrefs is a big advantage only if you're organized about how you use xrefs. Suppose that an architect creates a plan drawing showing a building's walls and other major features that are common to the architectural, structural, plumbing, and electrical plan drawings. The architect then tells the structural, plumbing, and electrical drafters to xref this "background" plan into their drawings, so that everyone is working from a consistent and reusable set of common plan elements. If the architect decides to revise the wall locations and updates the xrefed drawing, everyone will see the current wall configuration and be able to change their drawings. But if the architect absent-mindedly adds architecture-specific objects, such as toilets and furniture, to the xrefed drawing or shifts all the objects with respect to 0,0, then everyone else will have problems. If different people in your office share xrefs, you should have a protocol for who is allowed to modify which file when, and what sort of notification needs to take place after a shared xref is modified.

Becoming attached to your xrefs

Attaching an external reference is easy. Just use the following steps:

1. **Choose Insert⇨Xref Manager from the menu bar to start the XREF command.**

   The Xref Manager dialog box appears (see Figure 15-4).

2. **Click Attach.**

   The Select Reference File dialog box appears.

3. **Browse to find the file you want to attach, select it, and then click Open.**

   The External Reference dialog box appears.

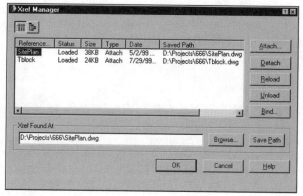

4. Specify the parameters for the xref in the dialog box.

Parameters include the insertion point, scaling factors, and rotation angle. You can set these parameters in the dialog box or specify them on-screen, just as you can do when inserting a block, as described earlier in this chapter.

You can choose the Attachment or Overlay radio button to tell AutoCAD LT how to handle the xref. The choice matters only if you create a drawing that uses xrefs, and then your drawing is in turn used as an xref. Attachment is the default choice, and it means that the xrefed file will always be included with your drawing when someone else uses it as an xref. Overlay, the other choice, means that you see the xrefed drawing, but someone who xrefs your drawing won't see the overlaid file. By choosing Overlay, you can xref in a map, for instance, to your drawing of a house, but not have the map show up when someone else xrefs your house drawing. (That person can xref the map, if need be.)

5. Click OK.

The externally referenced file appears in your drawing.

Layer-palooza

When you attach or overlay an xref, AutoCAD LT adds new layers to your current drawing that correspond to the layers in the xrefed DWG file. The new layers are assigned names that combine the drawing name and layer name; for instance, if you xref in layers from the drawing MYSCREW.DWG that have the names GEOMETRY, TEXT, and so on, the xrefed layers will be named MYSCREW|GEOMETRY, MYSCREW|TEXT, and so on. By creating separate layers corresponding to each layer in the xrefed file, LT eliminates the potential problem we warned you about with blocks when layers have the same name but different color or linetype in the two drawings.

AutoCAD LT also creates new linetypes, text styles, dimension styles, and block definitions for each of these items in the xrefed file — for example, MYSCREW I DASHED, MYSCREW I NOTES, MYSCREW I A-DIMS, and MYSCREW I LOGO.

Creating an external reference file

To create a file that you can use as an external reference, just create a drawing and save it (or use the WBLOCK command to create a new DWG from geometry in the current drawing). That's it. You can then start up a new drawing and create an external reference to the previous one. The xrefed drawing appears in your parent drawing as a single object, like a block insert. In other words, if you click any object in the xref, AutoCAD LT selects the entire xref. You can measure or object snap to the xrefed geometry, but you can't modify or delete individual objects in the xref — you must open the xref drawing in order to edit its geometry.

Managing xrefs

The Xref Manager dialog box includes many more options for managing xrefs after you attach them. Important dialog box options include:

- ✔ **List of external references:** You can change between a List and a Tree view of your drawing's external references just by clicking the appropriate button at the top of the dialog box. You also can resize the columns by dragging the column dividers or re-sort the list by clicking the column header names, just as in other Windows dialog boxes.

- ✔ **Detach:** Completely removes the reference to the external file from your drawing.

- ✔ **Reload:** Causes AutoCAD LT to re-read the xrefed DWG file from the disk and update your drawing with its latest contents. This feature is handy when you share xrefs on a network and someone has just made changes to a drawing that you've xrefed.

- ✔ **Unload:** Makes the xref disappear from the on-screen display of your drawing and from any plots you do of it, but retains the pointer and attachment information. Use the Reload button to redisplay an unloaded xref.

- ✔ **Bind:** Converts the xref into your drawing as a block.

None of these options affects the xrefed drawing itself; it continues to exist as a separate DWG file. If you need to delete or move the DWG file that the xref refers to, do so quickly, before you forget!

The fact that the xrefed drawing is a separate file is a potential source of problems when you send your drawing to someone else; that someone else needs *all* the files that your drawing depends on, or it will be useless to the receiving party. Make sure to include xrefed files in the "package" with your drawing. See the "Package and go" section of Chapter 8 for a procedure.

 When you attach an xref, AutoCAD LT normally stores the xref's path along with the filename (as you can see in the Saved Path column of the Xref Manager dialog box). If the child and parent drawing are in different folders, AutoCAD LT needs the path information in order to locate the xrefs the next time you load the parent drawing. If you send the drawings to other people who don't use exactly the same drive letters and folder structure as you did, AutoCAD or LT probably won't be able to locate the xrefs on their systems. You can avoid this problem by always keeping parent and child drawings in the same folder.

 Don't panic if you open a drawing and find that only part of an xref appears. AutoCAD (but not AutoCAD LT) includes an additional xref feature called *xref clipping.* The AutoCAD XCLIP command enables users to "clip" an externally referenced file so that only part of it appears in the parent drawing. AutoCAD LT doesn't include the XCLIP command, but if you open a drawing containing an xref that was clipped in AutoCAD, the clipped view will be preserved.

 AutoCAD (but not AutoCAD LT) includes another xref-like feature: the ability to attach *raster,* or bit-mapped, images to drawings. This feature is useful for adding a raster logo to a drawing title block or placing a photographed map or scene "behind" a drawing. AutoCAD LT can open, view, and plot drawings containing raster images that an AutoCAD user has attached, but LT can't do the attaching. So if you need a raster image in your drawing, ask an AutoCAD user to place it there for you.

Blocks, Xrefs, and Drawing Organization

Both blocks and xrefs are useful for organizing sets of drawings so that they take advantage of repeated elements and so that you can update those repeated elements quickly and completely. It's not always clear, though, when to use blocks and when to use xrefs.

Common applications for xrefs include:

- The parts of a title block that are the same on all sheets in a project.

- Reference elements that need to appear in multiple drawings (for example, wall outlines, site topography, column grids).

- Assemblies that are repeated in one or more drawings, especially if the assemblies are likely to change together (for example, repeated framing assemblies, bathroom layouts, modular furniture layouts).

✔ Pasting up several drawings (for example, details or a couple of plans) onto one plot sheet.

✔ Temporarily attaching a background drawing for reference or "tracing" purposes.

On the other hand, blocks remain useful in simpler circumstances. Remember that every xref requires keeping track of a separate file. Some situations in which you might stick with a block are

✔ Components that aren't likely to change.

✔ Small components.

✔ A simple assembly that's used repeatedly, but in only one drawing. (You can easily update a block in one drawing by inserting it in a blank area, exploding and editing it, and then redefining it with the BLOCK command.)

✔ Any time you want to include *attributes* (that is, variable text fields) that you can fill in each time you insert. Blocks let you include attribute definitions, while xrefs don't.

It's important that everyone in a company or workgroup be reasonably consistent about whether, when, and how to use blocks and xrefs. Check with your coworkers to see whether guidelines exist for using blocks and xrefs in your office. If so, follow them, and if not, suggest strongly that it would be a good idea to develop some guidelines.

Part IV
The Part of Tens

The 5th Wave — By Rich Tennant

GUS & LILY'S DOG GROOMING
NOW USING AutoCAD IT Software

In this part . . .

"Tens" sounds a lot like "tense," and tense is how AutoCAD LT may make you feel sometimes. But never fear — help is on the way! This Part of Tens features two lists that help you do the right thing and feel more comfortable with AutoCAD LT. The first list tells you how to avoid harming — and maybe even more importantly, how to improve — drawings when you work on them. The second list points you to a host of resources that you can use to extend your knowledge of the big, wide CAD world.

Chapter 16

Ten Ways to Do No Harm

*H*ippocrates of Greece is famous for many things, not least of which is the Hippocratic Oath sworn by doctors. It begins "First, do no harm." This is not a bad approach to take when editing existing drawings with AutoCAD LT; although you'll need several days to accomplish several days of productive work, you can accidentally undo days or weeks of work by yourself and others in minutes. (Of course, you also can *purposefully* undo days or weeks of work by yourself and others in minutes, but we can't give much advice to stop you if you want to do that!)

Follow these guidelines to avoid doing harm to the hard work of others and the productive potential of yourself.

Be Precise

Throughout this book, we remind you that using precision techniques such as snap, object snaps, and specific, typed-in coordinates is a fundamental part of good CAD practice. Don't try to use AutoCAD LT like an illustration program, in which you "eyeball" locations and distances. Use one of the many LT precision techniques *every* time you specify a point or distance.

Control Properties by Layer

As we describe in the "Objects Own Properties" section of Chapter 10, AutoCAD LT gives you two different ways of controlling object properties such as color, linetype, and lineweight: by layer and by object. Unless you have a *really* good reason to assign properties by object — such as instructions from your company's CAD manager or client — use the by-layer method: Assign colors, linetypes, and lineweights to layers, and let objects inherit these properties from the layer on which the objects reside. Don't assign explicit color, linetype, or lineweight to objects.

Work from Copies of Drawings

If you have any doubt at all about whether you should be editing the original version of a drawing, make a copy and do your work in the copy. Be sure to save your copy someplace "out of the way" so you don't confuse it with the latest and greatest version of your drawing.

Making lots of copies of the same drawing file as you work on it does have a downside: You or someone else might have trouble figuring out which is the "right" version. ("Hmm, I wonder whether House37.dwg or HouseNew.dwg is correct?") Multiple copies increase the odds that different people — or even the same absent-minded person — will unknowingly make changes to different versions. If you're going to create copies of drawings, you need to have a naming and filing scheme that keeps things straight. If you work on drawings with others, make sure that everyone understands the scheme and uses it consistently. Your office may already have guidelines in place.

Freeze Instead of Erase

It's common to start with an existing drawing from another discipline when you want to add, say, an electrical system to a floor plan. But if you remove the landscaping around a building because you don't need it for the wiring, you may cause a great deal of rework when the landscaping information is needed again. And what if the person who did the landscaping work has, in the meantime, decided to leaf? (Sorry. . .)

Unless you know for sure that objects are no longer needed, use the AutoCAD LT Freeze or Off layer setting to make objects invisible without completely obliterating them. You'll find these settings in the Layer Properties Manager dialog box, as described in the "Objects Own Properties" section of Chapter 10.

Know Your Drawing Scale Factor

The "Weigh your scales" section in Chapter 9 describes the importance of choosing an appropriate drawing scale factor when you set up a drawing. It's equally important to know the drawing scale factor of any drawing that you're working on — whether you set it up or not. You'll need this number in order to calculate lots of scale-dependent objects, such as text, dimensions, and hatching. The "Scaling: To fit or not to fit?" section in Chapter 4 includes tips for figuring out the drawing scale factor of an existing drawing.

Don't Cram Your Geometry

It's okay that you used to cram for your geometry test, but don't cram geometry, dimensions, text, or anything (and everything) else into your drawings. There's a real temptation to put a lots of stuff into every square inch of your drawing, using AutoCAD LT's flexible panning and zooming capabilities to really work over all the available space. Unfortunately, the resulting drawing can be extremely hard to update and to use when you finally print it.

Instead of cramming stuff onto the sheet, use white (empty) space to surround areas of dense geometry. Put details on separate sheets. Attach a page of notes instead of putting a ton of text onto your drawing. It's easier to manage a reasonable number of drawings with less on them than to have two or three killer sheets crammed with every drawing and every fact regarding a project.

Explode with Care

The EXPLODE command makes it easy to explode polylines (Chapter 10), dimensions (Chapter 13), hatches (Chapter 14), and block inserts (Chapter 15) into their constituent objects. The only problem is that someone probably grouped those objects together for a reason. So until you understand that reason and know why it no longer applies, leave the dynamite alone.

Use Industry Standards

Take advantage of resources and approaches that are standard for the discipline in which you work. Become knowledgeable about industry standards for how work is done and how drawings are put together in your discipline. Follow these standards throughout your office and ask other companies that you work with to follow them as well. By following standards consistently, you can apply your creativity, expertise, and energy to the interesting and novel parts of the task at hand rather than arguing about which hatching patterns to use. And if you find that things are a mess in your company because no one else pays much attention to industry standards, well, knowing those standards makes you very employable as well.

Using Office Standards

Although industry standards may save you time and money, office standards help even more. That's because you can standardize a great many more things, from layer names (which may be partly covered already by industry standards in your discipline) right down to processes such as deciding what scale to use and how and when to use color in your company's drawings. Every time you make a big decision on a drawing, consider whether that decision can contribute to setting a standard for some or all of the drawings created in your company.

Recycling: Don't Refuse to Re-Use

Aretha Franklin once sang, "Thank you, I'll do it myself." This is a typical and very human attitude, but one you usually should avoid in your CAD work. Using an existing drawing as a starting point is one form of re-use. Blocks and xrefs, described in Chapter 15, are another. When you sit down to draw, take a minute to consider which elements of your drawing are repeated from other drawings, or within the drawing. Start grabbing pieces from elsewhere and specifying block definitions. You may find yourself 80 percent done in an hour or two.

On the other hand, know when to start over, too. Recycling is a great idea unless what you're recycling is garbage! If that earlier drawing wasn't done right or doesn't quite fit your current situation, you'll get better results and may even save time by starting over. Gradually build up a pool of well-done drawings from which you can borrow with confidence.

Chapter 17

Ten Great AutoCAD LT Resources

● ●

In This Chapter

▶ Going online for help

▶ Checking out resources on the World Wide Web

▶ Browsing the Autodesk Web site and newsgroups

▶ Thumbing through *CADALYST* and *CADENCE* magazines

▶ Exploring the AutoCAD Resource Guide

▶ Getting involved with local users' groups

▶ Joining AUGI

▶ Training at the AutoCAD Training Centers

▶ Calling Autodesk

▶ Keeping in touch with your dealer

● ●

*H*ere, in no particular order, are ten handy AutoCAD LT resources for you to use. Try them all; it's important to develop sources of support for those times when you have a question you just can't otherwise find the answer to (or a wiseacre remark about AutoCAD LT that you just have to tell someone).

Using AutoCAD resources in LT

Because AutoCAD LT 2000 is identical to "full" AutoCAD 2000 in so many respects, most of the resources for full AutoCAD will be helpful to you, the LT user, as well. In fact, you'll find that most resources are aimed at users of AutoCAD, because they're bigger spenders and many of them have been using CAD longer. Don't be shy about tapping into these resources for LT's bigger brother — just ignore the relatively few AutoCAD-specific parts in those resources.

Add-on programs, 3D model creation, and programming using tools such as AutoLISP are the main things in "full" AutoCAD but not in LT. In fact, some AutoCAD-based advice is actually more likely to work as is in LT, because LT doesn't run most AutoCAD add-on programs that can muddy the waters by requiring that you modify certain procedures or steps. In that way, LT is "purer" than full AutoCAD (but thereby less useful in some cases as well).

In using the resources in this chapter, filter out the things that don't work in LT and use all the rest. Don't be afraid to experiment in LT — most AutoCAD information will work fine.

Online Help

The most overlooked resource for help with your AutoCAD LT questions is the online help and documentation. Hundreds and hundreds of pages of AutoCAD help and information are part of the LT program. You get more on the Learning Assistance CD-ROM that comes free with AutoCAD LT. There's even a Support Assistance program available on the LT Help menu. It contains a wide variety of support information, including explanations of error messages and a library of technical documents. You can access even more information on the Web: Choose Help⇔Autodesk on the Web to get started finding it. Look in the online help first!

The World Wide Web

The World Wide Web is a hot topic of conversation, well, worldwide, and it's becoming a great resource for CAD use (and has now overtaken CompuServe, which had long been the top stop online for AutoCAD users). You really need Web access to be an effective CAD user — you'll miss out on too many support and information resources if you don't have it. Almost all the information on the Web is for "full" AutoCAD; you'll have to filter out parts that don't apply to LT, as described earlier in this chapter.

Autodesk Web Site and Newsgroups

The Autodesk Web site (www.autodesk.com) is a good source of product information, technical assistance, tips, software patches, and other official AutoCAD LT resources. The main AutoCAD LT page's address is www.autodesk.com/products/acadlt/index1.htm.

One of the better resources on the Autodesk Web site is the collection of Autodesk-supported AutoCAD LT newsgroups, which you'll find at www.autodesk.com/support/discsgrp/acadlt.htm. For AutoCAD information, much of which is applicable to AutoCAD LT as well, use www.autodesk.com/support/discsgrp/acad.htm.

The AutoCAD LT 2000 newsgroup's address is news://adesknews.autodesk. com/autodesk.autocadlt.2000general. Here you can post questions or comments, get feedback from Autodesk employees and other LT users, and generally stay abreast of tips, tricks, techniques, bugs, and other LT information.

CADALYST and CADENCE Magazines

Although AutoCAD is no doubt responsible for billions of dollars in sales of PC hardware and related software, most of the computer press tends to ignore AutoCAD. *CADALYST* and *CADENCE* are the leading magazines devoted exclusively to CAD, with an ongoing focus on AutoCAD and other Autodesk products, but covering other CAD programs as well. Both magazines provide tips and tricks, tutorials, technical columns, and hardware and software reviews, all specifically for CAD users. (There's an occasional article specifically about LT as well.)

To subscribe to *CADALYST,* call 800–949–6525. To subscribe to *CADENCE,* call 800–486–4995.

The *CADALYST* Web site (www.cadonline.com/) contains a number of CAD management columns by one of the authors of this book (look in the Solutions section under CAD Management). The *CADENCE* magazine Web site is at www.cadence-mag.com.

AutoCAD Resource Guide

This handy little manual includes an overview of the different AutoCAD versions and supporting computer platforms, third-party add-on applications and their developers, peripheral devices, books and training products, a directory of users' groups, and a directory of Autodesk Training Centers (ATCs). Many of the software products listed are for full AutoCAD only, but most of the other resources apply at least in part to LT.

The book also contains a CD-ROM version with additional product information, device drivers, and more. (The information is also available on the Autodesk Web site, but having the printed version handy when you need it is nice.) To get the AutoCAD Resource Guide in online form, go to the Autodesk Resource Guide Web site at www.argonline.com. You can order the printed version from the Autodesk Resource Guide online site or call Autodesk customer information at 800-964-6432.

Local Users' Groups

Local users' groups are the heart and soul of the AutoCAD community. One of the authors has been co-chairman of the San Francisco AutoCAD Users Group; the other has attended several and remembers a meeting of the Silicon Valley AutoCAD Power Users group, in San Jose, California, as the biggest and best-organized user's group meeting he has ever attended. And *CADALYST* magazine, described earlier in this chapter, started out as the newsletter of the Vancouver, British Columbia AutoCAD Users Group. We have found that in the CAD world, even more than in other areas of personal computer hardware and software, users' groups are a key resource.

Find out where the users' group nearest you meets and go to a few meetings. Users' groups are almost always looking for new members and will be glad to have you, LT or no. Call Autodesk at 800–964–6432 or look in the AutoCAD Resource Guide to locate the group nearest you.

AUGI

No, "AUGI" isn't what you yell after a basketball hits you in the wrong spot. The Autodesk User Group International is administered by Autodesk, but it's a real users' group made up of real users, dealers, and other concerned individuals. AUGI sponsors an annual learning conference (Autodesk University), a newsletter, software, and more. To join, see its Web site at www.augi.com or call the User Group Hotline at 415–507–6565.

AutoCAD Training Centers

AutoCAD Training Centers, or ATCs, are Autodesk-authorized deliverers of AutoCAD training. Courses are expensive, but then, so is ignorance. Check the AutoCAD Resource Guide, call Autodesk, or check out the Autodesk Web site for the number of the ATC nearest you. Training from AutoCAD dealers, consultants, or local community colleges are other options. Most training is for full AutoCAD rather than LT, so make sure that the curriculum doesn't stray too far into AutoCAD-only features.

Autodesk

In our experience, Autodesk is more accessible than most big companies. Its main numbers are 415-507-5000 and 800-964-6432. Call and tell someone there what you're looking for; you're pretty likely to reach a friendly and helpful reception person who connects you to another friendly and helpful person who gives you the information you need or tells you where to find it.

The AutoCAD Dealer

The first and foremost line of support for AutoCAD users is the dealer from whom they bought AutoCAD. For LT, it's a little different — support resources for you depend on where you got the program. If you did buy it from a dealer, that dealer may be able to help you with questions or problems.

Dealer support policies and areas of expertise differ, but the dealer who is your group's main source for AutoCAD and, possibly, AutoCAD LT as well, may be your best starting point for AutoCAD and AutoCAD LT support and information.

If you're using AutoCAD LT within a multiuser, networked setup, find out whether someone in your company has been designated as the first line of defense for technical support and other information. Contact that person first with your questions.

Part V

Appendix

The 5th Wave   By Rich Tennant

"WE SHOULD HAVE THIS FIXED IN VERSION 2."

In this part . . .

In your body, an appendix is something that's unnecessary at best and hazardous to your health at worst. The appendix in this book, however, is meant to be more helpful — and certainly less harmful — than that other kind. AutoCAD LT has a vocabulary all its own, and the glossary in the appendix should help you cross the bridge from English to the language of CAD.

Appendix

Glossary of AutoCAD LT Terms

*T*he definitions that appear in this appendix are ours only; they are informal and describe the terms in the way that this book uses them. For more complete and general definitions, see the AutoCAD LT online or printed documentation — especially the glossary at the end of the AutoCAD LT 2000 *Getting Started Guide.*

ANSI: American National Standards Institute, a leading standards body.

AUGI: Autodesk User Group International, the worldwide user group for AutoCAD and other programs from Autodesk.

AutoCAD DesignCenter: That's not a typo; Autodesk really has munged "Design" and "Center," two perfectly respectable words that do plenty of heavy lifting in English, into a single made-up word. (Possibly so that Autodesk can trademark it.) AutoCAD DesignCenter lists components within a drawing, such as blocks, xrefs, linetypes, text styles, and layers, so that you can import them into other drawings.

A special circle of linguistic Hell may be reserved for the inventor and the users of *intercaps,* capital letters stuck in the middle of words such as AutoCAD and DesignCenter. For some reason, the generally sensible computer industry has made a habit of using intercaps in various names. Use them at your own risk.

bounding rectangle, bounding window: A rectangle surrounding objects. When you select objects with a bounding window, AutoCAD LT includes only objects that are fully enclosed within the window. See also ***crossing window.***

CAD: Computer-Aided Drafting or Design. Also known as CADD, or Computer-Aided Design and Drafting. The term CAD is now used to describe activities that include computer-aided design, computer-aided drafting, or both.

chamfer: A straight line that connects two other lines short of the point where they would intersect.

command line: A specific area of the AutoCAD LT screen, usually at the bottom, in which LT prompts you for the information it needs, and you enter commands and options. Many menu choices in AutoCAD LT also cause commands to appear on the command line.

command-first editing: Modifying the current drawing by entering a command and then selecting the objects that the command affects. The opposite of *selection-first editing.* See also ***Noun/Verb Selection.***

coordinate entry: Locating a point in the drawing by entering numbers on the command line that represent the point's coordinates. See also ***cursor coordinates.***

crossing window: A selection window that includes any objects it encloses as well as any objects that cross the window's boundaries. See also ***bounding window.***

cursor coordinates: The location of the cursor as represented by its horizontal, or X, coordinate and its vertical, or Y, coordinate.

dimension: An AutoCAD LT object, consisting of lines, numbers, and additional symbols and text, used to indicate the distance between two points.

dimension line: The line that shows the extent of a dimension.

dimension scale factor: The number by which the size of the text and arrowheads in a dimension are scaled in order for them to appear correctly in the final printout of a drawing. You usually should set the dimension scale factor to equal the drawing scale factor. See ***drawing scale factor.***

dimension text: The text that denotes the actual measurement of a dimension (for example, length or angle).

direct distance entry: An efficient way of picking a point that lies a particular direction and distance from the previous point. You simply point the cursor in the desired direction (usually with ortho mode turned on), type a distance at the command line, and press Enter.

direct manipulation: Entering or modifying data by using the mouse to move or change an on-screen representation. Clicking an AutoCAD LT line and then stretching it by moving one of its endpoint grips, for example, is direct manipulation.

displacement: Fancy word for the X and Y distance between two points.

donut: AutoCAD LT object consisting of two concentric circles with the space between them filled in (the favorite concentric-circle pastry of police officers).

Draw toolbar: A toolbar that enables you to start commonly used drawing commands quickly. Usually found on the far left side of the drawing area.

drawing area: The part of the AutoCAD LT screen on which you can actually draw. It's an all-too-small area wedged between the menus, toolbars, and command line.

drawing scale: A relationship expressed in the form 1:10 or ¼ = 1'–0" that tells how lengths on the plotted drawing correspond to lengths of real objects that the drawing represents.

drawing scale factor: A multiplier that represents the drawing scale (see *drawing scale*). You use this multiplier to determine many important AutoCAD LT settings for each drawing, including text height, dimension scale factor, hatch scales, and linetype scale.

extension line: In dimensioning, a line connecting one end of the dimension line to one end of the object being dimensioned.

geometry: The drawn objects that make up a drawing, not including additional elements such as dimensions and text.

grid, grid mode: A grid is a visible array of dots used to indicate distances on-screen. The grid is intended to serve as a kind of flexible graph paper in which the user can, at any time, redefine the size of the grid. Grid mode is either on (that is, grid dots displayed) or off (grid dots not displayed). AutoCAD LT never plots the grid — it's for display purposes only.

grid interval: The distance between grid points. See also *grid, grid mode.*

grip editing: Editing an object by dragging one of the handles, or grips, that appear on an object after you select it. See also *grips — hot, warm, cold.*

grips — hot, warm, cold: A hot grip is the grip that you can directly manipulate; it appears on-screen in red. A warm grip is any other grip on a currently selected object. A cold grip is a grip on an unselected object. Warm and cold grips appear on-screen in blue.

hatch, boundary hatch, associative boundary hatch: A hatch is a pattern placed in the interior of an area enclosed by objects. A boundary hatch is a hatch that is begun by calculating the boundary from among the objects surrounding an empty space. An associative boundary hatch is a hatch that updates automatically if you modify one or more of the objects that make up its boundary.

ISO: International Standards Organization, a leading standards body.

layer: An organizational tool for grouping objects that are associated for purposes of displaying, plotting, editing, and controlling properties (color, linetype, lineweight, and plot style).

layout: A particular paper space arrangement. AutoCAD LT 2000 drawings can have more than one paper space layout. See also *paper space.*

leader: A pointer that connects a dimension or note to an object.

linetype: The pattern of dashes, dots, and spaces used to display certain objects.

model space: The space in which you create your drawing geometry — the AutoCAD LT objects representing the real-world thing that you're drawing. See also *paper space.*

Modify toolbar: A toolbar that enables you to start commonly used editing commands quickly. Usually found on the left side of the drawing area, just inside the Draw toolbar.

named objects: Nongraphical elements such as layers, block definitions, linetypes, text styles, and dimension styles that live in each drawing and provide properties and other characteristics of graphical objects.

Noun/Verb Selection: An option that allows most commands to operate on an existing selection set. With Noun/Verb Selection turned off, the commands you enter ignore any existing selection set, and you must select one or more objects after entering the command. See also *selection-first editing.*

object: A single item that you can select and edit separately. In older versions of AutoCAD, objects were called *entities.*

Object Properties toolbar: A toolbar that enables you to view and specify object properties, such as layer and linetype, with little or no keyboard entry.

object snap: Makes certain points on an object act like magnets so that clicking near a point is the same as clicking the point itself.

ortho, ortho mode: A setting that forces lines to be drawn horizontally or vertically only.

pan: Panning is moving the drawing around (without changing the zoom factor) so that a different part of the drawing appears on-screen in the current viewport.

paper space: The space in which you compose a plotted view of your drawing, complete with title block. Paper space also can present different views and plotting styles of the same drawing. See also *layout* and *model space.*

polygon: What your 3-year-old says when your parrot dies. (Groan!) Seriously, any closed shape made up of three or more line segments. Triangles, rectangles, pentagons, hexagons, and other multisided shapes are examples of polygons.

polyline: A single object made up of multiple line or arc segments.

raster image: An image made up of a bunch of dots, as opposed to the typical CAD *vector* image, which is made up of a bunch of lines. A scanned photograph is an example of a raster image.

real-time pan and zoom: A way of panning and zooming in AutoCAD LT whereby your view of the drawing changes smoothly as you drag the mouse around in the drawing area.

redraw: Clears the screen and quickly redisplays all objects in the drawing.

regeneration (REGEN): Clears the screen and uses the drawing database to recalculate and then redisplay all objects in the drawing. A *regen,* as it is referred to, can take from a fraction of a second on simple drawings to many minutes on complex drawings.

selection set: A set, or group, of objects that you have selected.

selection settings: Options that affect how selections are made and treated, such as Press and Drag and Noun/Verb Selection.

selection window: A window used to create a selection. Bounding windows and crossing windows are the types of windows used to create a selection. See also *bounding window* and *crossing window.*

selection-first editing: Editing by first creating a selection and then entering a command that affects the selected objects. Opposite of *command-first editing.*

snap, snap mode: A mode that causes the cursor to be attracted to points on-screen that are a specified distance apart.

snap grid: If snap mode is on, the snap grid is the array of imaginary points that the cursor jumps to, based on the *snap interval.*

snap interval: The distance between snap points if snap mode is on.

solid fill: Your trustworthy friend, Philip. Also, a type of hatch pattern that fills an area with a color.

spline: A flexible type of curve that has a shape defined by control points.

Standard toolbar: A toolbar with icons for commonly used functions such as opening a file. Usually found near the top of the screen, between the menu bar and the Object Properties toolbar.

status bar: A toolbar, always positioned at the bottom of the screen, that displays information about the current AutoCAD LT session, such as the current coordinates of the cursor and whether ortho mode is in effect. You can also change many options (such as model space versus paper space) by clicking or right-clicking the status bar's icons.

system variable: A setting that controls the way a particular aspect of AutoCAD LT works. You can change system variables by typing their names at the command line, or, less obtusely, by choosing various dialog box options that are linked to the system variables.

tangent: A tangent point on a circle is the only point at which a line at a specific angle to and direction from the circle can touch the circle.

template drawing: An AutoCAD drawing that serves as a starting point for new drawings. When you create a new drawing from a template drawing, AutoCAD LT creates a new drawing using the contents and settings of the template file.

third-party application: A program that works with or within AutoCAD. Most third-party applications don't work with AutoCAD LT, because they require the customization interfaces that LT lacks.

title bar: The strip across the top of the program window that displays the name of the program and the currently active drawing if it is maximized.

title block: An area on a drawing that is set aside for descriptive information about the drawing, such as the company name, project name, drafter's name, and so on.

ToolTip or tooltip: A descriptive word or phrase that appears on-screen if you hold the cursor over an icon for a brief period of time.

TrueType fonts: A kind of font that is standard within Microsoft Windows. TrueType fonts first appeared in AutoCAD Release 13 and are also supported, with better performance, in AutoCAD 2000 and LT 2000.

viewport: A window that displays part of a drawing.

zoom: Zooming is moving the viewpoint closer to or farther from the drawing so that more or less of the drawing appears on-screen.

Index

WWW.DUMMIES.COM

Discover Dummies Online!

The Dummies Web Site is your fun and friendly online resource for the latest information about *For Dummies*® books and your favorite topics. The Web site is the place to communicate with us, exchange ideas with other *For Dummies* readers, chat with authors, and have fun!

Ten Fun and Useful Things You Can Do at www.dummies.com

1. Win free *For Dummies* books and more!
2. Register your book and be entered in a prize drawing.
3. Meet your favorite authors through the IDG Books Worldwide Author Chat Series.
4. Exchange helpful information with other *For Dummies* readers.
5. Discover other great *For Dummies* books you must have!
6. Purchase Dummieswear® exclusively from our Web site.
7. Buy *For Dummies* books online.
8. Talk to us. Make comments, ask questions, get answers!
9. Download free software.
10. Find additional useful resources from authors.

Link directly to these ten fun and useful things at
http://www.dummies.com/10useful

For other technology titles from IDG Books Worldwide, go to
www.idgbooks.com

Not on the Web yet? It's easy to get started with *Dummies 101*®: *The Internet For Windows*® *98* or *The Internet For Dummies*® at local retailers everywhere.

Find other *For Dummies* books on these topics:

Business • Career • Databases • Food & Beverage • Games • Gardening • Graphics • Hardware
Health & Fitness • Internet and the World Wide Web • Networking • Office Suites
Operating Systems • Personal Finance • Pets • Programming • Recreation • Sports
Spreadsheets • Teacher Resources • Test Prep • Word Processing

IDG BOOKS WORLDWIDE BOOK REGISTRATION

Register This Book and Win!

We want to hear from you!

Visit **http://my2cents.dummies.com** to register this book and tell us how you liked it!

- ✔ Get entered in our monthly prize giveaway.

- ✔ Give us feedback about this book — tell us what you like best, what you like least, or maybe what you'd like to ask the author and us to change!

- ✔ Let us know any other *For Dummies*® topics that interest you.

Your feedback helps us determine what books to publish, tells us what coverage to add as we revise our books, and lets us know whether we're meeting your needs as a *For Dummies* reader. You're our most valuable resource, and what you have to say is important to us!

Not on the Web yet? It's easy to get started with *Dummies 101*®: *The Internet For Windows*® *98* or *The Internet For Dummies*® at local retailers everywhere.

Or let us know what you think by sending us a letter at the following address:

For Dummies Book Registration
Dummies Press
10475 Crosspoint Blvd.
Indianapolis, IN 46256

™

BESTSELLING BOOK SERIES